Tourism Product and Services

TOURISM PRODUCT AND SERVICES

Development Strategy and Management Options

JITENDRA KUMAR SHARMA

KANISHKA PUBLISHERS, DISTRIBUTORS
NEW DELHI-110 002

KANISHKA PUBLISHERS, DISTRIBUTORS
4697/5-21A, Ansari Road, Daryaganj
New Delhi -110 002
Phones : 2327 0497, 2328 8285
Fax : 011-2328 8285
E-mail : kanishka_publishing@yahoo.co.in

Tourism Product and Services:
Development Strategy and Management Options
First Published: 2007
Edition: 2021

ISBN : 978-81-7391-987-9

PRINTED IN INDIA

Published by Madan Sachdeva for Kanishka Publishers, Distributors, 4697/5-21A, Ansari Road, Daryaganj, New Delhi-110 002, Typeset by Sunshine Graphics, Delhi, and Printed at Rajdhani Printers, Delhi.

Preface

This book entitled "Tourism Product and Services: Development Strategy and Management Options" has been written keeping in mind the uniqueness of the subject and its growing significance in contemporary age. The main purpose of tourism product development is to enhance the quality of services involving various tourism products. Capacity-building through knowledge creation, education and training of tourism and hospitality related work force is therefore the key factor. Visitor satisfaction in all possible ways is the prime target. In other words, tourism product development mainly seeks to support in maintenance, development and enhancement of the tourism product. The required services, therefore, include sustainable tourism product planning and development, presentations, seminars, campaigns and strategies for destination marketing organizations, individual operators and agencies. Stakeholder identification, analysis and networking with local community are the key steps, while balancing public and private sector interests in ever-growing tourism industry is the key challenge. The service providers in this regard are also growing and specialize in attaining the desired tourism product.

Tourism product development strategies include factors like increasing competitiveness, incorporating inclusiveness, bringing growth in income, and suggesting changes to meet the future requirements of tourism industry locally, nationally internationally over the short, medium and long-terms. It also inculcates quality management in this service sector by introducing international standards benchmarks in the form of ISOs and eco-marks, etc. Besides, product improvement is undertaken by tourism training on a regular basis. Finally, tourism product development also helps in bringing-up product diversification by serving as a channel, facilitator and controller of development through adventure sports and local-community based development with focus on culture — tourism, heritage tourism and eco-tourism.

So, while tourism product development is all about the process of new product building and development in the area of travel and tourism, new product design and its operation efficiently, and maintaining a good or product or services as per the international standards. On the other hand, tourism product management is primarily responsible for critical day-in-day-out tourism product decisions that dictate the very success of tourism planning and strategy. Without effective tourism product management, tourism product development is prone to guess work. With world-class tourism product management, the product and services companies in the field of travel, tourism, hotel and hospitality proceed with tourism product development in the knowledge that markets and goods are intimately understood. However, one must remember that this insight into the ingredients of successful product is not without its challenges. This is mainly because of the fact that a tourism product's functionality is created for the user via product planning efforts, and product value is presented to the customer via product marketing activities. A tourism product manager has to deal carefully the closely-related functions like tourism product planning, tourism product marketing, tourism programme management and tourism project management. The main challenge, therefore, becomes the retention of synergy among the aforementioned functions.

This book covers the subject area of tourism product development and management in 6 chapters, besides providing the very user-friendly list of acronyms, glossary of related terms, appendix, bibliography and index. Chapter 1 gives and introductory overview of contemporary tourism service industry and tourism product with focus on trends, tourism vision 2020 and product management, community development, etc. Chapter 2 highlights the various issues facing tourism product development today and the options available. It deals with various select tourism products, such as, group tourist accommodation; heritage tourism product development; pricing tourism products and services; etc. Model case studies area presented to better understand the process of tourism product development and its management. Chapter 3 focusses on the key are of evolution of steps towards the sustainable marketing of tourism products mainly by promotion of responsible tourism destinations across the world. Key concepts and functions, such as, marketing sustainable tourism products; marketing tourism planning; total destination management; and recent declaration for responsible tourism destinations; are covered in detail. Chapter 4 reflects briefly on the concepts, principle and system standards with respect to the all important issue of quality management in tourism. The ISO systems in particular the 9000 series, 14000 series and 26000 series are discussed. The ways and means of increasing eco-efficiency in the whole process is also covered. Chapter 5 provides a detailed overview of sustainable tourism certification and training. It also analysis the international recommendations in this regard, particularly by the World Tourism Organization, Department of Economic and Social Affairs Commission, the International Chamber of Commerce and the World Travel and Tourism Council. A detailed world-wide analysis of global eco-tourism guidelines and code of ethics has been conducted, so as to perceive sustainable tourism product development and management in an inclusive framework. The 'Green Evaluation Programme' has been presented, so is the option for developing consultancy services in environmental training. Finally, the last Chapter 6 provides readers with an indepth understanding of tourism product development strategy, tourism product management and tourism product research. Select model case studies are given, especially focusing on nature and culture tourism. The criteria for resort-development is also discussed in the required framework. In sum, this book can be used as a reference book in the subject area tourism product development and management, in both theoretical and practical terms.

Author

Contents

List of Acronyms

ABC	:	Affiliates, Benchmarking and Certification
AIDS	:	Acquired Immune Deficiency Syndrome
AITO	:	Association of Independent Tour Operators
ASATA	:	Association of South African Travel Agents
ASTA	:	American Society of Travel Agents
CASS	:	Continuous Assessment
CAST	:	Caribbean Alliance for Sustainable Tourism
CBD	:	Convention on Biological Diversity
CI	:	Conservation International
CR	:	Customer Relations
CSD	:	Commission on Sustainable Development
CST	:	Certificate of Sustainable Tourism
DO	:	Developmental Outcome
EC	:	European Commission
EMS	:	Economic and Management Sciences
ETOA	:	European Tour Operators Association
EU	:	European Union
FET	:	Further Education and Training
FTO	:	UK Federation of Tour Operators
FTTSA	:	Fair Trade Tourism South Africa
GD	:	Green Deal
GDP	:	Gross Domestic Product
GET	:	General Education and Training
GG21	:	Green Globe 21
GMT	:	Greenwich Mean Time
GRI	:	Global Reporting Initiative
GSA	:	GSA Travel Marketing Magazine (previously known as the GSA Travel Agents' Sales Guide)
HIV	:	Human Immunodeficiency Virus
ICC	:	International Chamber of Commerce
ICT	:	Costa Rican Tourism Institute
IH&RA	:	International Hotel & Restaurant Association

IHEI	:	International Hotels Environment Initiative
IIED	:	International Institute for Environment and Development
IKS	:	Indigenous Knowledge Systems
ILO	:	International Labour Organization
IM	:	Internal Management
ISO	:	International Organization for Standardization
IYE	:	International Year of Ecotourism
NCS	:	National Curriculum Statement
NEAP	:	National Ecotourism Accreditation Programme
NGO	:	Non-Governmental Organization
NQF	:	National Qualifications Framework
OBE	:	Outcomes-Based Education
ODI	:	Overseas Development Institute
PATA	:	Pacific Asia Travel Association
PMD	:	Product Management and Development
PPT	:	Pro-Poor Tourism
SADC	:	Southern African Development Community
SAQA	:	South African Qualifications Framework
SCM	:	Supply Chain Management
SIDS	:	Small Island Developing States
STSC	:	Sustainable Tourism Stewardship Council
SV	:	Smart Voyager
TOI	:	Tour Operator's Initiative
TUI	:	Touristik Union International
UN	:	United Nations
UNCED	:	United Nations Conference on Environment and Development
UNEP	:	United Nations Environment Programme
UNESCO	:	United Nations Educational, Scientific and Cultural Organization
UNGASS	:	United Nations General Assembly Special Session
UTC	:	Universal Time Co-ordinate (same as Greenwich Mean Time)
WHO	:	World Health Organization
WTO	:	World Tourism Organization
WTTC	:	World Travel and Tourism Council
WWF	:	World Wildlife Fund

List of Glossary

Aspect

An environmental aspect is an element of an *organization's* activities, products or services that can interact with the *environment.*

Audit

An Environmental Management System Audit is a systematic and documented verification process of objectively obtaining and evaluating evidence to determine whether an organization's *environmental management system* conforms to the environmental management system audit criteria set by the *organization,* and for communication of the results of this process to management.

Attraction

Attraction is a place, event, building or area which tourists want to visit.

Biodiversity

A variety of wildlife in an area.

Business Plan

An action plan that entrepreneurs draw up for the purpose of starting a business; a guide to running one's business.

Component

A constituent part.

Continual Improvement

Continual Improvement is the process of enhancing the *environmental management system* to achieve improvements in overall environmental *performance* in line with the organization's environmental *policy*.

Environment

An environment is described as surroundings in which an organization operate, including air, water, land, natural resources, flora, fauna, humans, and their interrelation.

Culture

People's customs, clothing, food, houses, language, dancing, music, drama, literature and religion.

Destination

The end point of a journey.

Diversity

Variety, multiplicity, range, assortment.

Domestic

Within one's own country. A domestic tourist is a person who engages in tourism in his/her own country; domestic flights are those within the airline's own country.

Economy

Wealth of resources of a community.

Eco-system

An area where living and non-living things interact.

Eco-tourism

A combination of tourism and the environment (e.g. planning before development; sustainability of resources; economic viability of a tourism product; no negative impact on either the environment or local communities; responsibility for the environment from developers, the tourism industry and tourists; environmentally-friendly practices by all parties concerned and economic benefits flowing to local communities).

Endangered Species

In severe danger of becoming extinct in the near future unless immediate steps are taken to protect the species.

Environment

The diverse community activities and cultures of a country's inhabitants, as well as its scarce and sensitive natural resources.

Environmental Management System (EMS)

The Environmental Management System (EMS) is the part of the overall management system that includes organizational structure, planning activities, responsibilities, practices, procedures, processes, and resources for developing, implementing, achieving, reviewing and maintaining the environmental *policy*.

Event

An occurrence of importance.

Excursionist

A temporary visitor, staying less than 24 hours, including cruise travellers but excluding travellers in transit.

Fauna

All the animals of a particular area.

Flora

All the plants of a particular area.

Gateway

The point of access to a country or region, usually an airport or seaport, although certain frontier points and railway stations can be given the designation.

Global

Worldwide.

Greenwich Meridian

The meridian of longitude that passes through Greenwich (London) and from which all other meridians are numbered; also known as the prime meridian or the zero meridian.

Heritage Site

A place that capitalizes on its connection with heritage.

Heritage

A very broad expression that describes anything that has a link with some past event or person (e.g. cultural heritage refers to past customs and traditions with the unspoken implication that these are worthwhile or creditable).

Human-made Attraction

An attraction created by people.

Icon

A symbol representing something.

Impact

An environmental impact is any change to the *environment,* whether adverse or beneficial, wholly or partially resulting from an *organization's* activities, products or services.

Inbound Tourist

Tourist coming into a country from another country.

Interested Party

The Interested Party is the individual or group concerned with or affected by the environmental *performance* of an *organization.*

International Tourist

Tourist travelling to and between foreign countries.

Itinerary

The written details of a customer's travel arrangements in the form of dates, times and destinations.

Local

Belonging to a particular place or region.

Macro Business

A large, formal business that employs many people.

Micro Business

A small, often informal, business that employs very few people.

Natural Attraction

A tourist attraction that has not been made or created by people.

Natural Disaster

A destructive force (e.g. earthquake, flood, volcanic eruption).

Objective

An Environmental Objective is the overall environmental goal, arising from the environmental *policy*, that an *organization* sets itself to achieve, and which is quantified where practicable.

Organization

The organization is defined as the company, corporation, firm, enterprise, authority or institution, or part or combination thereof, whether incorporated or not, public or private, that has its own functions and administration.

Outbound Tourist

A tourist departing to a destination beyond the borders of the country of residence.

Performance (*Environmental*)

Environmental Performance is measurable results of the *environmental management system*, related to an *organisation's* control of its environmental *aspects*, based on its environmental *policy*, *objectives* and *targets*.

Policy (*Environmental*)

The Environmental Policy is a statement by the *organization* of its intentions and principles in relation to its overall environmental *performance* which provides a framework for action and for the setting of environmental *objectives* and *targets*.

Prevention of Pollution

Prevention of Pollution is defined as the use of processes, practices, materials or products that avoid, reduce or control pollution, which may include recycling, treatment, process changes, control mechanisms, efficient use of resources and materials substitution.

Profitability

Capacity to make profit.

Region

An area of land having more or less definable boundaries.

Sector

A part or branch of the whole industry that provides particular goods and/or services.

Service Delivery

The manner in which customer needs are met.

Service Provider

A person or company that supplies a particular service.

Service

Work done for the benefit of another.

Souvenir

A product purchased by a tourist as a reminder of a holiday.

Sustainable

Something which can be kept in the same or a better condition for the future.

Target (*Environmental*)

An Environmental Target is a detailed *performance* requirement, quantified where practicable, applicable to the *organization* or parts thereof, that arises from the environmental *objectives* and that needs to be set and met in order to achieve those objectives.

Tourism Geography

The knowledge of countries, regions, major cities, gateways, famous icons, monuments, building structures, and geographical features such as rivers, seas, mountains, deserts and time zones.

Tourism Industry

A group of businesses that provide services and facilities for consumption by tourists.

Tourism Infrastructure

Roads, railway lines, harbours, airport runways, water, electricity, other power supplies, sewerage disposal systems and other utilities to serve not only the local residents but also the tourist influx (suitable accommodation, restaurants and passenger transport terminals form the superstructure of the region).

Tourism Product

Different things to the various members of the tourism industry. To the hotel it is 'guest-nights.' To the airline it is the 'seats flown' and the 'passenger miles.' To the museum, art gallery or archaeological site, the product is measured in terms of the number of visitors. For the tourist the product is the complete experience resulting from the package tour or travel facility purchased, from the time they leave home until their return.

Tourism

The all-embracing term for the movement of people to destinations away from their place of residence for any reason other than following an occupation, remunerated from within the country visited, for a period of 24 hours or more.

Tourist Facility

A feature created for utilization by tourists.

Tourist Route

A route developed to attract tourists to an area to view or experience something unique to that area (e.g. wine route, whale route, heritage route, battlefield route).

Tourist Trend

A general tendency to visit a country, region or destination or to pursue a specific tourist activity.

Tourist

One who travels for a period of 24 hours or more in a place other than that in which he or she usually resides, whose purpose could be classified as leisure (whether for recreation, health, sport, holiday, study or religion), business, family, mission or meeting.

World Heritage Site

A site designated by UNESCO as being of special historical, cultural or natural importance.

1

Contemporary Tourism Service Industry and Tourism Product: An Introduction

Tourism is the act of travel for predominantly recreational or leisure purposes, and also refers to the provision of services in support of this act. According to the *World Tourism Organization*, tourists are people who "travel to and stay in places outside their usual environment for not more than one consecutive year for leisure, business and other purposes not related to the exercise of an activity remunerated from within the place visited." The distance between a place of origin and a tourism destination is immaterial to this definition. Tourism has become an extremely popular, global activity. In 2004, there were over 763 million international tourist arrivals.

As a service industry, tourism has numerous tangible and intangible elements. Major tangible elements include transportation, accommodation, and other components of a hospitality industry. Major intangible elements relate to the purpose or motivation for becoming a tourist, such as rest, relaxation, the opportunity to meet new people and experience other cultures, or simply to do something different and have an adventure.

Tourism is vital for many countries, due to the income generated by the consumption of goods and services by tourists, the taxes levied on businesses in the tourism industry, and the opportunity for employment and economic advancement by working in the industry. For these reasons NGOs and government agencies may sometimes promote a specific region as a tourist destination, and support the development of a tourism industry in that area. The contemporary phenomenon of mass tourism may sometimes result in overdevelopment, however alternative forms of tourism such as eco-tourism seek to avoid such outcomes by pursuing tourism in a sustainable way.

The terms *tourism* and *travel* are sometimes used interchangeably. In this context travel has a similar definition to tourism, but implies a more purposeful journey. The terms *tourism* and *tourist* are sometimes used pejoratively to imply a shallow interest in the cultures or locations visited by tourists.

DEFINITION, CLASSIFICATION AND REQUIREMENTS

General Definition

One of the earliest definitions of tourism was provided by the Austrian economist Hermann Von Schullard in 1910, who defined it as, "sum total of operators, mainly of an economic nature, which directly relate to the entry, stay and movement of foreigners inside and outside a certain country, city or a region."

Hunziker and Krapf, in 1941, defined tourism as "the sum of the phenomena and relationships arising from the travel and stay of non-residents, insofar as they do not lead to permanent residence and are not connected with any earning activity."

In 1976 Tourism Society of England defined it as "Tourism is the temporary, short-term movement of people to destination outside the places where they normally live and work and their activities during the stay at each destination. It includes movements for all purposes."

In 1981 International Association of Scientific Experts in Tourism defined Tourism in terms of particular activities selected by choice and undertaken outside the home environment.

United Nations Definition

United Nations classified three forms of tourism in 1994 in its Recommendations on Tourism Statistics as follows:

1. Domestic tourism, involving residents of the given country travelling only within this country;
2. Inbound tourism, involving non-residents travelling in the given country; and
3. Outbound tourism, involving residents travelling in another country.

UN also derived different categories of tourism by combining the three basic forms of tourism:

1. Internal tourism, which comprises domestic tourism and inbound tourism;
2. National tourism, which comprises domestic tourism and outbound tourism; and
3. International tourism, which consists of inbound tourism and outbound tourism.

Prerequisites of Tourism

Before people are able to experience tourism they usually need at least:

1. disposable income, i.e. money to spend on non-essentials,
2. leisure time, and
3. tourism infrastructure, such as transport and accommodation.

Individually, sufficient *health* is also a condition, and of course the inclination to travel. Furthermore, in some countries there are legal restrictions on travelling, especially abroad. Certain states with strong governmental control over the lives of citizens (notably established Communist states) may restrict foreign travel only to trustworthy citizens. The United States prohibits its citizens from travelling to some countries, for example, Cuba.

HISTORY

Wealthy people have always travelled to distant parts of the world to see great buildings or other works of art, to learn new languages, to experience new cultures, or to taste new cuisine. As long ago as the time of the Roman Republic places such as Baiae were popular coastal resorts for the rich.

The terms *tourist* and *tourism* were first used as official terms in 1937 by the League of Nations. Tourism was defined as people travelling abroad for periods of over 24 hours.

Health Tourism and Leisure Travel

The history of European tourism can perhaps be said to originate with the medieval pilgrimage. Although undertaken primarily for religious reasons, the pilgrims in the Canterbury Tales quite clearly saw the experience as a kind of holiday (the term itself being derived from the 'holy day' and its associated leisure activities). Pilgrimages created a variety of tourist aspects that still exist-bringing back souvenirs, obtaining credit with foreign banks (in medieval times utilising international networks established by Jews and Lombards), and making use of space available on existing forms of transport (such as the use of medieval English wine ships bound for Vigo by pilgrims to Santiago De Compostela). Pilgrimages are still important in modern tourism—such as to Lourdes or Knock in Ireland. But there are modern equivalents—Graceland and the grave of Jim Morrison in Père Lachaise Cemetery.

During the seventeenth century, it became fashionable in England to undertake a Grand Tour. The sons of the nobility and gentry were sent upon an extended tour of Europe as an educational experience. The eighteenth century was the golden age of the Grand Tour, and many of the fashionable visitors were painted at Rome by Pompeo Batoni. A modern equivalent of the Grand Tour is the phenomenon of the backpacker, although cultural holidays, such as those offered by Swann-Hellenic, are also important.

Health tourism has always existed, but it was not until the eighteenth century that it became important. In England, it was associated with spas, places with supposedly health-giving mineral waters, treating diseases from gout to liver disorders and bronchitis. Bath was the most fashionable resort, but Buxton, Harrogate, and Tunbridge Wells, amongst others, also flourished. Of course, people visited these places for the balls and other entertainments, just as much as 'the waters'. Continental Spas such as Karlsbad attracted many fashionable travellers by the nineteenth century.

It could be argued that Britain was the home of the seaside holiday. In travelling to the coast, the population was following in the steps of Royalty. King George III made regular visits to Weymouth when in poor health. At the time, a number of doctors argued the benefits of bathing in sea water, and sea bathing as a widespread practice was popularised by the Prince Regent (later George IV), who frequented Brighton for this purpose.

Leisure travel was associated with the industrialisation of United Kingdom—the first European country to promote leisure time to the increasing industrial population. Initially, this applied to the owners of the machinery of production, the economic oligarchy, the factory owners, and the traders. These comprised the new middle class. Cox and Kings were the first official travel company to be formed in 1758. Later, the working class could take advantage of leisure time.

The British origin of this new industry is reflected in many place names. At Nice, one of the first and best-established holiday resorts on the French Riviera, the long esplanade along the seafront is known to this day as the *Promenade des Anglais;* in many other historic resorts in continental Europe, old well-established palace hotels have names like the *Hotel Bristol,* the *Hotel Carlton* or the *Hotel Majestic*—reflecting the dominance of English customers.

Winter Tourism

Winter sports were largely invented by the British leisured classes, initially at the Swiss village of Zermatt (Valais), and St Moritz in 1864. The first packaged winter sports holidays took place in 1902 at Adelboden, Switzerland. Winter sports were a natural answer for a leisured class looking for amusement during the coldest season.

Organized sport was well established in Britain before it reached other countries. The vocabulary of sport bears witness to this: rugby, football, and boxing all originated in Britain, and even tennis, originally a French sport, was formalized and codified by the British, who hosted the first national championship in the nineteenth century, at Wimbledon.

Mass Travel

Mass travel could only develop with two crucial features:

1. improvements in technology allowed the transport of large numbers of people in a short space of time to places of leisure interest, and
2. greater numbers of people began to enjoy the benefits of leisure time.

The pioneer of modern mass tourism was Thomas Cook who, on 5 July, 1841, organized the first package tour in history. He arranged for the rail company to charge one shilling per person for a group of 570 temperance campaigners from Leicester to a rally in Loughborough, eleven miles away. Cook was paid a share of the fares actually charged to the passengers, as the railway tickets, being legal contracts between company and passenger, could not have been issued at his own price. There had been railway excursions before, but this one included entrance to an entertainment held in private grounds, rail tickets and food for the train journey. Cook immediately saw the potential of a convenient 'off the peg' holiday product in which everything was included in one cost. He organized packages inclusive of accommodation for the Great Exhibition, and afterwards pioneered package holidays in both Britain (particularly in Scotland) and on the European continent (where Paris and the Alps were the most popular destinations).

He was soon followed by others (the Polytechnic Touring Association, Dean and Dawson etc.), with the result that the tourist industry developed rapidly in late Victorian Britain. Initially it was supported by the growing middle classes, who had time off from their work, and who could afford the luxury of travel and possibly even staying for periods of time in boarding houses.

The Bank Holidays Act, 1871 introduced a statutory right for workers to take holidays, even if they were not paid at the time. By the last quarter of the nineteenth century, the tradition of the working class holiday had become firmly established in Britain. These were largely focussed upon the seaside resorts.

The spread of the railway network in the nineteenth century resulted in the growth of Britain's seaside towns by bringing them within easy distance of Britain's urban centres. Blackpool was created by the construction of a line to Fleetwood, and some resorts were promoted by the railway companies themselves—Morecambe by the Midland Railway and Cleethorpes by the Great Central Railway. Other resorts included Scarborough in Yorkshire, servicing Leeds and Bradford; Weston-super-Mare in Somerset, catering for the inhabitants of Bristol; and Skegness, patronised by the residents of the industrial East Midlands. The cockneys of London flocked to Southend-on-Sea, mainly by Thames Steamer, and the South Coast resorts such as Broadstairs, Brighton, and Eastbourne were only a train ride away, with others further a field such as Bournemouth, Bognor Regis and Weymouth.

For a century, domestic tourism was the norm, with foreign travel being reserved for the rich or the culturally curious. A number of inland destinations, such as the English Lake District, and Snowdonia appealed to those who liked the countryside and fine scenery. The holiday camp began to appear in the 1930s, but this phenomenon really expanded in the post-war period. Butlins and Pontins set this trend, but their popularity waned with the rise of overseas package tours and the increasing comforts to which visitors became accustomed at home. Towards the end of the 20th century this market has been revived by the up market inland resorts of Dutch company Center Parks.

Cox & Co, the forebear of Cox & Kings were in existence from 1758 largely entwined with the travel arrangements for the British Army serving around the Empire. While acting as 'agents' for various regiments, they organized the payment, provision, clothing and travel arrangements for members of the armed forces. In the 19th century their network of offices contained a banking and also travel department. The company became heavily involved with affairs in India and its Shipping Agency had offices in France and the Middle East.

Other phenomena that helped develop the travel industry were paid holidays:

- 1.5 million manual workers in Britain had paid holidays by 1925
- 11 million by 1939 (30% of the population in families with paid holidays)

Outside Britain

In the USA, the first great seaside resort, in the European style, was Atlantic City, New Jersey.

In Continental Europe, early resorts included Ostend (for the people of Brussels), and Boulogne-sur-Mer (Pas-de-Calais) and Deauville (Calvados) (for Parisians).

International Mass Tourism

Increasing speed on railways meant that the tourist industry could develop internationally.

To this may be added the development of sea travel. By 1901, the number of people crossing the English Channel from England to France or Belgium had passed 0.5 million per year. Shipping companies were anxious to fill cabin space that was under utilized. For example, P & O found that the majority of their passengers for India and the Far East joined the ship at Marseilles. Consequently, they marketed holidays based upon sea trips from London to Lisbon and Gibraltar. Other companies diverted their older ships to operate cruises in the summer months.

However, the real age of international mass travel began with the growth of air travel after Second World War. In the immediate post-war period, there was a surplus of transport aircraft, such as the popular and reliable Douglas Dakota, and a number of ex-military pilots ready to fly them. They were available for charter flights, and tour operators began to use them for European destinations, such as Paris and Ostend.

Vladimir Raitz pioneered modern package tourism when on 20 May, 1950 his recently founded company, Horizon, provided arrangements for a two-week holiday in Corsica. For an all inclusive price of £32.10s.-, holiday makers could sleep under canvas, sample local wines and eat a meal containing meat twice a day—this was especially attractive due to the continuing austerity measures in post-war United Kingdom. Within ten years, his company had started mass tourism to Palma (1952), Lourdes (1953), Costa Brava (1954), Sardinia (1954), Minorca (1955), Porto (1956), Costa Blanca (1957) and Costa del Sol (1959).

However, it was with cheap air travel in combination with the package tour that international mass tourism developed. The post-war introduction of an international system of airline regulation was another important factor. The bilateral agreements at the heart of the system fixed seat prices, and airlines could not fill blocks of empty seats on underused flights by discounting. But if they were purchased by a tour operator and hidden within the price of an inclusive holiday package, it would be difficult to prove that discounting had taken place—even though it was obvious that it had! This was the origin of the modern mass package tour.

These developments coincided with a significant increase in the standard of living in Britain. At the end of the 1950s, Harold Macmillan could say "you've never had it so good."

Another significant development also happened at the end of this decade. The devaluation of the Spanish peseta made Spain appear a particularly attractive destination. The cheapness of the cost of living attracted increasing numbers of visitors. Mass package tourism has at times been an exploitative process, in which tour operators in a country with a high standard of living make use of development opportunities and low operating costs in a country with a lower standard of living. However, as witness the development of many tourist areas in previously poor parts of the world, and the concomitant rise in standards of living, when there is equality of bargaining power, both parties can gain economic benefits from this arrangement.

Spain and the Balearic Islands became major tourist destinations, and development probably peaked in the 1980s. At the same time, British tour operators developed the Algarve in Portugal. The continuing search for new, cheaper, destinations spread mass tourism to the Greek Islands, Italy, Tunisia, Morocco, parts of the coast of Turkey, and more recently Croatia.

For the worker living in greater London, Venice today is almost as accessible as Brighton was 100 years ago. Consequently, the British seaside resort experienced a marked decline from the 1970s onwards. Some, such as New Brighton have disappeared. Others have reinvented themselves, and now cater to day trippers and the weekend break market.

RECENT DEVELOPMENTS

There has been a discernible up market trend in tourism over the last few decades, especially in Europe where international travel for short breaks is commonplace. Tourists have higher levels of disposable income and greater leisure time. They are also better educated and have more sophisticated tastes. There is now a demand for a better quality product in many quarters. This has resulted in the following trends:

- The old 'sun, sea and sand' mass market has fragmented. People want more specialized versions of it, such as 'Club 18-30', quieter resorts with select hotels, self-catering, etc.
- People are taking second holidays in the form of short breaks/city breaks, ranging from British and European cities to country hotels.
- There has been a growth in niche markets catering for special interests or activities, including growth of destination hotels.

The developments in technology and transport infrastructure (particularly the advent of jumbo jets) have placed some types of holiday in the affordable mainstream:

- The development of a mass cruise holiday market.
- The advent of affordable holidays to long-haul destinations such as Thailand or Kenya.
- The phenomenon of the low budget airline, utilizing a new generation of small regional airports.

There have also been changes in lifestyle, which may call into question the current definitions of tourism. Some people (particularly the 45+ and retired) may be adopting a tourism lifestyle, living as a tourist all the year round—eating out several times a week, going to the theatre, day tripping, and indulging in short breaks several times a year.

Much of this results in impulse purchasing. This is facilitated by internet purchasing of tourism products. Some sites have now started to offer dynamic packaging, in which an inclusive price is quoted for a tailor-made package requested by the customer upon impulse.

There have been a few setbacks in tourism, such as the September 11, 2001 attacks and terrorist threats to tourist destinations such as Bali and European cities. Some of the tourist destinations, including the Costa del Sol, the Baleares and Cancún have lost popularity due to shifting tastes. In this context, the excessive building and environmental destruction often associated with traditional "sun and beach" tourism may contribute to a destination's saturation and subsequent decline. This appears to be the case with Spain's Costa Brava, a byword for this kind of tourism in the 1960s and 1970s. With only 11 per cent of the Costa Brava now unblemished by low-quality development (Greenpeace Spain's figure), the destination now faces a crisis in its tourist industry.

Sustainable tourism is becoming more popular as people start to realize the devastating effects tourism can have on communities.

Receptive tourism is now growing at a very rapid rate in many developing countries, where it is often the most important economic activity in local GDP.

In recent years, second holidays or vacations have become more popular as people's discretionary income increases. Typical combinations are a package to the typical mass tourist resort, with a winter skiing holiday or weekend break to a city or national park.

On December 26, 2004 a tsunami, caused by the 2004 Indian Ocean earthquake hit Asian countries bordering the Indian Ocean, and also the Maldives. Tens of thousands of lives were lost, and many tourists died. This, together with the vast clean-up operation in place, has stopped or severely hampered tourism to the area.

TRENDS

The World Tourism Organization (UNWTO) forecasts that international tourism will continue growing at the average annual rate of 4 per cent. By 2020 Europe will remain the most popular destination, but its share will drop from 60 per cent in 1995 to 46 per cent. Long-haul will grow slightly faster than intraregional travel and by 2020 its share will increase from 18 per cent in 1995 to 24 per cent.

With the advent of e-commerce, tourism products have become one of the most traded items on the internet. Tourism products and services have been made available through intermediaries, although tourism providers (hotels, airlines, etc.) can sell their services directly. This has put pressure on intermediaries from both on-line and traditional shops.

Space tourism is expected to "take off" in the first quarter of the 21st century, although compared with traditional destinations the number of tourists in orbit will remain low until technologies such as a space elevator make space travel cheap.

Technological improvement is likely to make possible air-ship hotels, based either on solar-powered airplanes or large dirigibles. Underwater hotels, such as Hydropolis, expected to open in Dubai in 2006, will be built. On the ocean tourists will be welcomed by ever larger cruise ships and perhaps floating cities.

Some futurists expect that movable hotel "pods" will be created that could be temporarily erected anywhere on the planet, where building a permanent resort would be unacceptable politically, economically or environmentally.

Special Forms of Tourism

For the past few decades other forms of tourism, also known as niche tourism, have been becoming more popular, particularly:

- *Adventure tourism*—tourism involving travel in rugged Oregions, or adventurous sports such as mountaineering and hiking (tramping).
- *Agritourism*—farm based tourism, helping to support the local agricultural economy.
- *Ancestry tourism* (also known as genealogy tourism) is the travel with the aim of tracing one's ancestry, visiting the birth places of these ancestors and sometimes getting to know distant family.
- *Armchair tourism* and *virtual tourism* not travelling physically, but exploring the world through internet, books, TV, etc.

- *Audio tourism* includes *audio walking tours* and other audio guided forms of tourism including museum audio guides and audio travel books.
- *Bookstore tourism* is a grassroots effort to support independent bookstores by promoting them as a travel destination.
- *Cultural tourism* includes urban tourism, visiting historical or interesting cities, and experiencing their cultural heritages. This type of tourism may also include specialized cultural experiences, such as art museum tourism where the tourist visits many art museums during the tour, or opera tourism where the tourist sees many operas or concerts during the tour.
- *Dark tourism* is the travel to sites associated with death and suffering. The first tourist agency to specialize in this kind of tourism started with trips to Lakehurst, New Jersey, the scene of the Hindenburg airship disaster.
- *Disaster tourism*—travelling to a disaster scene not primarily for helping, but because it is interesting to see. It can be a problem if it hinders rescue, relief and repair work.
- *Drug tourism*—travel to a country to obtain or consume drugs, either legally or illegally.
- *Ecotourism*—sustainable tourism which has minimal impact on the environment, such as safaris (Kenya), Rainforests (Belize) and hiking (Lapland), or national parks.
- *Educational tourism* may involve travelling to an education institution, a wooded retreat or some other destination in order to take personal-interest classes, such as cooking classes with a famous chef or crafts classes.
- *Extreme tourism*—tourism associated with high risk.
- *Free independent traveller*—a sector of the market and philosophy of constructing a vacation by sourcing one's own components e.g., accommodation, transport.
- *Gambling tourism,* e.g. to Atlantic City, Las Vegas, Palm Springs, California, Macau or Monte Carlo for the purpose of gambling at the casinos there.
- *Garden tourism*—visiting botanical gardens famous places in the history of gardening, such as Versailles and the Taj Mahal.
- *Heritage tourism*—visiting historical (Rome, Athens, Cracow) or industrial sites, such as old canals, railways, battlegrounds, etc.

- *Health tourism*—usually to escape from cities or relieve stress, perhaps for some 'fun in the sun', etc. Often to Sanatoriums or "health spas."
- *Hobby tourism*—tourism alone or with groups to participate in hobby interests, to meet others with similar interests, or to experience something pertinent to the hobby. Examples might be garden tours, amateur radio DX-peditions, or square dance cruises.
- *Inclusive tourism*—tourism marketed to those with functional limits or disabilities. Referred to as "Tourism for All" in some regions. Destinations often employ Universal Design and Universal Destination Development principles.
- *Medical tourism*, e.g.:
    - for what is illegal in one's own country, such as abortion or euthanasia
    - for advanced care that is not available in one's own country
    - in the case that there are long waiting lists in one's own country
    - for use of free or cheap health care organizations
    - *Pop-culture tourism*—tourism by those that visit a particular location after reading about it or seeing it in a film.
- *Perpetual tourism*—wealthy individuals always on vacation; some of them, for tax purposes, to avoid being resident in any country.
- *Pilgrimage tourism*—pilgrimages to ancient holy places (Rome and Santiago de Compostela for Catholics, Temples and stupas of Nepal for the Hindus and Buddhist, Mount Athos or Painted churches of northern Moldavia for the Orthodox), religious sites such as mosques, shrines, etc.
- *Sex tourism*—travelling solely for the purpose of sexual activity, usually with prostitutes.
- *Solo travel*—travelling alone.
- *Sport travel*—skiing, golf and scuba diving are popular ways to spend a vacation. This could also include travelling to a major international sporting event such as the FIFA World Cup or following a tour such as the Ashes or British and Irish Lions.

- *Space tourism*—travelling in outer space or on spaceships.
- *Vacilando* is a special kind of wanderer for whom the process of travelling is more important than the destination.
- *Wine tourism*—the visiting of growing regions, vineyards, wineries, tasting rooms, wine festivals, and similar places or events for the purpose of consuming or purchasing wine.

Adventure Tourism and Recreation

Adventure tourism and recreation, like the accommodation sector, is growing fast. Changing trends in travel and tourism, where clients request active, recreational experiences or travel adventures where they can learn about nature and/or culture, are driving the growth. This sector includes everything from bird watching to salmon fishing, horseback riding to white water rafting, golf to wilderness trekking. Adventure tourism and recreation draws those who want to experience Canada as a place that is natural and unspoiled, and those who want active, unusual vacations. Because activities often mean clients need transport, hotel rooms and restaurants, other tourism sectors also benefit.

There are over eighty different occupations in the adventure tourism and recreation sector. The opportunities for small business owner/operators are limited only by the creativity of the operators. Total Canadian employment in this sector in 1997 was 71,100 and this was expected to grow to 90,000 by 2005.

Types of Businesses

The major areas of this sector are:

Outdoor Adventure and Ecotourism

Many travellers seek adventure, challenge and excitement in an outdoor setting. Canada is blessed with a wide diversity of relatively unspoiled wilderness areas that support these types of activities. Hiking, cycling, mountaineering, canoeing, kayaking, sailing, horseback riding, river rafting, scuba diving, sky diving, snowmobiling, and nature/wildlife viewing are just some of the activities included in this portion of the sector. In addition, there are many Canadian businesses dedicated to fishing our lakes and oceans, and hunting or photographing wild animals.

Outdoor adventure and ecotourism businesses require staff who have a love and knowledge of the outdoors. They often need technical proficiency and expertise in the activity that the business focuses on. In addition, in order to ensure the long-term viability of the business, they must respect the environment and help others to respect it as well. As with all tourism occupations, employees must enjoy working with people and be skilled at understanding and meeting individual needs.

Ski Resorts

Over two million Canadians regularly ski or snowboard. There are nearly 300 alpine ski areas in Canada and hundreds of ski clubs to serve them. Canada's top five resorts enjoy steady growth. These resorts attract skiers and boarders from across the country, and large numbers of foreign travellers from around the world, especially from Japan, Britain and Germany.

Eleven per cent of Canadians cross-country ski. Enthusiasts travel to recreation areas, such as the site of the 1988 Olympic cross-country ski trails in Canmore, Alberta, to experience the tracks and the outdoors.

Ski-related jobs are numerous. They are available at ski resorts, hills and clubs, and in those businesses that support the industry, like lodges and ski shops.

Golf and Tennis Facilities

Almost five million Canadians golf. Annual industry revenue is almost $1 billion. There are 1800 golf courses in Canada and golf holidays are becoming increasingly important to the economy.

Another popular summer sport is tennis. Many clubs and resorts offer tennis courts, tennis lessons and tennis gear. This is also an important part of the industry, with revenue earned through the sale of clothing and gear, the rental of courts, the training of players and the maintenance of equipment.

Golf and tennis pros, those who fix equipment and maintain courts and greens, those who work in industries that support the golfers and tennis players—all work in this area of the adventure tourism and recreation sector.

Parks

There are 38 national parks and 792 national historical sites in Canada. In addition, all provinces and territories have regional parks, and most urban and rural municipalities have parks and habitat protection areas. Many people are involved in planning, maintaining, promoting, patrolling and interpreting these areas. Positions are as varied as the sector.

Marine Facilities

Across Canada, water and water-based activities are popular with Canadians and visitors alike. Activities include fishing, swimming, sailing, windsurfing, water-skiing, canoeing and sea-dooing. Related businesses include marinas, tour boat excursions, sport fishing lodges, fly-in fishing camps and boat rental operations. On both the east and west coasts, there are thriving marine businesses ranging from whale-watching tours to deep-sea fishing adventures.

As in all portions of this sector, instructors are an important part of the industry. Those who have mastered an activity to a point where they can teach others to do it can market these abilities to employers in this sector.

TOURISM VISION 2020

Tourism 2020 Vision is the World Tourism Organization's long-term forecast and assessment of the development of tourism up to the first 20 years of the new millennium. An essential outcome of the *Tourism 2020 Vision* are quantitative forecasts covering a 25 years period, with 1995 as the base year and forecasts for 2010 and 2020.

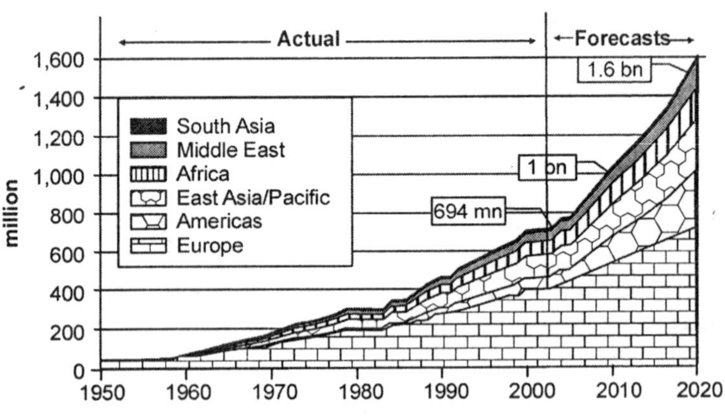

Although the evolution of tourism in the last few years has been irregular, UNWTO maintains its long-term forecast for the moment. The underlying structural trends of the forecast are believed not to have significantly changed. Experience shows that in the short-term, periods of faster growth (1995, 1996, 2000) alternate with periods of slow growth (2001 to 2003). While the pace of growth till 2000 actually exceeded the *Tourism 2020 Vision* forecast, it is generally expected that the current slowdown will be compensated in the medium to long-term.

UNWTO's *Tourism 2020 Vision* forecasts that international arrivals are expected to reach nearly 1.6 billion by the year 2020. Of these worldwide arrivals in 2020, 1.2 billion will be intraregional and 378 million will be long-haul travellers.

The total tourist arrivals by region shows that by 2020 the top three receiving regions will be Europe (717 million tourists), East Asia and the Pacific (397 million) and the Americas (282 million), followed by Africa, the Middle East and South Asia.

East Asia and the Pacific, South Asia, the Middle East and Africa are forecasted to record growth at rates of over 5 per cent year, compared to the world average of 4.1 per cent. The more mature regions Europe and Americas are anticipated to show lower than average growth rates. Europe will maintain the highest share of world arrivals, although there will be a decline from 60 per cent in 1995 to 46 per cent in 2020.

	Base Year	*Forecasts*		*Market share (%)*		*Average annual growth rate (%)*
	1995	*2010*	*2020*			
		(Million)		*1995*	*2020*	*1995-2020*
World	565	1006	1561	100	100	4.1
Africa	20	47	77	3.6	5.0	5.5
Americas	110	190	282	19.3	18.1	3.8
East Asia and the Pacific	81	195	397	14.4	25.4	6.5
Europe	336	527	717	59.8	45.9	3.1
Middle East	14	36	69	2.2	4.4	6.7
South Asia	4	11	19	0.7	1.2	6.2

Long-haul travel worldwide will grow faster, at 5.4 per cent per year over the period 1995-2020, than intraregional travel, at 3.8 per cent. Consequently the ratio between intraregional and long-haul travel will shift from around 82:18 in 1995 to close to 76:24 in 2020.

Overview

This illustration aims to provide comprehensive information on international tourism worldwide. It offers among others a selection of the *latest available statistics on International Tourist Arrivals, Tourism receipts and expenditure.*

"Facts & Figures" includes also the following areas:

UNWTO Tourism Highlights

Concise overview of international tourism in the world based on the results for the year 2005. It includes statistics and analysis on international tourist arrivals, international tourism receipts, a summary of tourism results by region, top tourism destinations by arrivals and receipts, outbound tourism by generating region and the ranking of the top tourism spenders.

Tourism Market Trends

Tourism Market Trends is the World Tourism Organization regular series of reports whose objective is to present international tourism trends in the world as well as in each region, sub-region and country.

UNWTO World Tourism Barometer

Latest available statistics and a short-term overview, aimed at monitoring the evolution of tourism and providing the sector with adequate and timely information.

TOURISM AS ECONOMIC DEVELOPMENT

Somewhere centuries ago a community decided to celebrate, and a festival was born. Vendors sensed that people would gather and be in a mood to buy their wares. Townsfolk realized that visitors from afar would need places to rest. Someone knew enough to organize the event and, if that person was a visionary, he knew that revellers would pay to watch the sun go down, that is if accompanying food and music were provided.

Visitors beat new paths to the community. Paths turned into roads. Vendors decided that the festival was sustainable, so they stayed on, calling the place where they gathered to do business the market. The community now had a commercial centre. Dwellings that offered hospitality became inns and eating-places. The sun was reliable in its setting. This was the place where tourism was born.

The model described has not changed over time. It is a simple model of tourism development. Add the production of the goods that the vendors offer for sale; then create a strategy for community development that includes local manufacturing; and the practice of economic development, as we know it today, becomes definitive.

Tourism developers are marketers. The elements of their marketing activities include recruiting, as well as the creation of products that entice visitors to linger and seek leisure activities that will part them from their money. For all practical purposes, tourism development and tourism promotion are the same things. Promotion is an element of marketing.

Economic developers are marketers also. In areas of the world where the Industrial Age has ended, there is only a semantic distinction between tourism developers and economic developers, in terms of how they function to serve prospects. In fact, industrial developers in North America only began to change their identity to "economic developers" about 25 years ago. Most people worldwide still think of economic development in terms of industrial development.

Economic developers oriented towards industrial development often refer to themselves as community developers when they are engaged in activities related to building local infrastructure. Economic developers often refer to themselves as product developers when they are oriented towards tourism development and similarly engaged in readying their communities. Separating economic development activities into "industrial" or "tourism" is of little importance until it causes confusion for those who own opportunities and have decisions to make that affect locations or expansions or start-ups. The smaller the community, the more important it is that the local economic developer be capable of addressing the needs of all types of prospects.

Entrepreneurs are more likely to be involved in tourism-related product development than are corporate executives responsible for relocating or expanding operations. Entrepreneurs are also more likely to be unfamiliar with the nuances of the economic development process as it relates to finding resources and assistance. In addition to entrepreneurs, investors and property or project developers are generally what make up a "whole" tourism-related prospect.

During the times of industrial development opportunity, communities promote and recruit for prospects that come neatly prepackaged, as compared to times of development opportunity for tourism product, which are primarily commercial opportunities. Industrial prospects generally challenge a community with a standardized set of criteria that place it in a competitive position against other communities. Commercial prospects generally challenge a community to produce evidence of market potential. In essence, a community competes with itself in commercial development. If entrepreneurs seek assistance from economic developers, it is generally because they want help in putting their packages together so that they can become a whole prospect. When they call upon economic developers they often want assistance in finding sources of capital (investors) and people who can make a concept work (developers).

In order to find a starting point for guiding those who want to maintain their communities in a position to grow as commercial centres, as well as for guiding those who are business leaders with opportunities to bring to communities, I wrote this paper as a recap of what I recently learned about tourism product. The time of my learning surrounds the 1996 Summer Olympic Games, which took place in Atlanta, Georgia, USA. The "Atlanta Olympics" was my opportunity to be exposed to all facets of tourism-related product at one time. It was a time in my career as an economic developer when I participated in the greatest variety of projects. I was on the scene before, during and after the event as a consultant with product development responsibilities that extended beyond the metropolitan area of Atlanta throughout the state of Georgia, and into the whole region of the Southeastern United States as well. I was involved with prospects interested in capturing the market created by the event in Atlanta, as well as prospects interested in developing permanent markets in rural areas. I was forced to define tourism product and carefully consider its process when confronted with any opportunity that would affect its development.

What is Product Development?

All of the definitions of tourism-related product that I have yet heard have an obvious common thread. A promotional brochure has been defined to me as product. An event, such as a family reunion, has been described to me as product. Organizing tours to give city people an opportunity to experience rural life is regularly suggested at tourism conferences as a product worthy of development. The common thread woven through all of these points is that product must appeal to travellers and people seeking leisure-time activities.

Alvin Rosenbaum of the National Centre for Heritage Development (formerly the National Coalition for Heritage Areas) said, "Tourism product supported by public agencies is a blend of conservation, community and economic development." He said this at the annual meeting of the American Association of Museums in 1997.

Earlier at a Cultural Tourism Leadership Forum in Chapel Hill, North Carolina, Jerold Kappel raised the issue of how to define product. Mr. Kappel, who is the American Association of Museums' (AAM) director of development, included a need to interpret what product is among five challenges to its development. In later correspondence to my wife and business partner he explained and emphasized the importance of considering product development within the context of the whole community. He wrote that tourism product is community-based. He wrote, "...what makes cultural tourism unique is that people go to absorb and experience the culture of a place." He earlier defined "place" as a destination with a story to tell to a visitor.

Both the imaginary model that introduces this paper and the Atlanta Olympics model can be identified as "market models." The first was presented as a permanent market that formed from an event. The latter was an established market that was enhanced by an event. Market is critical to product development. In Atlanta, it was necessary to build a sports infrastructure to support the Olympics. The right product in the right place, at the right time, is critical to turning a commercial development opportunity into a reality.

Prior to the 1996 Summer Olympic games, Atlanta developed an infrastructure to appeal to sports fans. That infrastructure was tested for its market potential, long before the Olympics came along. The state provided the city with a conference and trade show centre that was the foundation for building an infrastructure to accommodate the business traveller. The movie, *Gone With The Wind*, gave Atlanta its major historic theme, and support from people who made money from successful Atlanta based businesses such as Coca-Cola helped build a foundation for its appeal to visitors with cultural interests.

If you analyze Atlanta from a historic point of view, you arrive at a point in time when there was a rural community in its place. If you analyze Atlanta from a cultural point of view, you see that, at exactly the right time in its development, it embraced all the elements of its culture and heritage.

If you analyze Atlanta from the standpoint of its most recent landmark event in tourism development, the 1996 Summer Olympic Games, you see that its cultural and heritage position had to be established ahead of time. The fact that an infrastructure for sports-related tourism had to be created in recent times is more obvious than the fact that government and business working together in partnership was the key to making the event, itself, successful in its chosen location.

Scaling the Atlanta Olympics model back in its application as a model for even a small, rural community, makes a clear case for establishing a tourism market based on heritage and cultural appeal. Consider the fact that Atlanta's Olympic heritage is now a part of its history.

At the beginning of the third chapter, "Product Development: Increasing Attractiveness to Tourists," of her book, *Partnerships for Prosperity—Museums and Economic Development*, Dr. Peggy Wireman wrote these words: "From the point of view of economic development, a museum is a product—something that attracts visitors...."

Relatively few traditional museums are operated as "for-profit" enterprises; nevertheless, they are important as economic development entities that complete the formula for success in attracting visitors to most communities. Dr. Wireman's definition of product from the cultural and heritage point of view, coupled with Mr. Kappel's suggestion that product is a place of interest to tourists, helps underscore what my imaginary model is meant to convey—the whole community must be given consideration as a product to develop. Consider the fact that Walt Disney World is a master-planned community, designed as a whole, to be nothing more than a tourist attraction. There are many facets to its success, not the least of which is its unified presentation as a community.

Using what I learned from Dr. Wireman and Mr. Kappel, I stress another important point that is directly aimed at the practice of economic development. Practitioners, professional and volunteers alike, must be willing to take on projects for not-for-profit cultural and heritage-related operations, such as museums, if they are to play a role in preparing their communities to attract visitors.

My point is strengthened by the example of the site selection project for the Mighty Eighth Air Force Heritage Museum near Savannah, Georgia. The museum was opened in early 1996 as a 90,000 of facility and an investment of more than $12 million—a location prize by comparison to any comparable manufacturing project. It is a noteworthy example also because the location project was a national site search conducted with the assistance of the American Association of Museums (AAM).

The Mighty Eighth's site search team targeted one community where the local economic development office simply showed no interest, apparently because it was not oriented towards assisting with the location of museum projects. I learned about the situation directly from a member of the site selection team, but it was later borne-out by my personal experience in the same community where there was inept handling of a second museum project. As of the writing of this paper, the latter project is still active with four locations under consideration, so I have chosen not to identify it. My point is to stress the importance for communities to orient their economic development towards the full spectrum of opportunities.

In order not to weigh my pursuit of a definition for tourism product totally towards the cultural and heritage interests, I turned to Bill Hardman, Sr., former president of the Southeast Tourism Society, and asked the question, "What is product?" He first defined tourism as the movement of people from one place to another for the purpose of occupying their leisure time in combination with the "...art of entertaining; the promotion of points of interest; and, accommodations for (those) seeking recreation and pleasure." In 1995 Mr. Hardman stated that "tourism product is whatever is put into the promotion." His examples of tourism product ranged from fulfilment pieces to trade shows. He also mentioned that it could be a whole community or an individual facility, such as a park (a site) or a hotel (a property). His definition included events as well as individual efforts to be hospitable and ranged from natural settings to man-made attractions and from public conveyances to pathways.

Mr. Hardman indicated those efforts to put tourism product in place, such as finding a site or property and developing it, are not product development! He said that, instead, "Once the product is in place, the efforts to promote it and put it to use in accordance with [his] tourism definition is product development." He emphatically stated that economic development is the process used to put product in place.

Gail R. Trussell, a commercial development specialist with the University of Missouri Extension Service, once defined tourism product as a place in a community where a cash register rings because a visitor from out-of-town has brought in money. After giving consideration to what various people, including those named above, have said and written about tourism product and its development, I concluded that it is what interests travellers and people seeking leisure-time activities. I also divided product into five categories, which are defined as follows:

- *events*: current and historic or cultural
- *locations*: man-made and natural environments (places with all their components sufficiently in place to attract the visitors)
- *properties*: sites and facilities
- *materials*: guides, books, maps (fulfilment pieces and promotional give-aways)
- *operations*: controlled functions and activities that attract and/or accommodate people.

Product development is the progression from idea to the realization of anyone of the categories listed above. My definition incorporates the activities that take place before a product is actually in place; therefore, for practical purposes it includes all of the elements that make it the same as economic development. Expanding on what Mr. Trussell said, tourism product development is setting up and getting ready to ring a cash register with new dollars brought into a community by visitors.

I see product development as a component of economic development. I also see commercial development, community development and industrial development as its components for the purpose of stressing the importance of the whole community as a place for economic development. I believe my argument is strengthened by examination of a definition of economic development from outside of my experience in the business.

This paper was written to serve both the community seeking to develop new business operations of interest to travellers and people seeking leisure-time activities, as well as business people who have decisions to make about starting-up new ventures—

people who need information and resources to help them with decision-making. It examines definitions and gives examples that are intended to stir creativity and guide towards decision within the economic development process. I am providing eight guiding statements in closing for...

Communities that want to develop infrastructure to attract tourists—For the community and its development leaders, this paper presents key words and phrases throughout. It is a general guide, but the key words and phrases are offered as specific things that I believe every economic development practitioner needs to know in order to be a leader in guiding his community in the development of an infrastructure to attract tourists. I offer the following words and phrases that I think are important to keep in mind:

- The *whole community* must be developed as a *tourist attraction.*
- Understanding the market and its potential is critical to tourism development.
- The most likely *prospects* for future business development *are local.*
- Entrepreneurs become complete prospects when *investors* Rand *developers* are added.
- First-time entrepreneurs and those opening new markets are *high-risk prospects.*
- Building relationships with *resource providers* and *allies* in *associations* is the most effective *strategy for recruiting* outside a community.
- *Not-for-profit attractions* can be *prospects* just like any other.
- Public/private *partnerships* put communities into the prospect formula.

I am also offering eight guiding statements for...

Entrepreneurs who need resources and cooperation from communities—The key words and phrases written into this paper are meant to serve the entrepreneur or business leader who has decisions to make about a community or market he has under consideration. I believe that we are in a time of change when economic development organizations are seriously gearing up to provide complete services to all prospects that offer opportunities to their communities. Prospects need to accept a role in shaping the community economic development organization. I offer the following key words and phrases that I hope will be helpful:

- The real estate industry owns the *lead position* in *commercial* economic development.
- Savvy economic developers work with local *real estate professionals*.
- When seeking community information, ask for an *economic development profile*.
- When seeking community information, ask for a checklist for starting-up a new business.
- Tell community leaders what local *economic impact* you expect your project to make.
- Tell economic developers what you want them to guard as *confidential information*.
- Work through trade *association(s)* to *find* economic development *contacts*.
- *Network* with economic developers who participate in your trade *association(s)*.

TOURISM AS PRODUCT

In marketing, a *product* is anything that can be offered to a market that might satisfy a want or need. It is of two types: *Tangible* (physical) and *Intangible* (non-physical). Since services have been at the forefront of all modern marketing strategies, some intangibility has become essential part of marketing offers. It is therefore the complete bundle of benefits or satisfactions that buyers perceive they will obtain if they purchase the product. It is the sum of all physical, psychological, symbolic and service attributes, not just the physical *merchandise*. All products offered in a market can be placed between Tangible (Pure Product) and Intangible (Pure Service) spectrum.

A product is similar to goods. In accounting, goods are physical objects that are available in the marketplace. This differentiates them from a service, which is a non-material product. The term *goods* is used primarily by those that wish to abstract from the details of a given product. As such it is useful in accounting and economic models. The term *product* is used primarily by those that wish to examine the details and richness of a specific market offering. As such it is useful to marketers, managers, and quality control specialists.

A service is a non-material or intangible product—such as professional consultancy, waitressing, or an entertainment experience.

Three Aspects

There are three aspects to any product or service:

1. Core Benefit
   - In-use benefits
   - Psychological benefits (e.g., self-image enhancement, hope, status, self worth)
   - Problem reduction benefits (e.g., safety, convenience)
2. Tangible Product or Service
   - Product attributes and features
   - benefits and useability of market
3. Intangible Product or Service

Classifying Products

Product management involves developing strategies and tactics that will increase product demand (referred to as primary demand) over the product's life cycle. One useful technique in understanding a product is the *Aspinwall Classification System*. It classifies and rates products based on five variables:

1. Replacement rate (how frequently is the product repurchased?)
2. Gross margin (how much profit is obtained from each product?)
3. Buyer goal adjustment (how flexible are the buyers' purchasing habits with regard to this product?)
4. Duration of product satisfaction (how long will the product produce benefits for the user?)
5. Duration of buyer search behaviour (how long will they shop for the product?)

Types of Products

There are several types of products:

- *Specialty goods*: extensive comparisons with other goods and a lengthy information search. Specialty goods are generally items that would fall into another category, but the seller of these goods has chosen a specific niche market and is extremely narrowly focused. An example would be a cigarette and tobacco shop, or a shop that only sold items with owl pictures on, or a shop that only sells books and magazines.

- *Unsought goods*: e.g., cemetery plots, insurance. These are products that we need but which we do not actively seek out to buy. They usually require a hard sell approach by the seller. Example, "what will happen to your family if you die and do not have life insurance?" The fear of leaving the family destitute makes us buy almost against our will, even though we know that it is the intelligent thing to do. Certain legal services such as drawing up a will, will also fall into this category.
- *Perishable goods*: goods that will deteriorate quickly even without use.
- *Durable goods*: goods that survive multiple use occasions, often further subdivided into 'white goods'.
- *Non-durable/consumption/consumable goods*: goods that are used up in one occasion.
- *Capital goods*: installations, equipment and buildings.
- *Parts and materials*: goods that go into a finished product.
- *Supplies and services*: goods that facilitate production.
- *Commodities*: undifferentiated goods (e.g., wheat, gold, sugar).
- *By-products*: a product that results from the manufacture of another product.

PRODUCT MANAGEMENT

Product management is an organizational function within a company dealing with the product planning or product marketing of a product or products at all stages of the product lifecycle.

Product management is also a collective term used to describe the broad sum of diverse activities performed in the interest of delivering a particular product to market.

From a practical perspective, product management is an occupational domain which hold two professional disciplines: product planning and product marketing. This is because the product's functionality is created for the user via product planning efforts, and product value is presented to the buyer via product marketing activities.

Product planning and product marketing are very different but due to the collaborative nature of these two disciplines, some companies erroneously perceive them as being one discipline, which they call product management. Done carefully, it is very possible to functionally divide the product management domain into product planning and product marketing, yet retain the required synergy between the two disciplines.

Product planning typically deals with these activities:

- Defining new products and gathering market requirements
- Product lifecycle considerations
- Product portfolio management
- Product differentiation.

Product marketing typically deals with these activities:

- Product positioning and outbound messaging
- Promoting the product externally with press, customers, and partners
- Bringing new products to market.

Product management typically deals with these closely-related functions:

- Product planning
- Product marketing
- Programme management
- Project management.

ECONOMICS AND ACCOUNTING

A good in economics is any object or service that, upon consumption, increases utility, and therefore can be sold at a price in a market.

If an object or service is sold for a positive price, then it is most likely a good since the purchaser considers the utility of the object or service more valuable than the money. Some objects are very rarely traded, such as air: it can be difficult to determine if such an object is a good or not.

In macro-economics and accounting, a good is contrasted with a service. A good here is defined as a physical product capable of being delivered to a purchaser and involves the transfer of ownership from seller to customer, as opposed to an intangible service. In micro-economics this distinction is rarely made.

Utility Characteristics of Goods

A good is an object whose consumption increases the utility of the consumer, for which the quantity demanded exceeds the quantity supplied at zero price. Goods are usually modeled as having decreasing marginal utility. The first car an individual purchases is very valuable; the fourth is much less useful. Thus, in these and similar goods, the marginal utility of additional units approaches zero as the quantity consumed increases. Assuming that one cannot re-sell it, there is a point at which a consumer would decline to purchase an additional car, even at a price very near zero. This is the consumer's satiation point.

In some cases, such as the above example of a car, the lower limit of utility as quantity increases is zero. In other goods, the utility of a good can cross zero, changing from positive to negative through time. This means that what initially is a good can become a bad if too much of it is consumed. For example, shots of vodka can have positive utility, but at some point for all consumers, additional units make the consumer less happy and can be injurious to the consumer's health.

In economics a bad is the opposite of a good. Ultimately, whether an object is a good or a bad depends on each individual consumer, and therefore, it is important to realize that not all goods are good all the time, and not all goods are goods to all people.

Types of Goods

Goods can be defined in a variety of ways, depending on a number a characteristics, these are listed in the table below:

collective good (*social good)*—private good— common good—common-pool resource—club good— public good rivalrous good and non-excludable good complement good vs. substitute good free good vs. scarce good, positional good durable good—non-durable good—intermediate good (*producer good*)—final good—consumer good—capital good. inferior good—normal good—ordinary good—Giffen good—luxury good—Veblen good—superior good search good—(post-) experience good—merit good— credence good—demerit good

TOURISM AND COMMUNITY DEVELOPMENT

Applied Research Clearinghouse

This applied research clearinghouse is designed to serve the needs of community development professionals and applied researchers working on tourism-related issues throughout the Lake States region. At this time, the clearinghouse of annotated resources has a focus on *economic impact analysis* and *recreation conflict.* Other modules will be developed at a later date.

Follow the link for the *Recreation Conflict* clearinghouse, an affiliated project which is sponsored by the Wisconsin Department of Natural Resources.

Economic Impact Analysis in Tourism

The core issues involved in economic impact analysis are the manner in which income is created and how this income flows through the local economy. It is hoped that this clearinghouse assists communities to better understand the impact of tourism on the local and regional economy. We have relied almost exclusively on tourism research, but in some cases good Lake States examples exist in other fields. With that in mind, the organization of the applied economic impact analysis literature is designed for two different types of users:

1. The practitioner wanting to learn more about the methodology of tourism economic impact analysis.
2. The practitioner wanting to see examples of how economic impact analysis has been applied to different components of the tourism industry in the Lake States.

We have not applied a strict definition of economic impact analysis and this clearinghouse includes much research that falls outside of many definitions of economic impact analysis. Community development practitioners are less concerned with definitions and more interested in answering questions. We conducted a thorough review of the economic impact analysis literature, but reviewed other subjects less comprehensively. This clearinghouse is designed to assist the practitioner in finding the right methodology or find examples of how their question has been tackled by other researchers. Not all studies are included in each inventory.

The clearinghouse is an update of the Regional Economic Impact Assessments: An Annotated Bibliography of Selected Wisconsin Studies completed by the Centre for Community Economic Development.

Methodology-Based Clearinghouse

Tourism Economic Impact Analysis

- Multipliers
- Input-Output Analysis
- Social Accounting Matrix
- Computable General Equilibrium
- Tourism Satellite Accounts
- "Hallmark" Events
- Other Methods
- Specific Issues
  - Conversion
  - Data Collection
  - Income Distribution
  - Employment, Seasonality and Distribution
  - Factor Analysis
  - Taxation and Fiscal Balance

Non-Market Goods Valuation

- Stated Preferences
  - Willingness to Pay
  - Contingent Valuation
- Revealed Preferences
  - Travel Cost Method
  - Hedonic Pricing Method
- Cost-Benefit Analysis

Tourism Demand

- Demand Forecasting Accuracy
- Forecasting—Quantitative Methods
  - Times-Series Models

- Exponential Smoothing
- Econometric Modelling
- Other Quantitative Methods

Forecasting—Qualitative Methods

- Delphi Method
- Judgement—Aided

Recreational Demand

Tourism Supply

Elements of Tourism Production

- Supply Metrics
- Market Structure
- Recreation Supply
- Spatial Description

Activity-Based Clearinghouse

Agritourism

Bed and Breakfasts

Arts Tourism

Cultural and Heritage Tourism

Destination Tourism

Fairs, Events and Conferences ("Hallmark Events")

Sports Teams and Venues

Recreation

- ATVs and Snowmobiling
- Canoeing, Kayaking and Whitewater Rafting
- Boating
- Hunting
- Lodges and Camping
- Parks and Trails
- Recreational Housing
- Sport Fishing
- Winter Recreation
- Wildlife Viewing

Community Wide Impacts

TOURISM INDUSTRY AS A SERVICE INDUSTRY

A couple of years ago a former state tourism minister claimed that Australia earned as much from a Japanese honeymoon couple holidaying in Australia for a week as it did from selling 50 tonnes of coal.

There is an old saying that comparisons are odious and in this instance I tend to agree. For a start, I doubt whether Japanese people particularly appreciate being compared to lumps of coal. Imagine New Zealand claiming that an Australian's five-day business trip to the Shakey Isles contributes as much to the Kiwi economy as the export of 10,000 lamb chops.

The point of these comparisons is, of course, is to prove that tourism is an important industry in the Australian economy. But I wonder whether it is not time to question the impact of the "cargo cult" mentality that grips much of the debate over tourism in Australia. Tourism has become the industry of hype. Our vision may becoming blurred as we perceive the world in terms of what is good for tourism and what is bad for tourism.

Let me give one example. You may have read in the newspapers a couple of weeks ago of the professional baseball team from Korea who were undergoing spring training on the Gold Coast. They were robbed on four separate occasions. Racist slurs were painted on the walls of their training centre. The Australian newspaper ran the following headline: "Racism puts Korean tourism at risk." The journalist assigned to this story was not, as you may expect, the newspaper's social affairs reporter but its tourism writer. In other words, the thrust of the story was not about the act of racism but about the impact of that act upon tourism. The issues of who the culprits might have been and why they might have perpetrated the act, were not raised. Local tourism officials, not the police, were interviewed.

The extent to which this incident reflects broader community attitudes toward the importance of tourism I will leave to your judgement. I, for one, however, feel that we have a problem when racist attacks on foreign guests are reported less as crimes and symptoms of social dysfunction but rather as impediments to the smooth growth in inbound tourism from an emerging market.

Clearly, the promotion of tourism as a major Australian industry over the past few years has been a success. But have we gone too far? Has our unrequited love affair with unbridled tourism blurred our reason and our objectivity?

For example, tourism is often touted as our fastest growing employment sector. We were told at the beginning of the 1990s by industry leaders and the Federal Government that tourism will generate 200,000 jobs during this decade.

Even the government would have to admit the chances of this figure being reached are slim. Moreover, the type of employment opportunities available are limited. Tourism is an industry typified by low-skill, part-time and poorly paid positions. The Department of Tourism admitted as such in a 1992 document which stated: "The industry's...capacity to employ those most affected by structural employment, such as unskilled and part-time, are industry attributes."

Similarly, the March 1993 issue of Bureau of Tourism Research (BTR)'s Tourism Update newsletter, draws the following conclusion: "Recent data indicate that employment changes in tourism industries over the past year have been more in line with rest of the economy, in that the number of persons in full-time employment is decreasing, while part-time employment is increasing." According to the BTR, two-thirds of employment in the 'restaurants, hotels and accommodation' sector, and ninety per cent in the airline industry, is attributable to tourism. Moreover, in 1992, the number of full-time employees in 'restaurants, hotels and accommodation' industry declined.

Debate over the tourism industry is fraught with methodological landmines. The first concerns the definition and quantification of the tourism industry; the second relates to the nature of tourism as a service industry. I will now turn to these two issues.

Defining the "Tourism" Industry

In 1992, the Commonwealth Government released a national tourism strategy under the title, "Tourism: Australia's Passport to Growth." Then Minister of Tourism, Alan Griffiths, in his preface to the report, stated that tourism "has matured into a prominent, sophisticated industry...".

But what is the tourism industry? And who are its participants? The Australian Bureau of Statistics does not recognise tourism as a discrete industry and has no definition for "tourism". This should not surprise since tourism is not an industry to begin with. Rather it is an amalgam of diverse industries or sectors that directly or indirectly cater to the needs of the tourist.

It is this diversity that has proved the biggest stumbling block in the tourism industry's battle over the past ten years to legitimate itself in the eyes of the Australian public and governments (federal, state and local). Factors such as the diversity and geographical spread of the tourism product, as well as the competing interests among tourism sectors, are the main reasons for this constant struggle for recognition.

The Australian Travel Industry Association, or ATIA, lists five direct commercial sectors under the tourism umbrella: accommodation, transport carriers, attractions, tour operators and wholesalers, promotions and distributions, and retail services. Yet even these categories are arbitrary. For example, the 1993 ATIA Award for "Best Major Attraction" was awarded to the National Art Gallery and the runner-up was Warner Bros. Movie World. Considering that Uluru falls under the attraction label, the definitions of tourist product types can become fuzzy indeed.

Tourism is our biggest foreign exchange earner but neither AUSTRADE nor JETRO has the expertise or capabilities to support tourism operators in the Japanese market. There are two reasons for this: first, tourism services are not consumed in Japan and therefore, the benefits are less readily visible, and second, the Australian Tourist Commission is perceived as the government agency that assist tourist "exporters" in selling to foreign markets. But I ask the question: Is the geographical location of the transaction sufficient reason for government agencies to withhold assistance to Australian tourism operators? I would like to turn to the characteristics of the industry that we call "tourism."

Characteristics of Tourism as a Service Industry

The tourism industry, and the products and services that fall under its wide umbrella, are complex indeed. There are a number of features that make it unique.

Tourism is a subjective experience and an amalgam of products and services not a single product

- Tourism products, like all services, are intangible. A Sydney Harbour cruise, a stroll through a North Queensland rainforest or a champagne dinner at Uluru at sunset are intangibles. They cannot be seen, touched, felt or sampled before purchase.

  The selling of tourism is the selling of images. The Australian Tourist Commission in Japan does not sell

Australian tourism products, it sells what we may call a shifting generic image of Australia. Today's images of Australia are the Great Barrier Reef and happy, smiling Aboriginals. A few years ago it was Paul Hogan's "throw another shrimp on the barbie." Next came Greg Norman who urged foreigners to swing on down to Australia. While the ATC sells images of Australia to attract Japanese to our shores, the delivery of the tourist product depends on the individual tourism operators and marketers. I will return to this subject later.

- The tourism product is not a homogeneous product. We cannot standardize a service. Hotels attempt to standardize their room and service delivery as efficiently as possible through staff training and quality control procedures, but the human ingredient complicates the equation. As most services require interaction between the producer and consumer, each with their own set of expectations, it is highly unlikely that any product can ever be perceived equally by all customers. External factors can also affect the tourist experience. A bumpy flight can spoil an overseas trip and rain can ruin a Gold Coast stay.
- Tourism products are perishable. An unsold Park Grand hotel room, an unused Qantas aircraft seat and a vacant Opera House concert seat is revenue lost. They cannot be stored for later use, as can tangible products. Hence, the prevalence of discounting in services.
- This leads to the major problem confronting the tourism operator: namely, demand fluctuation. Tourism is perhaps more vulnerable than any other industry to seasonal fluctuations in demand. Demand fluctuation can be unseen, sometimes due to natural causes, others man-made. Acts of God include climate and natural disasters (Guam was devastated by a typhoon and an earthquake within the space of a few weeks). Acts of man include strikes (domestic pilots' strike) and international events (Gulf War) and murders (tourist murders in Florida). In the Australia-Japan context, you will remember the case of the disappearing honeymoon bride in Sydney and the enormous concerns that generated among those involved in Japanese travel to Australia.

Small Business Industry

Tourism has been described as the classic small-business industry. According to the Department of Tourism, for example, more than 70 per cent of businesses in the hospitality sector employ less than ten persons. One of the reasons for the small business concentration is the ease of entry into the industry. Anyone with a yacht, a farm, or a four-wheel drive can set up business targeting tourists. A very successful new entrant in the Sydney tourism scene is the company that takes tourists for city sight-seeing tours on the back of a Harley-Davidson.

Decentralized Industry

Tourism is a diversified and decentralized industry, as I mentioned earlier. The commercial imperatives that drive tourism change according to the location; as do the environmental, social and cultural impacts of tourism on particular communities. Different tourism product have different trade associations, such as hotels, marine parks or inbound operators. Regional, as well as urban, areas have their own associations, as disparate as the North Queensland Conservation Council and the Darling Harbour Authority. Professional associations involved in tourism, such as the Professional Tour Guide Association of Australia, represent another interest group. And the list goes on.

Private-Sector Driven

Governments provide relatively little assistance to the tourism industry. The hotel industry has staged a long, hard battle to gain recognition as a service exporter such that it can be deserving of export grants. In general, the entrepreneur is left to fend for himself or herself. Having said that, it is governments that shape the environment in which the industry operates. They provide much of the infrastructure and services used by tourists and the industry generally—these include promotion and information services, the provision of roads, airports, railways and harbours, the management of national parks, visas and customs services, research and statistical data, education and training programmes and various public amenities. Similarly, the ATC plays the critical role of promoting travel to Australia in overseas markets. No single private tourism operation, with exception of Qantas, could afford to market directly to the foreign consumer.

The Problem of Over-Consumption

Tourism must be one of the few industries in which too many customers can be detrimental. This can apply to the social and environmental impact on local communities, as this quote from the Economist indicates.

> *"There is some consensus that crude numbers are not a good indication of the contribution of tourism to a local economy. The more tourists you have the more expensive infrastructure you have to provide for them, the quicker your environment will be degraded past a point of diminishing returns."— Economist*

The argument can be extended to other areas. It is well-known that several leading hotels and resorts in Australia have a policy of restricting the number of Japanese guests in their properties. The concern of course is that the property will be seen as "too Japanese." Let me add hastily that Japanese travel companies often support such policies because Japanese travellers themselves often complain of seeing too many other Japanese.

High Inter-dependency Among Sectors

A feature of tourism is its high degree of inter-relatedness. For example, resort or hotel development cannot begin without adequate airports and roads to bring tourists to those properties. The explosive development of Cairns, for example, was sparked by the purchase of the airport by a private consortium with vision. This situation is a classic chicken-and-egg scenario. A topical example is the development of the Northern Territory as a northern gateway into Australia and as a tourism attraction in its own right. In Darwin, tourist infrastructure is insufficient for large numbers of tourists from Japan and investment in accommodation facilities in the Top End will depend heavily on strong signs of demand.

Tourism and Profitability

An irony of the hype surrounding tourism is that many sectors under the tourism umbrella complain of poor profits. A 1991 survey of hotels around the world by consultants Horwath and Horwath showed that Australia's hotels had the worst profit record. Australian hotels returned –3.3 per cent on funds invested, Asian hotels had 27.1 per cent, Europe 16.6 per cent and even a high-cost country such as Canada had 12.1 per cent.

Ross Woods, one of the most respected analysts in tourism development was quoted in the Business Review Weekly as arguing that the Australia tourism industry still has not tackled the three issues that most affect profitability. These are: firstly, higher building costs than Asia or the US, such that the capital outlay per room or bed is much higher; secondly, hotel and resorts operating costs are too high, especially compared with competing resorts in Asia and the Pacific; thirdly, Australian hotels and resorts have very seasonal and highly unpredictable occupancies and cash flows.

The investment disasters of the 1980s were chastening experiences, to say the least, for local banks who became involved in the tourism industry. Since then, banks have become extremely wary about any project that smacks of tourism. A couple of years ago a function was held in Sydney to raise the problem of a lack of investment funds in the tourism industry. Government officials and financial executives were invited. No banks or institutions attended. When asked why he did not attend, a finance executive said his organization was not prepared to spend $68 to attend the seminar because "it was not willing to invest this much on tourism."

The Department of Tourism, in an attempt to coax institutional investors back into the muddied waters of tourism investment, established the Tourism Forecasting Council in 1993. Its primary aim is to convince bankers that tourism has a future and a profitable one.

The Australian tourism industry today the biggest buzz word is "yield." Many operators are concerned that the increase in inbound tourists, for example, has not been paralleled by a rise in revenue and profits. One senior tourism executive coined the phrase "profitless volume" to describe this situation. Concerns over yield are not limited to Australia. In Japan the big wholesalers such as JTB face a similar predicament.

Seller's Market

Two tourism academics make the interesting observation that tourism is one of the last industries to experience the change from a seller's to a buyer's market. As a result, they argue, "marketing techniques... are still less advanced than those in branded goods industries, where managers have been accustomed to a fastidious and discriminating customer for years." Plainly, in the Japanese outbound market, the shift from a seller's to a buyer's market is taking place right now. Japanese travellers' interests and needs are changing rapidly and the major wholesalers are struggling to respond effectively. Increasingly, today's Japanese traveller wants to make his or her decision about tourist activities, wants more free time and less expensive accommodation. As a result, the wholesalers are finding their market shares under threat from emerging discount travel companies.

Marketing Australian Tourism to the Japanese

This discussion about the shift in consumer preferences leads me to the issue of how we market Australia tourism products to the Japanese.

Tourism is a relatively young industry and the learning curve for many practioners is understandably steep. There are only a handful of tourism practioners in Australia with more than a few years experience in the Japanese market. These men and women have extensive contacts in Japan, which they visit regularly; they are sensitive to the needs of their Japanese customers, both the consumer and the wholesaler, and they are open-minded to change and to new ideas. For the relative newcomer, however, things are tougher.

The challenge facing the industry problem is the lack of marketing orientation by tourism promoters and suppliers. Here I identify several main areas. First, there is an emphasis on sales and promotion at the exclusion of a thorough understanding of the distribution systems in outbound Japanese tourism. Second, fierce price competition among individual suppliers, particularly in the hotel sector, is widespread. Third, there is an underutilization of market research into the changing trends in Japanese tourism to Australia. The Japanese market is fundamentally different from our other major inbound markets. Different questions need to be asked, different solutions need to be found. Fourth, there is a reliance on simplistic forms of demographic segmentation, such as honeymooners, OLs and silver market. Tourism managers need to adopt more sophisticated approaches to market segmentation that bundle together travellers' interests and motivations.

The second issue about marketing to the Japanese traveller concerns what I call the "black box" phenomenon. The Australian Tourist Commission (ATC) promotes Australia to the Japanese through visual images. The ATC's primary role to get the Japanese traveller to decide to travel to Australia. In so doing, the ATC takes no responsibility for either price or the delivery and quality of tourism products; it does assume some responsibility for distribution. It remains the task of the individual suppliers to satisfy the needs of Japanese travellers once that decision to travel to Australia has been made.

Here a problem arises. Since tourism is a small business industry, most tourism operators do not have the financial or managerial capability to take full advantage of the opportunities in the rapidly diversifying Japanese travel market. There is a yawning marketing gap between ATC's promotional activities and the capability of Australia to offer Japanese, and indeed any international visitor, the full range of tourism product available around Australia. I believe we need an intermediary promoting body in Australia that is charged with the responsibility of ensuring the offer and delivery of quality tourism product to all international travellers, including the Japanese. The state tourism organizations have entered into an agreement with the ATC under a scheme called Partnership Australia to jointly promote Australia overseas and in Australia, but it remains to be seen how effective it is in overcoming resistance to cooperative marketing by our leading tourism states of NSW and Queensland.

Finally, I would like to offer some observations about trends in Japanese travel to Australia.

Overseas travel was the last industry in Japan to be affected by the current Japanese recession. Japanese outbound growth turned negative from late 1992 through the first half of 1993. Since August last year, however, growth has recovered. (While the first six months of last year saw a 5.3 per cent drop in outbound travel, the second half was up 7.3 per cent on the same period in 1992.)

Travel to Australia, however, has remained firm throughout. In 1993, 671,000 Japanese travelled to Australia, an increase of some 6.5 per cent over 1992. Although this is less than the ATC's bullish target of a 16 per cent increase for Japan, the good news is that Australia managed to increase its market share of the total outbound market (5.3 per cent to 5.6 per cent).

In closing let me say that the future of Japanese travel to Australia remains bright. The economic benefits accruing to Australia through international tourists such as the Japanese are undeniable, even if some of the claims made about tourism are overly optimistic. My concern is that we are in danger of losing sight of the more qualitative benefits of tourism, namely, increased cultural understanding through greater human interaction.

Australia and Japan have always had a complementary relationship. Before World War II, we supplied wool for the Japanese textile industry. After the war we supplied raw materials for Japan's value-added products. Now in the 1990s, we are supplying tourism and leisure products for Japanese tourists.

Hopefully neither side will forget that tourism relies, ultimately, on people. It is people who produce and deliver tourist products and services and it is people who consume them. In that interaction lies the great challenge for tourism managers. And in that interaction lies the potential of a memorable tourism experience for Japanese and indeed all travellers to this land of ours.

NEW PATHS FOR INTERNATIONAL TOURISM

When delegates at the 1992 Rio Earth Summit drafted their long-range blueprint for action, *Agenda 21*, they made little reference to the environmental and social impacts of one of the world's most rapidly growing industries—tourism.

Since Rio, international concern about the sustainability of tourism has grown steadily. Countries have endorsed declarations on a wide range of related topics, including tourism and sustainable development, the social impact of tourism, tourism and biodiversity, and tourism and ethics. In 1996, in an effort to integrate tourism into broader sustainability discussions, the World Tourism Organization, the World Travel and Tourism Council, and the Earth Council released their own action-plan, *Agenda 21 for the Travel and Tourism Industry*, outlining key priorities for governments, the industry and others.

International discussion about tourism's impacts has taken on even greater momentum in 2002, as the U.N.-declared "International Year of Ecotourism" gets underway. The year will be marked by a series of multi-stakeholder meetings and a World Ecotourism Summit in Quebec in May 2002.

Tourism will also be an important topic at the upcoming World Summit on Sustainable Development in Johannesburg. It is a particularly relevant area of focus for the conference's "type two" initiatives—partnership agreements that will identify areas for practical, action-oriented cooperation among key stakeholders, including industries, governments, international institutions and non-governmental groups.

The importance of addressing tourism's impacts worldwide cannot be understated. By some estimates, tourism is now the world's largest industry—in 2000, it generated an estimated $3.6 trillion in economic activity and accounted for one in every 12 jobs worldwide. Tourism is especially important in the developing world—it is the only economic area where developing countries consistently run a trade surplus. But the industry's rapid growth has placed a heavy burden on local economies, cultures, and environments. Uncontrolled tourism development is stressing many of the planet's most sensitive locations.

As the World Summit negotiations begin, Worldwatch encourages participants to work together to develop practical initiatives to minimize tourism's negative impacts while boosting its benefits for local communities and the environment.

The Tourism Industry

Many tourism businesses are beginning to take positive steps to become more environmentally and socially responsible. But long-term sustainability will require deeper changes in the way the industry operates. Self-interest may very well drive this shift: while declines in environmental quality can hit industry pocketbooks directly, evidence is accumulating that adopting more sensitive practices and helping to make destinations more attractive can lower costs and boost profits over the long-term.

Priorities for Action:

- Restructure management and operations along environmental lines, including reducing consumption of water, energy, and other resources and improving management, handling and disposal of waste.
  Between 1988 and 1995, Inter-Continental Hotels reduced overall energy costs by 27 per cent. It saved $3.7 million in 1995 alone, cutting sulfur dioxide emissions by 10,670 kilograms and saving 610,866 cubic meters of water—an average water reduction of nearly 7 per cent per hotel, despite higher occupancies.
- Accelerate the transfer of environmentally sound technologies, practices, and management tools to the developing world, including desalination plants and other

water-saving systems, renewable energy technologies, and ecologically sound chemical management practices.

- Develop voluntary "codes of conduct" to regulate the environmental and social impacts of staff and clients, and ensure that compliance with these codes is adequately monitored.
  Under the International Association of Antarctic Tour Operators' voluntary code of conduct, the 40 member tour operators are required to land no more than 100 people per site at a time and to make sure that visitors do not disturb wildlife.
- Adopt and participate in voluntary certification schemes that grant a seal of approval to companies or destinations that demonstrate environmentally or socially sound practice.
  Europe's Blue Flag Campaign awards a yearly "eco-label" to some 2,750 beaches and marinas in 21 countries for their high environmental standards and safe, sanitary facilities.

Government

Governments will need to play a proactive role in supporting the growth of sustainable tourism. Regulatory and policy frameworks can be altered to support key environmental and social goals, without stifling incentives for investment.

Priorities for Action:

- Encourage tourism planning authorities at the national, regional, and local levels to incorporate key social and environmental goals.
  In 1997, the Council of Europe recommended that member governments limit tourism development to a level compatible with ecological and social carrying capacity, including supporting activities that benefit local communities and controlling coastal construction.
- Integrate the development of sustainable tourism projects and facilities into overall land-use plans.
  At Cuba's Cayo Coco, hotels must be no more than four stories high and are required to be set back from the beach. Each new building must go through an extensive government environmental impact assessment before construction is approved.

- Develop regulations and policies that support smaller-scale tourism initiatives that are actively planned and managed by local communities. For example, governments can boost local land and resource ownership and market access by offering incentives like tax breaks, special interest rates, or micro-enterprise loans, providing low-cost licensing, or offering training in languages, small business development and marketing.
The Namibian government allows local communities to assume legal responsibility for zoning their own agriculture, wildlife, and tourism activities in multiuse areas called conservancies. Residents oversee these activities and can derive direct financial benefit from them.
- Impose tourist quotas or encourage the use of taxes, entry fees, and other economic instruments that reflect the environmental and social costs of tourism services.
The Himalayan kingdom of Bhutan practices an official policy of "high-value, low-volume" tourism. It accepted only 7,500 visitors in the year 2000, at a cost of $250 each per day.
- Support and implement regional and global environmental treaties that relate to tourism, such as the climate change and biodiversity conventions.

Non-Governmental Organizations (NGOs) and International Institutions

Non-governmental players—such as citizen groups and grassroots activists—have played an important role in generating much of the pressure for more sustainable tourism. International institutions such as the World Bank and UNEP have also stepped up their support for sustainable tourism, including engaging in efforts to create benchmarks for sustainable tourism that will make it easier for governments and businesses to measure progress.

Priorities for Action:

- Discourage unsustainable and inappropriate tourism developments.
In April 2001, local and international activist groups helped convince the Mexican government to revoke permits for five hotel companies to build resorts, golf courses, and other facilities at a 165-hectare stretch of beach south of Cancun that is home to 40 protected species.

- Help raise awareness of tourism's negative impacts through information campaigns and training.
  The World Travel and Tourism Council has created a video series on tourism's environmental impact aimed at airlines and schools.
- Encourage tourists to engage in environmentally and culturally sensitive behaviour, including supporting businesses that are locally run and staffed, that seek to minimize their environmental and cultural impacts, or that donate a share of their profits to local community or conservation efforts.
  The Vermont-based International Ecotourism Society helps travellers choose responsible tour operators and guides and offers "green" travel advice on their website.

NOTES

1. World's top 25 tourist destinations. World Tourism (2005).
2. Werner Hunziker and Kurt Krapf (1941). *Grundriss der allgemeinen Fremdenverkehrslehre*. OCLC # 69064371.
3. *Long-term Prospects*: Tourism 2020 Vision. World Tourism (2004).

2

Tourism Product Development: Issues and Options

Tourism Product means different things to the various members of the tourism industry. To the hotel it is 'guest-nights'. To the airline it is the 'seats flown' and the 'passenger miles'. To the museum, art gallery or archaeological site, the product is measured in terms of the number of visitors. For the tourist the product is the complete experience resulting from the package tour or travel facility purchased, from the time they leave home until their return.

For example, the Chennai-based Locus Technologies has launched an online tourism product—eshubyatra—mainly for travel agents and chain of hotels. The ASP model will be leased out to prospective clients to help cut their initial investment. The product will be promoted by straight line marketing method of offering single user licence. The company aims to market 150 products within three years.

Past marketing literature have seldom reported the use of sophisticated marketing research tools to develop new products in the tourism sector. When Indian tourism sector is in the process of growth it is wise to look at the developments that are taking place in the field of marketing research. The authors in the current paper suggest a marketing research method dentified as conjoint analysis and show the power and flexibility of this technique in developing new tourism products. Conjoint analysis is described as an emerging dependence technique that has brought new sophistication to the evaluation of objects, whether they are new products, services or ideas. The strength of this method lies in its most direct application in new product or service development. This is efficiently done by allowing for the evaluation of complex products while maintaining a realistic decision context for the respondent.

GROUP TOURIST ACCOMMODATION AS PRODUCT

Tourist accommodation is the first product group for awarding the European Eco-label to a service. The consideration of a service as an Eco-label product group has been made possible by the new Regulation 1980/2000 which states that "products" are to include both "goods and services" (Art. 1.1). The feasibility study FEMATOUR (feasibility and market study for a European Eco-label for tourist accommodations), conducted by the CREM and CH2MHILL and finished in August 2000, recognizes the complexity of this product group which is composed by two basic elements: the tourist structure which offers the service and the service itself. For this reason this product group has a complexity which previous Eco-label product groups have not shown. The project carried out by ANPA in collaboration with the Greek Competent Body, ASAOS, aims to develop ecological criteria for the European Eco-label defining the contents of the product group tourist accommodation.

Product Group Definition

The product group "tourist accommodation" has been defined according to the Commission Decision 99/35/EC implementing the Council Directive 95/57/EC on the collection of statistical data in tourism. The Commission Decision defines tourist accommodation as *"any facility that regularly or occasionally provides overnight accommodation for tourists."* The Commission Decision defines the different types of tourist accommodations and identifies some services which they provide. From an analysis of the document it is clear that tourist accommodation implies the consideration of two elements: structure and service.

STRUCTURE, as can be inferred from the Commission Decision, stands for the disposition of the space and the facilities given to the guest. Structure determines the type of accommodation (hotels, youth hostels, Bed & Breakfast (B & B), farmhouses, campsites...).

The structure alone, however, does not make the "tourist accommodation." Always from the analysis of the Commission Decision, it can be said that accommodation implies the supply of services.

SERVICES represent the opportunities offered to the guest. They are the activities which give life to the structures.

The EC Regulation 1980/2000 is addressed to services which have a life cycle that consists in three phases: "purchase of the goods necessary to provide the service", "provision and use of the service" and "management of waste." The services offered by tourist accommodation structures are varied and each type of service has its environmental impacts. Deciding which services to include in the product group means to decide the sources of the environmental impacts that will be considered.

Finding the starting point to define the product group "tourist accommodation" is complex and it can stem from one of the above stated fundamental elements, the structure and the service, which brings to two different approaches: the "structure oriented approach" in which the focus point is the structure, the "service oriented approach" where the focus points the service.

Thus, the "service oriented approach" focuses on the main accommodation service common to all different types of structures (for the services present in tourist accommodation: sleeping common activities, recreational... cfr. Table 2.1), while the "structure oriented approach" focuses on all the services provided by a particular kind of accommodation (e.g. hotels, campsites, hostels, B & B, etc.).

These two approaches have been described in the first activity report. Regarding the service oriented approach, the service "sleeping" was pointed out as the main service common to all tourist accommodation structures (see Table 2.1).

Table 2.1: Consideration of Tourist by Structure and by Service

	Accommodation (Structure)					
Service use phases	*Hotels*	*Campsites (only bungalows)*	*Youth hotels*	*Alpine shelters*	*Agri-Tourism*	*Bed & Breakfast*
Sleeping	×	×	×	×	×	×
Food services	×					
Common services	×					
Recreational activities	×					
Transport activities	×					
Communication	×					

Source: ANPA, 2000.

Paragraph 4.4.1 of the first activity report points out some pro and contras of the two approaches.

The two different approaches were presented during the first AHWG meeting held in Rome on 26 November, 2000. Results coming from the discussion were that *it is necessary to consider both approaches in the product group definition* as the core of tourist accommodation lies in the union of the two aspects (structure and service). Therefore, the product group definition should be based on the integration of the two approaches.

The discussion focussed mainly on the activities which the service "sleeping" would include.

It is also important to remind that the European Eco-label is addressed to product and services and not to producers or productive sites such as for example the hotel structure.

These considerations have brought to the concept of lodging as product group.

Lodging in tourist accommodation is a service which is connected to the structure of accommodation. The definition of lodging for the European Eco-label product group which considers the Commission Decision and the AHWG discussion is:

> "the provision of sheltered overnight stay structured in rooms, with all their contents, including at least a bed fit for use, offered as main service to tourists behind a fee."

This definition points out the five dimensions in which the lodging concept can be identified:

1. Provision of a room.
2. Provision of a bed.
3. Being the main service of the accommodation.
4. Application of a fee for the service.
5. Being addressed to tourists.

These dimensions and their compliance with Regulation requirements are explained below:

Provision of a Room and a Bed Fit for Use

The first two dimensions relate to structure requirements and mainly identify the concept of lodging as service used by tourists. It is in the provision of a room and a bed which is the core of the service that the consumer may use and to which also lie most environmental impacts. Therefore, it is there that the improvements resulting from the adoption of Eco-label criteria could be greatest (requirement of Reg. 1980/2000, Art.1). In addition, as emerged from the AHWG discussion, the provision of the room and the bed constitutes the main income for the internal market from tourist overnight stay. Thus, the inclusion of the "room and bed" dimension further complies with Art. 2.2.a of Regulation 1980/2000.

Lodging as the Main Purpose of the Accommodation

The third dimension relates to the purpose of the tourist accommodation. There are some structures where the provision of lodging is secondary to other purposes. These are referred to by the Commission Decision as "specialized establishments" (beauty farms, conference centres, public means of transport). In order to comply with the Regulation requirements on the matters of purpose, use and consumer perception (Reg. 1980/2000, Art. 1.1) such structures should be excluded from consideration.

Fee Applied to the Lodging

There are instances where lodging is provided for free: in private accommodation for friends and relatives, for example, or instances where payment cannot be directly related to the lodging. Those cases should not be included in product group definition in that they do not fulfil the requirement of representing "a significant volume of sales and trade in the internal market" as required by Reg. 1980/2000, Art. 2.2.a.

Lodging be Addressed to Tourists

It is obvious that the service provided by tourist accommodation is mainly addressed to tourist. The Commission Decision defines the tourist as a visitor who stays at least one night in a collective or private accommodation of the place/country visited. This place is other than his/her usual environment, the stay does not last more than 12 months and the main purpose of the visit is not the exercise of an activity remunerated from within the place visited.

Product Group Description

According to the Commission Decision 35/99/EC, the types of tourist accommodation which would be included in the product group by considering the provision of lodging as the fulcrum of tourist accommodation are the following:

Collective Accommodation

- Hotels (including motels, beach hotels, tourist resorts and all those accommodation giving hotel services)

- Similar establishments (boarding houses, tourist residence, bed and breakfast, farmhouse)
- Other types of collective accommodation (campsites with bungalows, holiday houses, youth hostels, group accommodation in general).

Private Accommodations

- Rented rooms in family houses
- Dwellings rented from private individuals or professional agencies
- Other types of private accommodations.

In the heterogeneity of these structures the standard for criteria development is given by considering in each structure its main service: lodging.

It is of course important to define which services would be included in lodging.

In this respect, the most relevant services related to the provision of the "room" and the "bed fit for use" will be considered. This includes first of all consumer use of all that is inside the room, the use of sanitary facilities, the activities related to reception and information, and the cleaning of all facilities related to the provision of the sheltered overnight stay. Breakfast will be included as part of the lodging service, all other food service such as restaurant service will be excluded.

As regards to restaurant service it is important to point out that Eco-label does not include food products as possible product groups, so that in this area of activity only management activities could be considered. That information on Eco-label criteria were easily available for the consumer would be a requirement itself of the Eco-label.

All services will be considered in the three phases of their life cycle: purchase of the goods to provide the service, use of the service, management of waste.

Referring to the classification reported in Table 2.1, *the services which are included in the product group definition* are all those related to the following:

- "sleeping" (use of room, cleaning of room and private sanitary facilities)
- "reception service"
- "food services" including breakfast excluding restaurant service

- "common services" such as common sanitary facilities
- "communication" which includes all that takes place in the back office.

The accommodation structures considered would be all those complying with the definition of lodging, as reported in Table 2.2.

Then the identification of the product group would be renamed as: "LODGING IN TOURIST ACCOMMODATION," with lodging defined as above and including the above listed services.

Considering what other institutions have said about product group definition for tourist accommodation, it can be also reminded that:

- some Competent Bodies have expressed their opinion in favour of considering hotels as product group, or hostels, or farmhouses, as of Fematour conclusions;
- hotels certainly have a wide distribution and a great part of the market, however, the definition of lodging and the inclusion in the product group of all those structures which comply with that definition allows to consider a wider market share and, moreover, a share which is geographically more widely distributed and reaches a greater number of Small and Medium Enterprises;
- as far as hostels and farmhouses are concerned, their distribution is growing fast but for now it is certainly minimal compared to other accommodations and the effort of developing European Eco-label criteria may not be worthy;
- EEC was in favour of considering more accommodation structures following a wider approach;
- referring to the new product group definition it is important to point out that the exclusion of food service (restaurant service) and recreational services is due to the fact that these services are not the main purpose of the product group for the consumer and furthermore in consideration to the fact that they can be provided outside the tourist accommodation also from other specific tourist facilities (restaurants, sport centre, etc.). The award of the European Eco-label to these services when offered inside tourist accommodation could lead to the discrimination of those services which are provided outside tourist accommodation.

Table 2.2: Tourist Accommodations as Classified by Commission Decision Linked to the Concept of LODGING

Accommodation Type	*Rooms*	*Bed*	*Specific lodging fee*	*Main activity*	*Tourist as final consumer*
HOTELS					
Hotels	×	×	×	×	×
Motels	×	×	×	×	×
Apt. Hotels	×	×	×	×	×
Roadside inns	×	×	×	×	×
Beach hotels	×	×	×	×	×
Residential clubs	×	×	×	×	×
SIMILAR ESTABLISHMENTS					
Boarding houses	×	×	×	×	×
Tourist residence	×	×	×	×	×
B&B	×	×	×	×	×
Farmhouse	×	×	×	?	×
OTHER COLLECTIVE ACCOMMODATION					
Holiday houses (without hotel services)	×	×	×	×	×
Campsites (for tents, trailers and caravans)	some	×	×	×	×
Marinas	no	no	?	?	×
Youth hostels	×	×	×	×	×
Tourist dormitories	×	×	×	×	×
Group accommodation	×	×	×	×	×
Holiday homes for elderly, employees, workers, students	×	×	×	×	×
Mountain refuses	×	some	×	×	×
SPECIALIZED ESTAB.					
Health establishments	×	×	×	no	×
Work and holiday camps (scout, archeological, ecological, mountain	some	some	×	×	×
Public means of transport	×	×	×	no	×
Conference centres	no	no	no	no	×
PRIVATE ACCOMMODATION					
Rented rooms in family houses	×	×	×	?	×
Dwellings rented from private individuals or professional agencies	×	×	×	?	×
OTHER TYPES OF PRIVATE ACCOMMODATION					
Secondary residence (incl. time-sharing)	×	×	no	?	×
Accommodation provided without charge to friends and relatives	×	×	no	no	×

In Table 2.2, the compliance of different types of tourist accommodations, defined in accordance with the Commission Decision 35/99/EC, to the five points of the definition of lodging is reported.

HERITAGE TOURISM PRODUCT DEVELOPMENT

What is a tourism "product?" We usually consider products to be something a customer buys and takes home with them, and that is exactly what happens with effective heritage tourism—the customer buys an experience and takes home the memories. They may also take home souvenirs, clothes, and maybe a few extra pounds around the middle, but those are meaningless without being connected to the experience. The real heritage tourism product is the experience.

Heritage tourism products differ from many other tourism products in that they are based on the characteristics of a real, authentic place that already exists. You do not have to build Disney World. You may not have to build anything at all, so the cost to develop heritage tourism products is low compared to a resort or theme park.

When we think about heritage tourism product development we must think about developing experiences based on the characteristics of our communities and rural countryside that are meaningful to our potential customers. What are those experiences and how do we develop them into products? This chapter will answer those questions with real life examples.

Experience is the Product

Tourists want something different from their daily lives. Because most visitors come from modern cities, the experience of spending time in a small town or a rural area is attractive and meaningful to them. This is even more so if the area has a particular ethnic background, its history is well told, and its natural heritage is explained in a compelling way.

Fredericksburg, Texas, is a good example. Some people, including a few residents, may think things are overdone in Fredericksburg. However, Fredericksburg's tourism provides a strong economic base that maintains property values, personal incomes, and tax revenues. Although there are some negative impacts of tourism in Fredericksburg, critics should consider what the town would be like without its tourism economy.

What is the product of Fredericksburg—what experiences does the visitor have there that cause them to return and bring their friends? The most obvious experience is the sense of being in a Texas German Community of the 1800s. That experience comes from the architecture, the overall layout of the town, the special historic buildings, the German-theme shops, restaurants and festivals, and even hearing people speak German. All these offer a dramatic contrast to Houston or Dallas and provide memorable experiences. Imagine the surprise of visitors when they hear cowboys in a restaurant speaking German!

Fredericksburg has concentrated on heritage tourism development for more than thirty years, and it had a good head start with its strong ethnic background and well-maintained historic buildings. But is the tourism product limited to towns like Fredericksburg? No, every place can be interesting and can attract visitors. Remember, people go to ghost towns or even the sites of ghost towns! Every place has a story.

In fact, towns and rural areas should not try to become "tourist" places. Visitors want a sense of authenticity. If things are overly contrived visitors will be offended by the "tourist trap." Fayetteville, Texas, is a good example of a small farming community that attracts visitors by simply being itself, keeping things cleaned up, and being friendly to people. Fayetteville is a Czechoslovakian/Polish community off the main road between LaGrange and Columbus. Local bands play polkas on Saturday nights in the little ice cream parlour/tavem, where families have danced for generations and visitors are welcome. Some of the houses have been turned into bed-and-breakfasts and some have been purchased by out-of-towners as weekend/retirement places. All in all, the town looks like it did fifty or seventy years ago and local businesses are viable.

How can we apply the experiences of Fredericksburg, Fayetteville, and other towns? What are the essential elements of a heritage tourism product that can be found in virtually any small town? The primary parts of a heritage product are historical events, ethnicity, architecture, natural features, and the daily life of the community, but it is the story of these that makes them into an experience for the visitor. The following paragraphs suggest some ways to discover and use each of these essential elements.

- *Historical events*: Every place has a history. People came from somewhere and settled there for some reason. They started farms and businesses. They fought in wars and with each other. Some of them became famous and some infamous. We should not think of "history" as it is often taught in schools—the presidents, generals and battles. Instead, we should think of social history. Why did people come to this place and how did they live here? How did the town get its name? Where did they get their water? Did they build dams and mills on the river? How did they make their living? What kind of daily life did they have? What were their triumphs and tragedies? Did a fire, flood, or tornado destroy the town? How and why did the people rebuild? What happened when the railroad came? Did the town have to move to the railroad or did the town develop because of the railroad? These are the stories of the lives of people who made the town, and visitors are inherently interested in the human story.

- *Ethnicity*: In Texas, everyone came from somewhere else and therefore represents an ethnic heritage. "Native Americans" probably came from Mongolia. Hispanics, African Americans, French, Irish, Scots, English, Germans, Polish, Russians, Syrians, Lebanese, Czechoslovakians, Norwegians, Dutch, and on and on make up the people of Texas. Why did people come from Norway to Bosque County? What is the story of the Jewish people in many small towns? Why is Guadalupe, one of our most common Spanish names, based on the Arabic word "wadi?" All of these stories can fascinate visitors. The Institute of Texas Cultures in San Antonio is a treasure of information about the great variety of Texas ethnicity.
  Ethnicity becomes a product not just in the stories, but in how those stories are told. Festivals, dance, music, food, dress, architecture—all of these are ways that ethnicity is expressed.
- *Architecture*: Some small towns may not have a single building designed by a "real" architect, but that does not mean that there is no architecture there. On the contrary, every building is a piece of vernacular architecture—often much more interesting and creative than famous architecture, and certainly more representative of the place. Some of that vernacular architecture is now well-known. Clovis Heimsath's book *Pioneer Texas Buildings*

(University of Texas Press), celebrates Texas vernacular architecture. *Built in Texas* edited by Francis Edward Abemethy (Publications of the Texas Folklore Society, 42) and *Early Texas Architecture* by Gordon Echols (Texas Christian University Press) are also good references. Even mobile homes are part of the story. Why people choose to live in a double wide rather than a traditional adobe is an important story—adobe buildings are difficult and expensive to maintain. The buildings of a town make up what geographers call the "built environment." The stories of that built environment can be fascinating to visitors if told well.

- *Natural features*: Just as every place has a history, every place also has natural features. Maybe they are not as dramatic as the Grand Teton Mountains, but they are real and important. Without the land, water, air and sun there would be no life, so how do those things go together to make life in your town or region? What were the characteristics of those features before European settlement? How did the Native Americans use the natural features? How has modern culture changed them? Are there places with particularly scenic views or watchable wildlife? What kinds of agriculture are practiced in the region? Many people have never seen corn or cotton in the field, not to mention trees heavy with grapefruit. They do not understand grazing and range management or irrigation. All of these things, that may be so ordinary to local residents, can be memorable experiences for the visitor. Most of us who live in rural places forget that seeing a white tail deer is a major nature experience for someone from Houston or Dallas.
- *Daily life of the community*: The heritage, ethnicity, and architecture of Europe are major attractions, but so is daily life there. Millions of Americans go to Europe each year to sit in sidewalk cafes in Paris, live in rural villages in southern England, or ride mopeds in Rome (bless their souls!). In the same way, daily life in our Texas towns can be an attraction for visitors from cities. The livestock auction, the hardware store, the barbeque joint, the local rodeo, even six-man football, are all unique experiences for visitors. Tourists are people and like to be treated like

people—that is, with respect, consideration, and friendliness. Thus, one of the best tourism products you can provide is to simply be nice to your visitors. Talk to them. Let them ask you questions and give them respectful answers, even if the questions seem dumb. We Texans probably ask some pretty dumb questions in New York City. Ask them about themselves, show interest in them and they will feel they have made a friend in your community—hopefully they have.

Hospitality as Product

Hospitality—the eating and sleeping service offered to visitors—is another way to provide meaningful experiences based on the historic, ethnic, natural, and cultural characteristics of a community or rural area. Eating should be an experience. The barbecue restaurants in Lockhart and Luling are tourist destinations because they are authentic expressions of daily life in those towns. Restaurants do not have to be ethnic in order to express the character of a place and to provide a meaningful experience. They just have to be "local." They must show a connection to the place. This maybe expressed by the owner's collection of historic local photographs or their obvious support for the local school athletic teams. Even the chain restaurants can achieve this "localness" by choice of decor.

Lodging is as important as restaurants in expressing the local character of a place. The architecture should be consistent with the town and region. The decor should be consistent with the place. How often have you been in a motel in a desert region that was decorated with pictures of ocean scenes? That does not create a valuable product for the visitor. A meaningful product is a cohesive experience. Bed and breakfast establishments are especially important as overall heritage tourism products. The visitor is staying in someone's home and should have an experience that makes them feel like they have lived in the town, even for one night.

The Story is the Product

National and state parks, which have done heritage tourism for more than one hundred years, place major emphasis on what is called interpretation. Guided trails, ranger talks, booklets, videos, maps, and visitor centres are all part of the interpretive programmes of parks. Heritage tourism in small towns and rural areas must also provide interpretation because visitors will not see or understand most of the heritage tourism products described above unless someone "interprets" them to the visitors. While it would be difficult for someone not to be awestruck by the Rocky Mountains or the coast of Maine, the Rio Grande Valley takes a little explaining to help visitors recognize what is there and to have memorable experiences.

There is an entire profession of heritage interpretation. Many people make their living as interpreters. They may be formally trained or they may be self-taught. There is a professional association, the National Association for Interpretation (Interpnet.com.) that offers certification courses. But what is interpretation, how can people learn interpretive methods, and how can interpretation be used to develop heritage products in your town or region?

There are some formal definitions of interpretation, but basically interpretation is telling the stories of a place. Those stories may focus on history, ethnicity, architecture, natural characteristics, daily life, or all of these. The stories may be told by individuals talking to groups, or by music, drama, art, printed material, video and audio, signs, displays, and many combinations of such methods. But whatever the topic or method, *interpretation must speak to the needs and interests of the visitor and must stimulate their interest.*

Interpretation is not classroom teaching. It is not about conveying a certain set of facts to the audience. It is about arousing their interest and curiosity about the place by somehow connecting the characteristics of the place to their lives, background, and interests. The purpose of interpretation is to provide a memorable experience (product) to the visitor, not to prepare them to pass the final exam.

Interpretation is not difficult if you love your place and your visitors. You want to show your visitors a good time by sharing your excitement and understanding of the place they are visiting. Good interpreters do not have to have university degrees or high school diplomas. They do not have to be experts on history or zoology. Certainly they have to know some things, but they also have to knowhow to say they do not know, and stimulate the visitor to want to find out.

The following books are good sources on interpretive principles and methods. Most of these can be purchased from the National Association for Interpretation.

Beck, Larry and Ted Cable, 1998. *Interpretation for the 21st Century: Fifteen Guiding Principles for Interpreting Nature and Culture.* Champaign, IL: Sagamore Publishing.

Ham, Sam, 1992. *Environmental Interpretation: A Practical Guide for People with Big Ideas and Small Budgets.* Golden, Colorado: North American Press.

Knudson, Donald, Ted Cable and Larry Beck, 1995. *Interpretation of Cultural and Natural Resources.* State College, PA: Venture Publishing, Inc.

Regnier, Kathleen, Michael Gross and Ron Zimmerman, 1994. *The Interpreter's Guidebook: Techniques for programmes and presentations.* 3rd edition. Interpreter's Handbook Series. Stevens Point, WI: UW-SP Foundation Press, Inc.

Tilden, Freeman, 1977. *Interpreting our Heritage.* 3rd edition. Chapel Hill: The University of North Carolina Press.

Trapp, Suzanne, Michael Gross and Ron Zimmerman, 1994. *Signs, Trails and Wayside Exhibits.* 2nd edition. Interpreter's Handbook Series. Stevens Point, WI: UW-SP Foundation Press, Inc.

Veverka, John, 1994. *Interpretive Master Planning.* Tustin, CA: Acorn Naturalists.

Zehr, Jeffery, Michael Gross, and Ron Zimmerman, 1991. *Creating Environmental Publications: A guide to writing and designing for interpreters and environmental educators.* Interpreter's Handbook Series. Stevens Point, WI: UW-SP Foundation Press, Inc.

Chicken or the Egg—Product or Market?

Standard business practice says develop your product to meet a market demand. Research the market and give them what they want. Clearly, that is essential. You must have someone who will pay for your product. However, developing heritage tourism products does not follow the textbook practice. First, there are some major constraints on the kinds of products you can develop or want to develop. Texas will not be able to offer hiking on glaciers or the heritage of the Italian Renaissance—we just do not have those things, even if that is what the market wants. Likewise, many towns may not want to turn their ethnic heritage into a commodity and landowners may not want birdwatchers on their land. So the first step in product development is to determine what you have that may be a product and then determine if you want to offer it as a product.

After you identify your potential products, you have to determine if someone will pay for them and how much they will pay. This may be difficult because there are few comparables to use for analysis. For example, when Dan Brown decided to offer hummingbird watching on his ranch outside Christoval, Texas, he had almost no examples to draw on. He knew birdwatching was popular on the Texas coast, near a large population. How could anyone know if people would drive several hours to Christoval? Sometimes in heritage tourism product development you simply have to hope that if you build it, they will come, as they have with the Dan's Hummer house.

Part of the attraction of a heritage product is its uniqueness, but because the product is unique it may be very difficult to find comparables. This presents a major problem for financing heritage product development. Lenders need assurance that the business venture will be successful, but the lack of comparables can make it difficult to provide such assurance.

Resource Protection

There is an inherent danger in heritage tourism—the resources that make up your attractions can easily be overused so they are no longer attractive. In their long history of heritage tourism, the national and state park systems have emphasized resource protection. They have staff members at each park who monitor resource conditions and manage use to prevent damage. Unfortunately, most private sector heritage tourism sites do not have a resource protection staff. Many do not recognize the subtle but serious damage that can result from visitors. Resource damage is a moral and even legal issue, but it also strikes at the heart of the product. No business can survive if it destroys its ability to deliver its product.

Resource damage takes many forms. Visitors can damage historical artifacts and even steal them. They can frighten animals, destroy habitats and disrupt breeding seasons. Too many visitors or inappropriate behaviour can diminish the experience of other visitors. Tourists also have impacts on the entire community. Although they may bring economic benefits, many local residents are disturbed by traffic and the jostle of strangers in their town.

There are three basic ways to manage visitors to reduce resource damage. The first is to avoid excessive numbers of visitors. The second is to determine appropriate locations for various activities. The third is to manage the timing of visitors.

Avoid excessive numbers of visitors: We all know that too many visitors is not good, but how many is too many? A common concept in tourism resource management is "carrying capacity," which implies that there is a certain number of people that a site can accommodate. This concept came from range management, where it is generally considered that the carrying capacity is the number of domestic and native animals that will eat only half of the grass crop. Tourists and heritage sites are much more complicated than cattle on rangeland because there is usually not a clear measurement of impact, such as the amount of grass.

A more refined method to avoid excessive numbers of visitors is the concept of Limits of Acceptable Change (LAC). In the LAC method, the resource manager identifies factors that will be impacted and can be measured, such as the number of parking places or the wear and tear on a historic structure. The manager establishes baseline conditions for these factors, determines how much change can be tolerated (limit of acceptable change), monitors the conditions of the factors, and takes action when they approach the limit of acceptable change.

Appropriate locations for activities: Some visitor activities have greater impacts than others and some sites are more resistant to change than others. Thus, tourism activities should be planned so that higher impact activities take place in areas that are more resistant to impacts. For example, a ranch may have a canyon with a spring-fed stream that provides great habitat for watchable wildlife. The ranch family decides to accommodate overnight campers who want to watch wildlife and ride mountain bikes. Obviously, neither the camp sites nor the mountain bike trails should be built in the canyon. They should be located in places that are less vulnerable to impact and less valuable as attractions.

Timing of visitors: Tourists are like migratory animals, there are seasons when they are moving and seasons when they stay at home. Thus, most heritage tourism attractions have high and low seasons, and the high seasons may produce unacceptable impacts. One way to avoid this (and to smooth out income), is to develop products that appeal to niche markets throughout the year. Spring, fall, and even winter provide comfortable hiking weather in most of Texas. Retirees and empty-nesters can travel at those times, while families with children are more limited to summer and spring break. A variety of products aimed at niche markets can smooth out visitation throughout the year.

All of this management takes time and money. Unfortunately, many private heritage tourism enterprises are short on both of those. However, it is crucial that resources be handled with care because both the resources and the business that depends on them can be ruined. The best approach to resource protection is to build it into the initial product planning and development.

The heritage tourism product is the experience received by the visitors. This experience is the sum total of the historical events, ethnicity, architecture, natural features, daily life of the community, dining, lodging, and the stories told by all of these. Fortunately, these features are already present in virtually every town and region, and can be developed as heritage tourism products for very little cost. However, because these features are all fragile in their own ways, responsible product planning and development will include ways to protect the resources from unacceptable damage.

PRICING TOURISM PRODUCTS AND SERVICES

In general, tourism businesses appear to be in a highly competitive industry with limited flexibility to set prices. Either they sell at or below the established market price or see a rapid drop in sales. Establishing a firm's price under such circumstances is straightforward, although not always simple. All one needs to do is to identify what the competition is charging and price one's own product comparably.

Despite this apparent lack of flexibility, however, the uniqueness of tourism/recreation goods and services actually enables producers to establish prices. This uniqueness stems from a number of product attributes, including: business location, its natural environment, the types of facilities offered, the personal relationships that management and staff develop with customers, and real and perceived differences in the quality of the firm's products.

Because most tourism/recreation businesses have at least some flexibility to establish prices, this bulletin will address the key factors that should be considered in making pricing decisions. Keep in mind, however, that the same uniqueness which provides pricing flexibility also precludes development of a universally applicable formula for guiding pricing decisions. Furthermore, the goals of businesses in this industry vary widely and, because price is a major tool for achieving a business's goals, identical businesses under identical circumstances may logically establish different prices.

While it is not possible to prescribe a single formula for all price-setting decisions, it is possible to identify the primary components of a sound pricing strategy. These "ingredients" can be found in textbooks and by observing business pricing practices. Both sources are drawn upon here to provide you with the ingredients to make sound pricing decisions. Ultimately, you must fit them to your business goals and circumstances to arrive at the best prices for your products.

The Basics of Pricing

Price theory is a keystone of economics. Because of this central role, no economics text would be complete without one or more chapters devoted to pricing. Many books have been written on this single topic. Successful business people, whether from books or practical experience, have learned to use basic pricing concepts for their products and services. These elements are introduced briefly below.

Economists begin their introduction to pricing by explaining the concept of demand. In simple terms, demand means that consumers will purchase more of a good or service at a low price than at a high price. Therefore, demand is the economists' term to describe the relationship between the varying quantities of a product which can be sold over a range of prices. Demand can be expressed in at least three ways: (*a*) in tabular form; (*b*) as a mathematical relationship; or (*c*) as a graph.

Note that as the price charged decreases from $3 to $2, the quantity which can be sold increases from five to ten units. Based only on this information, the operator of this particular business would maximize sales revenue by establishing a price of $2 for the product. At that price, gross revenue would equal $2 × 10 units = $20. At a price of $3 or $1 gross revenue would equal only $15.

If the unit cost of producing these 5, 10 or 15 units was identical—for example, $0.50 per unit, net revenue would also be maximized by setting the price at $2. Net revenue (gross revenue – production cost = net revenue) at a $2 price would equal $15. Note, however, that while gross revenue is $15 at both the $1 and $3 unit price, net revenue is not equal. At a $3 price, net revenue is $12.50 while at a $1 price net revenue is only $7.50. This illustrates the need to account for both demand and cost when setting prices.

In addition, unit costs contain both fixed and variable elements. Fixed costs include such items as rent, insurance and managerial costs which must be paid to be in a particular business. The per unit fixed cost burden declines as output increases. Doubling output, for example, would reduce fixed costs per unit by half. Variable costs, on the other hand, vary directly with output. Examples of variable cost items include employee wages, laundry costs and supplies. Total variable costs increase as output increases but often will not be the same across all levels of output. Per unit variable costs typically are high at low levels of output and decline as output level expands because of economies of scale (e.g. volume discounts on large orders from suppliers).

With reasonably good projections of a business's fixed and variable costs, it is possible to establish the minimum price required in order for the business to earn a profit. This is often referred to as a break-even price. This is the price per unit for a given volume of output at which total revenue is exactly equal to total costs. This relationship can be expressed algebraically as follows:

$$P \times Q = F + (V \times Q)$$

where

P = price per unit sold
Q = quantity produced and sold
F = total fixed costs
V = variable cost per unit

Isolating price in the above expression yields the following:

$$P = \frac{F + (V \times Q)}{Q}$$

Even though fixed and variable costs and quantity may not be known precisely, calculation of an appropriate range of break-even prices can often be very revealing. Indeed, use of this simple business technique could keep you from inadvertently investing in products unlikely to be purchased at the price required for you to break-even on the quantity you could produce. Occasionally, however, there are circumstances in which a rational business person may deliberately establish a selling price below the break-even point.

Pricing in Practice

The real world which the commercial recreation/tourism business faces is far more complex than the highly simplified theoretical economic models which we have been discussing.

However, these models can help you to deal better with your real-world pricing problems and are a firm foundation upon which to build a more comprehensive tourism/recreation pricing strategy. When economists establish the price-quantity relationship which they refer to as demand, they mean it to apply to a single product which consumers perceive as being identical. Billions of dollars are spent each year on advertising with the single purpose of convincing consumers that apparently identical products in fact possess important differences. These advertising dollars are not wasted. The boom in sales of certain designer jeans, headache remedies, soft drinks, and fast foods reflect consumer perceptions of differences among the products available to them, whether or not these differences actually exist.

Even without the influence of advertising, consumers' perceptions of products and services in the tourism and recreation industry do differ greatly. These differences in perceptions are extremely important to a business's pricing strategy. In essence, these perceptions define the competition. From a prospective consumer's perception, for example, the competition for a modern campground along a major highway, may be nearby budget motels, rather than less-developed campgrounds on the same route. In such a setting, the modern campground owner might be able to price a night of camping considerably higher—near the level of nearby budget motels—than would be feasible if the competition was exclusively other campgrounds. Thus, a first step in developing a pricing strategy is to establish from the consumer's perspective what other products in your market compete most directly with your offering. Be sure to include all significant attributes of your product such as: location, facilities and services you offer, and significant attractions in the vicinity of your business.

Many tourism/recreation businesses offer multiple products and/or services to the consumer. A marina, for example, may rent boat slips, sell boats, fuel, and equipment, offer maintenance and storage services, and even operate a grocery/beverage outlet. In establishing a pricing strategy, the marina must not only focus on demand, production costs, and its competitors' prices, but also must consider the impact of slip rental prices on the attractiveness of its other products and services. The objective is to maximize profit across its entire product line. This might be achieved by charging slip rental fees below the competition and even below the break-even price. Grocery stores commonly employ such a pricing strategy for turkeys at holiday seasons, since all but the most conscientious shoppers are likely to purchase the rest of the ingredients for the holiday meal wherever, the best price on turkeys is offered. Restaurants with bars will often discount food prices in order to attract customers who will purchase drinks, which are a high profit product. Impact across a firm's product line is an important consideration in establishing pieces for an individual product offering.

Demand for tourism/recreation varies with the season and the day of the week. In some cases, demand may also vary across product offerings. For example, rooms with a scenic view or campsites near the water are in greater demand than others which a business may have to offer. These differences can be exploited, since greater demand provides an opportunity to charge higher prices. Variations in demand also suggest that lowering prices during non-peak periods can yield added revenue. As long as the price discounts offered are not excessive (i.e. the established price covers all variable costs), offering reduced rates can actually enhance a firm's profit. To the extent that differences in demand can be identified, differential pricing should be an ingredient in a firm's overall pricing strategy.

Pricing is often employed to attract new customers, to maintain good customer relations, to help a new business to become known, and to "wage war" on competition. The latter seldom makes sense for small businesses, especially those with limited capital or lines of credit.

Offering price discounts, however, can be effective in the other instances noted and is often feasible even for small businesses. For example, offering a price discount on occasion may yield more business than allocating an equivalent sum for advertising. On the other hand, a business in the hospitality industry must avoid the appearance of price gouging or risk loss of customers over the long haul.

This approach to making pricing decisions draws upon the concepts of demand and production costs. Break-even analysis reveals the minimum price to be charged in order for a firm to remain in business in the long run. In the "pricing in practice" section, we highlighted the importance of viewing your product from the consumer's perspective. Knowing the consumer's perspective helps identify your competitors. Assessing the impact of pricing decisions across your entire product line and using the concept of differential pricing were also noted as considerations in developing pricing strategies. Finally, the idea of discount pricing as a promotional strategy to attract new customers or to maintain good relations with old customers was noted as a possible use of pricing strategy.

One point remains to be made. Regardless of how much you read about pricing, both in theory and in practice, and how much research you undertake to support your decisions, it is necessary to monitor the results of your pricing decisions. Only through monitoring can you determine whether your pricing decisions are yielding the anticipated results. It is far better to adjust your strategy than it is to stick with a bad decision. Even good business people occasionally make bad decisions because of faulty information or incorrect analysis. The only way to determine what price to charge is to experiment. The ideas presented here should help you to narrow the focus of your experiments so that you can more quickly identify prices which are best for your business.

3

Towards Sustainable Tourism Products Marketing by Promoting Responsible Tourism Destinations

MARKETING SUSTAINABLE TOURISM PRODUCT

Within the framework of a 'Sustainable Consumption and Production' approach, the promotion and distribution of sustainable 'products' play a vital role. In the tourism sector, there are today many recognized leaders that have integrated sustainability in their core business, who, however are experiencing little 'market' reward for their efforts to integrate environmental and social practices. This in turns acts as a limiting factor for mainstreaming good sustainable practices.

UNEP's session on 'Marketing sustainable tourism products: challenges and opportunities' at the 4th Euro meeting (Florence, 5 November, 2004), organized by the United Nations Environment Programme, in co-operation with the Regione Toscana and the scientific support of the Leeds Metropolitan University, aimed at opening a debate on the main opportunities and challenges for the promotion and distribution of services that claim to be 'sustainable.'

MARKETING TOURISM PLANNING

It is amazing how many marketing plans totally miss the strategic analysis and positioning steps, and each year jump to the same list of activities the organization did the previous year. Our marketing plans always involve strategic analysis, market positioning and the tough decisions regarding resource allocation. If it does not take these important considerations it is just a "to do list" of activities and is not a strategy.

Most commonly requested marketing services are:

- Marketing Blueprint
- Marketing Support
- Marketing Audit.

TOTAL DESTINATION MANAGEMENT

We are an internationally recognized team of specialists in destination branding, tourism planning and marketing. We have 30 years of hands-on experience in all aspects of destination and community branding and marketing in over 20 countries.

Our clients are ambitious countries, cities, counties arid regions who want to stand out from competitors and be more prosperous through tourism, investment, increased exports, by recruiting the best people and being accepted in "the right circles."

We assist Destination Marketing Organizations (DMO), convention and visitor bureaus, chambers of commerce, economic development agencies, national tourism offices, governments, and resorts.

Our team has worked with over one hundred locations. We have created and managed award winning campaigns and brand, building for some of the world's leading tourism destinations. While awards are great, it is always the satisfaction of our clients with the results of our work that we are most proud of.

Years of experience in tourism planning and destination-branding has led us to create the '7A Place Branding and Planning Systems.' This consultative and systematic process has consistently yielded breakthrough results for our clients. '7A' simplifies the task of revealing the building blocks essential for places of all sizes to become market leaders.

Destination Branding

If there is any gap between the reality of your city or region, and the perceptions that are held in key markets, then you need a brand strategy.

Successful destination brands are those that are able to clearly differentiate themselves and simplify choices for customers. Experience has shown us that fundamental to developing a winning brand is recognizing that it is much more than a new logo, new graphic design, or "a fresh coat of paint." And a destination's brand is not simply a clever advertising theme or a tagline.

Our philosophy is that a destination brand is the totality of perceptions that a customer holds about the experiences associated with a place. Effective management of these perceptions and experiences can secure enduring value for the destination, its partners and customers. This means that the brand is built at every point of contact between customers and the destination. Each of these points before, during and after the visit has a vital role in building and delivering the experience embodied in the brand.

The logo and tagline serve as valuable reminders for the values inherent in the brand. Unless a destination brand is adopted, supported and given "life" by stakeholders and partners it will amount to nothing more than a mark on a piece of paper.

Strategic Planning

"Any road will take you there if you do not know where you are going", said The Mad Hatter in "Alice in Wonderland." The Mad Hatter's approach to planning is certainly one to avoid when it comes to the marketing of places and destinations. In today's competitive and over-crowded environment cities and regions cannot afford an ad hoc approach to marketing.

Visitors and customers are becoming more discerning, knowledgeable and experienced, and this is changing the way that cities and regions must cater to them. This means that they must consistently deliver outstanding experiences that exceed expectations from the first moment that visitors click on a web site or look at a brochure, to seeing a "Thanks for Visiting Us" sign as they leave town.

With so many stakeholders and partners with diverse objectives to satisfy and inspire, cities and regions must have a systematic and collaborative approach to planning.

The '7A Tourism Planning System'

Successful community-based planning requires a lot of listening, research, strategic analysis, creative thinking, tough decisions and careful refinement. That is why we have developed proven consultative techniques and systems that simplify the task of revealing the building blocks essential for destinations to become market leaders.

RESPONSIBLE TOURISM DESTINATIONS: THE CAPE TOWN DECLARATION

Shaping Sustainable Spaces into Better Places

We, representatives of inbound and outbound tour operators, emerging entrepreneurs in the tourism industry, national parks, provincial conservation authorities, all spheres of government, tourism professionals, tourism authorities, NGOs and hotel groups and other tourism stakeholders, from 20 countries in Africa, North and South America, Europe and Asia; having come together in Cape Town to consider the issue of Responsible Tourism in Destinations have agreed this declaration.

Mindful of the debates at the United Nations Commission on Sustainable Development in 1999, which asserted the importance of the economic, social and environment aspects of sustainable development and of the interests of indigenous peoples and local communities in particular.

Recognising the global challenge of reducing social and economic inequalities and reducing poverty, and the importance of New Partnership for Africa's Development (NEPAD) in the process.

Recognizing the importance of the World Tourism Organization's Global Code of Ethics, which aims to promote responsible, sustainable and universally accessible tourism and sharing its commitment to equitable, responsible and sustainable world tourism and its STEP initiative with UNCTAD, which seeks to harness sustainable tourism to help eliminate poverty.

Conscious that we are now ten years on from the Rio Earth Summit on Environment and Development, and that the World Summit on Sustainable Development taking place in Johannesburg will put renewed emphasis on sustainability, economic development, and in particular on poverty reduction.

Aware of the World Tourism Organization, World Travel and Tourism Council and the Earth Council's updated Agenda 21 for the Travel and Tourism Industry and the success achieved by a number of businesses, local communities and national and local governments in moving towards sustainability in tourism.

Aware of the work of the UNEP, and the Tourism Industry Report 2002, and work of UNESCO, and other UN agencies, promoting sustainable tourism in partnership with the private sector, NGOs, civil society organizations and government.

Aware of the guidelines for sustainable tourism in vulnerable ecosystems being developed in the framework of the Convention on Biological Diversity.

Conscious of developments in other industries and sectors, and in particular of the growing international demand for ethical business, and the adoption of clear Corporate Social Responsibility (CSR) policies by companies, and the transparent reporting of achievements in meeting CSR objectives in company annual reports.

Recognizing that there has been considerable progress in addressing the environmental impacts of tourism, although there is a long way to go to achieve sustainability; and that more limited progress has been made in harnessing tourism for local economic development, for the benefit of communities and indigenous peoples, and in managing the social impacts of tourism.

Endorsing the Global Code of Ethics and the importance of making all forms of tourism sustainable through all stakeholders taking responsibility for creating better forms of tourism and realizing these aspirations.

Relishing the diversity of our world's cultures, habitats and species and the wealth of our cultural and natural heritage, as the very basis of tourism, we accept that responsible and sustainable tourism will be achieved in different ways in different places.

Accepting that, in the words of the Global Code of Ethics, an attitude of tolerance and respect for the diversity of religious, philosophical and moral beliefs, are both the foundation and the consequence of responsible tourism.

Recognizing that dialogue, partnerships and multi-stakeholder processes—involving government, business and local communities—to make better places for hosts and guests can only be realized at the local level, and that all stakeholders have different, albeit inter-dependent, responsibilities; tourism can only be managed for sustainability at the destination level.

Conscious of the importance of good governance and political stability in providing the context for responsible tourism in destinations, and recognizing that the devolution of decision-making power to democratic local government is necessary to build stable partnerships at a local level, and to the empowerment of local communities.

Aware that the management of tourism requires the participation of a broad range of government agencies and particularly at the local destination level.

Recognizing that in order to protect the cultural, social and environmental integrity of destinations limits to tourism development are sometimes necessary.

Having, during the Cape Town Conference, examined the South African Guidelines for Responsible Tourism, tested them in a series of field visits, and explored how tourism can be made to work better for local communities, tourists and businesses alike, we recognize their value in helping to shape sustainable tourism in South Africa.

Recognizing that one of the strengths of the South African Guidelines for Responsible Tourism is that they were developed through a national consultative process, and that they reflect the priorities and aspirations of the South African people.

Recognizing that Responsible Tourism takes many forms, that different destinations and stakeholders will have different priorities, and that local policies and guidelines will need to be developed through multi-stakeholder processes to develop responsible tourism in destinations.

Having the following characteristics, Responsible Tourism:

- minimizes negative economic, environmental, and social impacts;
- generates greater economic benefits for local people and enhances the well-being of host communities, improves working conditions and access to the industry;
- involves local people in decisions that affect their lives and life chances;
- makes positive contributions to the conservation of natural and cultural heritage, to the maintenance of the world's diversity;
- provides more enjoyable experiences for tourists through more meaningful connections with local people, and a greater understanding of local cultural, social and environmental issues;
- provides access for physically challenged people; and
- is culturally sensitive, engenders respect between tourists and hosts, and builds local pride and confidence.

We call upon countries, multilateral agencies, destinations and enterprises to develop similar practical guidelines and to encourage planning authorities, tourism businesses, tourists and local communities—to take responsibility for achieving sustainable tourism, and to create better places for people to live in and for people to visit.

We urge multilateral agencies responsible for development strategies to include sustainable responsible tourism in their outcomes.

Determined to make tourism more sustainable, and accepting that it is the responsibility of all stakeholders in tourism to achieve more sustainable forms of tourism, we commit ourselves to pursue the principles of Responsible Tourism.

Convinced that it is primarily in the destinations, the places that tourists visit, where tourism enterprises conduct their business and where local communities and tourists and the tourism industry interact, that the economic, social and environmental impacts of tourism need to be managed responsibly, to maximize positive impacts and minimize negative ones.

We undertake to work in concrete ways in destinations to achieve better forms of tourism and to work with other stakeholders in destinations. We commit to build the capacity of all stakeholders in order to ensure that they can secure an effective voice in decision-making. We uphold the guiding principles for Responsible Tourism which were identified.

Guiding Principles for Economic Responsibility

- Assess economic impacts before developing tourism and exercise preference for those forms of development that benefit local communities and minimize negative impacts on local livelihoods (for example through loss of access to resources), recognizing that tourism may not always be the most appropriate form of local economic development.
- Maximize local economic benefits by increasing linkages and reducing leakages, by ensuring that communities are involved in, and benefit from, tourism. Wherever possible use tourism to assist in poverty reduction by adopting pro-poor strategies.
- Develop quality products that reflect, complement, and enhance the destination.
- Market tourism in ways which reflect the natural, cultural and social integrity of the destination, and which encourage appropriate forms of tourism.
- Adopt equitable business practises, pay and charge fair prices, and build partnerships in ways in which risk is

minimized and shared, and recruit and employ staff recognizing international labour standards.

- Provide appropriate and sufficient support to small, medium and micro enterprises to ensure tourism-related enterprises thrive and are sustainable.

Guiding Principles for Social Responsibility

- Actively involve the local community in planning and decision-making and provide capacity building to make this a reality.
- Assess social impacts throughout the life cycle of the operation—including the planning and design phases of projects—in order to minimize negative impacts and maximize positive ones.
- Endeavour to make tourism an inclusive social experience and to ensure that there is access for all, in particular vulnerable and disadvantaged communities and individuals.
- Combat the sexual exploitation of human beings, particularly the exploitation of children.
- Be sensitive to the host culture, maintaining and encouraging social and cultural diversity.
- Endeavour to ensure that tourism contributes to improvements in health and education.

Guiding Principles for Environmental Responsibility

- Assess environmental impacts throughout the life cycle of tourist establishments and operations—including the planning and design phase and ensure that negative impacts are reduced to the minimum and maximizing positive ones.
- Use resources sustainably, and reduce waste and over-consumption.
- Manage natural diversity sustainably, and where appropriate restore it; and consider the volume and type of tourism that the environment can support, and respect the integrity of vulnerable ecosystems and protected areas.
- Promote education and awareness for sustainable development—for all stakeholders.
- Raise the capacity of all stakeholders and ensure that best practice is followed, for this purpose consult with environmental and conservation experts.

We recognize that this list is not exhaustive and that multi-stakeholder groups in diverse destinations should adapt these principles to reflect their own culture and environment.

Responsible tourism seeks to maximize positive impacts and to minimize negative ones. Compliance with all relevant international and national standards, laws and regulations is assumed. Responsibility, and the market advantage that can go with it, is about doing more than the minimum.

We recognize that the transparent and auditable reporting of progress towards achieving responsible tourism targets and benchmarking, is essential to the integrity and credibility of our work, to the ability of all stakeholders to assess progress, and to enable consumers to exercise effective choice.

We commit to making our contribution to move towards a more balanced relationship between hosts and guests in destinations, and to create better places for local communities and indigenous peoples; and recognizing that this can only be achieved by government, local communities and business cooperating on practical initiatives in destinations.

We call upon tourism enterprises and trade associations in originating markets and in destinations to adopt a responsible approach, to commit to specific responsible practises, and to report progress in a transparent and auditable way, and where appropriate to use this for market advantage. Corporate businesses can assist by providing markets, capacity building, mentoring and micro-financing support for small, medium and micro enterprises.

In order to implement the guiding principles for economic, social and environmental responsibility, it is necessary to use a portfolio of tools, which will include regulations, incentives, and multi-stakeholder participatory strategies. Changes in the market encouraged by consumer campaigns and new marketing initiatives also contribute to market driven change.

Local authorities have a central role to play in achieving responsible tourism through commitment to supportive policy frameworks and adequate funding. We call upon local authorities and tourism administrations to develop—through multi-stakeholder processes—destination management strategies and responsible tourism guidelines to create better places for host communities and the tourists who visit. Local Agenda 21 programmes, with their participatory and monitoring processes, are particularly useful.

We call upon the media to exercise responsibility in the way in which they portray tourism destinations, to avoid raising false expectations and to provide balanced and fair reporting.

We all have a responsibility to make a difference by the way we act. We appreciate Calvia's (Spain) intention to host the second conference on Responsible Tourism in Destinations in May 2004; and recognize that this provides a focus for our work over the next two years. The Calvia Conference will focus on the roles of local authorities and tour operators in working to achieve responsible tourism.

We commit ourselves to work with others to take responsibility for achieving the economic, social and environmental components of responsible and sustainable tourism. The Calvia Conference will provide us with the opportunity to share further experience and to assess progress towards achieving better places for hosts and guests. We look forward to hearing about progress in South Africa in implementing its national responsible tourism policy and reviewing developments in other destinations.

Global Code of Ethics for Tourism

Introduction

1. The World Tourism Leaders convened by the World Tourism Organization at a meeting on the Social Impact of Tourism, in Manila (Philippines) on 22 May, 1997 committed themselves to "work towards the formulation and eventual adoption of a Global Code of *Ethics* for Tourism." This proposal appears in the draft programme of work of the Organization for the period 1998-99. It was based on the recommendation of the Quality Support Committee made at its second meeting (Madrid, 28-29 October, 1996) as a follow-up to suggestions from various member States which took part in the work programme survey.
2. It is fundamental to recall that in 1985 (Sofia, sixth General Assembly) WTO adopted the Tourism Bill of Rights and Tourist Code which basically focuses on the responsibility of States (including sections relating to "the populations constituting the host communities") and the travelling individual. It is also noteworthy that the political emphasis of this document was set on the rights to rest and leisure

and the freedom to travel while also advocating, as a second priority, the desired humane nature and content of tourism. Both domestic and international tourism as well as its environmental and social aspects were addressed.

3. The document was not legally binding and did not provide for a follow-up mechanism. It is supposed, however, that it was used by various governments and organizations and also inspired certain laws, regulations and tourism policy documents. The evidence is that on many occasions the WTO Secretariat had to furnish the document on demand to tourism policy makers and professional bodies as well as non-governmental organizations and that there are numerous references to it in literature. Nevertheless, its direct effective impact on tourism, practices may be considered as rather minor.
4. It also inspired WTO itself to develop a series of technical publications setting standards of environment protection, as well as a few tourism policy documents such as the Recommended Measures for Tourism Safety, Creating Tourism Opportunities for Handicapped People in the Nineties (Buenos Aires, 1991). Health Formalities and Information in International Travel (Bah, 1993), and the WTO Statement on the Prevention of Organized Sex Tourism (Cairo, 1995).
5. The latter document is an example of the new challenges that tourism development and society have to face. And there are many others that was seen especially in the environment area which prompted many tourism organizations to draw up environmental *codes* of *conduct*. Other approaches were developed at both national and international levels, such as attempts in 1990 to adopt a Code for Tourists by the European Commission, and a Model Municipal Tourism Policy by the then United States Travel and Tourism Administration. In each instance it was insisted that the resulting documents should be non-obligatory or for illustrative purposes.
6. More recent and current approaches aimed at corporate and business community at the national level are developed by NGOs, among others, in France by Group

Development and in the United Kingdom by Tourism Concern. In each case this work is carried out at the request of the business community concerned. Both groups have approached WTO with a view to contribute to WTO work in this area. This offer was also received from a coalition of non-governmental organizations operating in Western Europe called TEN which held a consultation in Madrid with the WTO Management right after the World Tourism Leaders' Meeting in Manila.

7. These and other developments at various levels, including the highest one such as the recent United Nations Conference on Agenda 21 which WTO addressed suggest that once again WTO is expected to take the lead and proceed to designing a firm, overall Code for Tourism which would establish global *ethics* in respect of the continuous and new challenges faced by tourism development which is also global. There are expectations that there should be a guiding and instrument authority for such development.

Content of the Global Code of Ethics for Tourism

8. The new instrument will be able to balance the responsibilities of all the social agents involved in tourism development:

   - States/Governments (including local administration)
   - Private Enterprise
   - The Travelling individual
   - The Host Community.

9. It can equally address the three inter-related aspects of tourism development:

   - environmental
   - social
   - economic.

The social aspect here is meant to cover tourism's accessibility, content and role for and in society, in particular its culture, religion, ways of life, traditions and customs, and the observance of human rights.

Implementation

10. In contrast with past *declarations* the Global Code of *Ethics* for Tourism is expected to allow for measuring its application. Without pretending to be another international convention demanding a legal machinery which traditionally tends to be heavy and bureaucratic—and often not even promising effective compliance, it could still have an ambition to make its provisions obligatory to the extent possible, although not legally binding. Leaving the new instrument without a measure to check on its implementation quite possibly would lead to its disregard and the failure to meet the existing expectations about the Code authority and applicability.
11. This can possibly be achieved or at least facilitated by introducing two elements to the Code:

    (*a*) appropriate language
    (*b*) implementation mechanism.

12. Before being formally passed by the WTO General Assembly, the instrument should have been consulted and received wide acceptance at the various levels, both public and operational. The aim would be not to impose it, but adopt a code already known and largely assumed by the principal agents and their representatives.

Language

13. It is necessary to depart from stereotyped, ceremonial and mentor-like language which is characteristic of so many past *declarations*. A combination of clear, measurable principles and the ready-to-use check-lists to be applied to tourism projects and developments could be an answer to this concern.
14. When establishing principles and check-lists, their operational meaning should be clearly defined to allow comprehension and assessment by ordinary citizens concerned about tourism development. In order to formulate principles, sometimes it may be necessary to support them by identifiable research. This is due to the fact that certain principles, although reflecting popular beliefs may be not taken for granted and at times questioned.

15. Given an international vocation of the Code, it is also important to use in it the terms and terminology to be understood to various cultures. Special care should therefore be given to its translation.

Implementation

16. Various simultaneous elements could be used to assist in the Code application:

    (*a*) receiving commitments to apply the Code by the bodies concerned (governments, tourism industry organizations, tourism investors, municipalities, etc.)
    (*b*) establishing an independent body to receive and deal with information on the application of the Code
    (*c*) cooperation with NGOs in the field to monitor the application of the Code
    (*d*) recognition and prizes awarded by the Organization in cooperation with other bodies for socially responsible tourism projects
    (*e*) involving travellers, in particular through consumer organizations and tourism clubs, in the Code implementation
    (*f*) introducing systematic reporting on the implementation of the Code according to established criteria.

Preparation of the Code by WTO

17. The 12th General Assembly of WTO could create a special Committee for the Preparation of the Code of *Ethics* for Tourism. This Committee would be related to the Quality Support Committee, a subsidiary, body of the Executive Council. The Committee would establish its own terms of reference (including time-table) and elect its president from among the personalities who would like to assist the Secretariat in preparing the draft Code. Those willing to voluntarily form part of the Committee may wish to notify it to the Secretary-General of WTO prior to the General Assembly. At the Secretariat level, the work will be coordinated by the Deputy Secretary-General.
18. Following the General Assembly, the preparation of the Code would regularly feature on the agenda of all Regional Commissions and would be systematically reviewed by

the Quality Support Committee and the Executive Council. In addition to the Special Committee members notified to the Secretary-General, the Commissions may designate their own representatives to this committee to ensure geographical balance.

19. The preparation of the first draft could be entrusted to an independent consultant who would take stock of the existing instruments already adopted or being prepared by other bodies at different levels. The consultant would take care of substantiating the respective provisions of the Code by research when necessary or would indicate where such research may be needed.
20. For reasons of economy and the need to use expertise where available, WTO could benefit, whenever feasible from the various meetings, organized by the Organizations or to which it is invited, to consult the draft with the bodies concerned. Such meetings could also be used to obtain acceptance of the provisions in point and to consult the possibility of commitments to apply the instrument by these bodies.

Global Codes of Ethics for Sustainable Tourism

[Article 1] Tourism's Contribution to Mutual Understanding and Respect between Peoples and Societies

1. The understanding and promotion of the ethical values common to humanity, with an attitude of tolerance and respect for the diversity of religious, philosophical and moral beliefs, are both the foundation and the consequence of responsible tourism; stakeholders in tourism development and tourists themselves should observe the social and cultural traditions and practices of all peoples, including those of minorities and indigenous peoples and to recognize their worth;
2. Tourism activities should be conducted in harmony with the attributes and traditions of the host regions and countries and in respect for their laws, practices and customs;
3. The host communities, on the one hand, and local professionals, on the other, should acquaint themselves with and respect the tourists who visit them and find out

about their lifestyles, tastes and expectations; the education and training imparted to professionals contribute to a hospitable welcome;

4. It is the task of the public authorities to provide protection for tourists and visitors and their belongings; they must pay particular attention to the safety of foreign tourists owing to the particular vulnerability they may have; they should facilitate the introduction of specific means of information, prevention, security, insurance and assistance consistent with their needs; any attacks, assaults, kidnappings or threats against tourists or workers in the tourism industry, as well as the willful destruction of tourism facilities or of elements of cultural or natural heritage should be severely condemned and punished in accordance with their respective national laws;
5. When travelling, tourists and visitors should not commit any criminal act or any act considered criminal by the laws of the country visited and abstain from any conduct felt to be offensive or injurious by the local populations, or likely to damage the local environment; they should refrain from all trafficking in illicit drugs, arms, antiques, protected species and products and substances that are dangerous or prohibited by national regulations;
6. Tourists and visitors have the responsibility to acquaint themselves, even before their departure, with the characteristics of the countries they are preparing to visit; they must be aware of the health and security risks inherent in any travel outside their usual environment and behave in such a way as to minimize those risks.

[Article 2] Tourism as a Vehicle for Individual and Collective Fulfilment

1. Tourism, the activity most frequently associated with rest and relaxation, sport and access to culture and nature, should be planned and practised as a privileged means of individual and collective fulfilment; when practised with a sufficiently open mind, it is an irreplaceable factor of self-education, mutual tolerance and for learning about the legitimate differences between peoples and cultures and their diversity;

2. Tourism activities should respect the equality of men and women; they should promote human rights and, more particularly, the individual rights of the most vulnerable groups, notably children, the elderly, the handicapped, ethnic minorities and indigenous peoples;
3. The exploitation of human beings in any form, particularly sexual, especially when applied to children, conflicts with the fundamental aims of tourism and is the negation of tourism; as such, in accordance with international law, it should be energetically combatted with the cooperation of all the States concerned and penalized without concession by the national legislation of both the countries visited and the countries of the perpetrators of these acts, even when they are carried out abroad;
4. Travel for purposes of religion, health, education and cultural or linguistic exchanges are particularly beneficial forms of tourism, which deserve encouragement;
5. The introduction into curricula of education about the value of tourist exchanges, their economic, social and cultural benefits, and also their risks, should be encouraged.

[Article 3] Tourism, a Factor of Sustainable Development

1. All the stakeholders in tourism development should safeguard the natural environment with a view to achieving sound, continuous and sustainable economic growth geared to satisfying equitably the needs and aspirations of present and future generations;
2. All forms of tourism development that are conducive to saving rare and precious resources, in particular water and energy, as well as avoiding so far as possible waste production, should be given priority and encouraged by national, regional and local public authorities;
3. The staggering in time and space of tourist and visitor flows, particularly those resulting from paid leave and school holidays, and a more even distribution of holidays should be sought so as to reduce the pressure of tourism activity on the environment and enhance its beneficial impact on the tourism industry and the local economy;
4. Tourism infrastructure should be designed and tourism activities programmed in such a way as to protect the

natural heritage composed of ecosystems and biodiversity and to preserve endangered species of wildlife; the stakeholders in tourism development, and especially professionals, should agree to the imposition of limitations or constraints on their activities when these are exercised in particularly sensitive areas: desert, polar or high mountain regions, coastal areas, tropical forests or wetlands, propitious to the creation of nature reserves or protected areas;

5. Nature tourism and ecotourism are recognized as being particularly conducive to enriching and enhancing the standing of tourism, provided they respect the natural heritage and local populations and are in keeping with the carrying capacity of the sites.

[Article 4] Tourism, a User of the Cultural Heritage of Mankind and Contributor to its Enhancement

1. Tourism resources belong to the common heritage of mankind; the communities in whose territories they are situated have particular rights and obligations to them;
2. Tourism policies and activities should be conducted with respect for the artistic, archaeological and cultural heritage, which they should protect and pass on to future generations; particular care should be devoted to preserving and upgrading monuments, shrines and museums as well as archaeological and historic sites which must be widely open to tourist visits; encouragement should be given to public access to privately-owned cultural property and monuments, with respect for the rights of their owners, as well as to religious buildings, without prejudice to normal needs of worship;
3. Financial resources derived from visits to cultural sites and monuments should, at least in part, be used for the upkeep, safeguard, development and embellishment of this heritage;
4. Tourism activity should be planned in such a way as to allow traditional cultural products, crafts and folklore to survive and flourish, rather than causing them to degenerate and become standardized.

[Article 5] Tourism, a Beneficial Activity for Host Countries and Communities

1. Local populations should be associated with tourism activities and share equitably in the economic, social and cultural benefits they generate, and particularly in the creation of direct and indirect jobs resulting from them;
2. Tourism policies should be applied in such a way as to help to raise the standard of living of the populations of the regions visited and meet their needs; the planning and architectural approach to and operation of tourism resorts and accommodation should aim to integrate them, to the extent possible, in the local economic and social fabric; where skills are equal, priority should be given to local manpower;
3. Special attention should be paid to the specific problems of coastal areas and island territories and to vulnerable rural or mountain regions, for which tourism often represents a rare opportunity for development in the face of the decline of traditional economic activities;
4. Tourism professionals, particularly investors, governed by the regulations laid down by the public authorities, should carry out studies of the impact of their development projects on the environment and natural surroundings; they should also deliver, with the greatest transparency and objectivity, information on their future programmes and their foreseeable repercussions and foster dialogue on their contents with the populations concerned.

[Article 6] Obligations of Stakeholders in Tourism Development

1. Tourism professionals have an obligation to provide tourists with objective and honest information on their places of destination and on the conditions of travel, hospitality and stays; they should ensure that the contractual clauses proposed to their customers are readily understandable as to the nature, price and quality of the services they commit themselves to providing and the financial compensation payable by them in the event of a unilateral breach of contract on their part;
2. Tourism professionals, insofar as it depends on them, should show concern, in co-operation with the public

authorities, for the security and safety, accident prevention, health protection and food safety of those who seek their services; likewise, they should ensure the existence of suitable systems of insurance and assistance; they should accept the reporting obligations prescribed by national regulations and pay fair compensation in the event of failure to observe their contractual obligations;

3. Tourism professionals, so far as this depends on them, should contribute to the cultural and spiritual fulfilment of tourists and allow them, during their travels, to practise their religions;
4. The public authorities of the generating States and the host countries, in cooperation with the professionals concerned and their associations, should ensure that the necessary mechanisms are in place for the repatriation of tourists in the event of the bankruptcy of the enterprise that organized their travel;
5. Governments have the right—and the duty—especially in a crisis, to inform their nationals of the difficult circumstances, or even the dangers they may encounter during their travels abroad; it is their responsibility however to issue such information without prejudicing in an unjustified or exaggerated manner the tourism industry of the host countries and the interests of their own operators; the contents of travel advisories should therefore be discussed beforehand with the authorities of the host countries and the professionals concerned; recommendations formulated should be strictly proportionate to the gravity of the situations encountered and confined to the geographical areas where the insecurity has arisen; such advisories should be qualified or cancelled as soon as a return to normality permits;
6. The press, and particularly the specialized travel press and the other media, including modern means of electronic communication, should issue honest and balanced information on events and situations that could influence the flow of tourists; they should also provide accurate and reliable information to the consumers of tourism services; the new communication and electronic commerce technologies should also be developed and used for this

purpose; as is the case for the media, they should not in any way promote sex tourism.

[Article 7] Right to Tourism

1. The prospect of direct and personal access to the discovery and enjoyment of the planet's resources constitutes a right equally open to all the world's inhabitants; the increasingly extensive participation in national and international tourism should be regarded as one of the best possible expressions of the sustained growth of free time, and obstacles should not be placed in its way;
2. The universal right to tourism must be regarded as the corollary of the right to rest and leisure, including reasonable limitation of working hours and periodic holidays with pay, guaranteed by Article 24 of the Universal Declaration of Human Rights and Article 7(d) of the International Covenant on Economic, Social and Cultural Rights;
3. Social tourism, and in particular associative tourism, which facilitates widespread access to leisure, travel and holidays, should be developed with the support of the public authorities;
4. Family, youth, student and senior tourism and tourism for people with disabilities, should be encouraged and facilitated.

[Article 8] Liberty of Tourist Movements

1. Tourists and visitors should benefit, in compliance with international law and national legislation, from the liberty to move within their countries and from one State to another, in accordance with Article 13 of the Universal Declaration of Human Rights; they should have access to places of transit and stay and to tourism and cultural sites without being subject to excessive formalities or discrimination;
2. Tourists and visitors should have access to all available forms of communication, internal or external; they should benefit from prompt and easy access to local administrative, legal and health services; they should be free to contact the consular representatives of their countries of origin in compliance with the diplomatic conventions in force;

3. Tourists and visitors should benefit from the same rights as the citizens of the country visited concerning the confidentiality of the personal data and information concerning them, especially when these are stored electronically;
4. Administrative procedures relating to border crossings whether they fall within the competence of States or result from international agreements, such as visas or health and customs formalities, should be adapted, so far as possible, so as to facilitate to the maximum freedom of travel and widespread access to international tourism; agreements between groups of countries to harmonize and simplify these procedures should be encouraged; specific taxes and levies penalizing the tourism industry and undermining its competitiveness should be gradually phased out or corrected;
5. So far as the economic situation of the countries from which they come permits, travellers should have access to allowances of convertible currencies needed for their travels.

[Article 9] Rights of the Workers and Entrepreneurs in the Tourism Industry

1. The fundamental rights of salaried and self-employed workers in the tourism industry and related activities, should be guaranteed under the supervision of the national and local administrations, both of their States of origin and of the host countries with particular care, given the specific constraints linked in particular to the seasonality of their activity, the global dimension of their industry and the flexibility often required of them by the nature of their work;
2. Salaried and self-employed workers in the tourism industry and related activities have the right and the duty to acquire appropriate initial and continuous training; they should be given adequate social protection; job insecurity should be limited so far as possible; and a specific status, with particular regard to their social welfare, should be offered to seasonal workers in the sector;
3. Any natural or legal person, provided he/she or it has the necessary abilities and skills, should be entitled to develop

a professional activity in the field of tourism under existing national laws; entrepreneurs and investors—especially in the area of small and medium-sized enterprises—should be entitled to free access to the tourism sector with a minimum of legal or administrative restrictions;

4. Exchanges of experience offered to executives and workers, whether salaried or not, from different countries, contributes to foster the development of the world tourism industry; these movements should be facilitated so far as possible in compliance with the applicable national laws and international conventions;
5. As an irreplaceable factor of solidarity in the development and dynamic growth of international exchanges, multinational enterprises of the tourism industry should not exploit the dominant positions they sometimes occupy; they should avoid becoming the vehicles of cultural and social models artificially imposed on the host communities; in exchange for their freedom to invest and trade which should be fully recognized, they should involve themselves in local development, avoiding, by the excessive repatriation of their profits or their induced imports, a reduction of their contribution to the economies in which they are established;
6. Partnership and the establishment of balanced relations between enterprises of generating and receiving countries contribute to the sustainable development of tourism and an equitable distribution of the benefits of its growth.

[Article 10] Implementation of the Principles of the Global Code of Ethics for Tourism

1. The public and private stakeholders in tourism development should cooperate in the implementation of these principles and monitor their effective application;
2. The stakeholders in tourism development should recognize the role of international institutions, among which the World Tourism Organization ranks first, and non-governmental organizations with competence in the field of tourism promotion and development, the protection of human rights, the environment or health, with due respect for the general principles of international law;

3. The same stakeholders should demonstrate their intention to refer any disputes concerning the application or interpretation of the Global Code of Ethics for Tourism for conciliation to an impartial third body known as the World Committee on Tourism Ethics.

Source: World Tourism Organization, 1999.

4

Quality Management in Tourism: Concepts, Principles and Systems Standards

QUALITY IN TOURISM: A CONCEPTUAL FRAMEWORK

In its work programme WTO is guided by the understanding of quality in tourism as "the result of a process which implies the satisfaction of all the legitimate product and service needs, requirements and expectations of the consumer, at an acceptable price, in conformity with mutually accepted contractual conditions and the underlying quality determinants such as safety and security, hygiene, accessibility, transparency, authenticity and harmony of the tourism activity concerned with its human and natural environment." Defined and modified by the WTO Quality Support Committee at its sixth meeting (Varadero, Cuba, 9-10 May, 2003).

The analysis of each term used in this definition suggests concrete actions which can be evaluated from the perspective of quality criteria.

"Result" implies that quality is attained and perceived at a given time. It cannot be in place without harmonious and active engagement of all the factors intervening in tourism experience. The result can be measured by consumer satisfaction as well as by social, environmental and economic effects of the tourism activity concerned.

"Process" means that a single undertaking is not sufficient to attain quality. Work towards quality always has to in place, it cannot discontinue because of the temporarily attained quality result. It also implies a seamless or flawless process in which it is possible to identify and do away with the constrains of a supply

which spoil the tourism product and are responsible for direct and indirect losses to the company or destination.

"Satisfaction" introduces the elements of subjectivity in quality perception. According to their characteristics, customers have different requirements and expectations. Informed quality-driven marketing caters to these characteristics and attempts to identify consumers according to the different types and levels of perceived quality.

"Legitimate" brings into the analysis the elements of rights and entitlement. Consumers cannot expect to receive more than what they remunerate by payment or what has been determined by social and environmental limits. The role of tourism planners and entrepreneurs is to relate quality types and levels to remuneration and external limitations.

The notion of *"needs"* follows on the concern for legitimacy and looks for satisfying people's basic and vital needs which should never be overlooked while bringing into tourism projects and programmes the other aspects with a view to introducing attractions, strengthening experiences, etc. The needs are primarily related to the underlying quality determinants, although over time the expectations related to the type and volume of basic needs change and usually increase. Basic needs of the past are not exactly the basic needs of today.

The notion of *"product requirements"* emphasizes a need to relate a single service and facility use to the whole product and the total tourism experience. One good quality service is not sufficient to give rise to tourism product quality perception, although an excellent service may positively impress the consumer to make him or her close their eyes to shortcomings and defects experienced elsewhere in the tourism product.

The term *"service requirements"* relates quality to its human, personal and personnel dimensions which are often intangible and apparently difficult to measure, evaluate and quantify in contrast with the physical attributes of tourism facilities which are used primarily in facility classifications or grading. However, certain service elements are quantifiable, for example waiting time, frequency of service (e.g., cleaning), the number and type of services included in the basic price, etc.

The term *"expectations"* relates to the requirement of positive communication and perception of the product characteristics to the potential consumer. There should be no negative surprises at the time of delivery of a service or supply of a product, the consumer must receive what has been promised (or even more). Expectations should also be legitimate, there are limits to expectations, some expectations cannot be fulfilled even at a very high price which can be offered.

The term "*consumer*" relates to individual (end) consumers, who may include groups of people (e.g. a family), corporate consumers (e.g. a company purchasing an incentive trip) and commercial intermediaries (e.g. a tour operator). The latter may request that the product quality be assessed and certified by its own representative or a recognized external third party.

"*Acceptable price*" suggests that the client's expectations reflected in the price cannot be attained at any cost, and that positive surprises should not be too generous, otherwise this may imply excessive allocation of resources which do not receive adequate remuneration. If quality is guaranteed and the product exceptional, there should be no expectation that it should be sold cheap.

"*Mutually accepted contractual conditions*" is an additional concept included in the definition by the WTO Quality Support Committee, at the indication of the private sector. It introduces the element of commercial and legal nature and is related to transparency. Acceptance can be explicit or tacit (implicit), depending on the regulations governing the tourism sector in a given country or the type of transaction. For example, some contracts may need to be signed, while other transactions would only require prior communication of the price on ordering a service.

"*The underlying quality determinants*" suggest that there should be common, irrevocable criteria of quality which are vital for the consumer independently of category or class of the product, establishment, facility or service sophistication. They establish the minimum level of consumer protection under which quality, or total quality, is impossible to achieve, or when failing to meet any of such determinants will significantly reduce the quality of tourism experience.

Safety and Security

A tourism product or service cannot represent danger to life, damage to health and other vital interests and integrity of the consumer (even if we talk about "adventure tourism"). Safety and security standards are normally established by law (e.g. by fire prevention regulations) and should be considered as quality standards per se.

Hygiene

For example, an accommodation facility just has to be safe and clean, one cannot pretend that such requirements are more important to high-class establishments. Food safety standards (often also established by law) must be met and be common to all types of food outlets, from street vendors to luxury gourmet restaurants to airline catering.

Accessibility

This determinant requires that physical, communication and service barriers must be done away with to allow, without discrimination, the use of mainstream tourism products and services by all people irrespective of their natural and acquired differences, including people with disabilities.

Transparency

It is a key element to provide for legitimacy of expectations and consumer protection. It relates to providing and effectively communicating truthful information on the characteristics and coverage of the product and its total price. It includes to state what is covered by the price and what is not in the product on supply.

Authenticity

In a commercial world, authenticity is the hardest and most subjective quality determinant to attain. It also has marketing and competition dimensions. Authenticity is culturally determined and one of its results is making the product markedly distinct from other similar products. Authenticity must meet consumer expectations. It diminishes and eventually terminates when the product loses its links with its cultural and natural background. In this sense, a "genuine" ethnic restaurant can never be entirely authentic in a place distinct from its original setting. This does not mean that such an establishment cannot be an attraction and that it cannot be assessed from the viewpoint of quality with respect to production (content and design), marketing, distribution, sale and delivery of the service concerned. A theme park representing other lands and far away cultures is a good example of an initially artificial tourism product which may create an authenticity and a quality image of its own. On the other hand, an authentic product can also develop and adapt to needs and expectations.

Harmony

Harmony with the human and natural environment pertains to sustainability which is a medium-and long-term concept. "Maintaining the sustainability of tourism requires managing environmental and socio-economic impacts, establishing environmental indicators and maintaining the quality of the tourism products and tourist markets" (WTO Guide for Local Authorities on Developing Sustainable Tourism). There can be no sustainability without quality.

QUALITY MANAGEMENT PRINCIPLES

This document introduces the eight quality management principles on which the quality management system standards of the revised ISO 9000: 2000 series are based. These principles can be used by senior management as a framework to guide their organizations towards improved performance. The principles are derived from the collective experience and knowledge of the international experts who participate in ISO Technical Committee ISO/TC 176, *Quality management and quality assurance,* which is responsible for developing and maintaining the ISO 9000 standards.

The eight quality management principles are defined in ISO 9000: 2000, *Quality Management Systems Fundamentals and Vocabulary,* and in ISO 9004: 2000, *Quality Management Systems Guidelines for Performance Improvements.*

This document gives the standardized descriptions of the principles as they appear in ISO 9000: 2000 and ISO 9004: 2000. In addition, it provides examples of the benefits derived from their use and of actions that managers typically take in applying the principles to improve their organizations' performance.

- Principle 1: Customer focus
- Principle 2: Leadership
- Principle 3: Involvement of people
- Principle 4: Process approach
- Principle 5: System approach to management
- Principle 6: Continual improvement
- Principle 7: Factual approach to decision-making

- Principle 8: Mutually beneficial supplier relationships
- The next step.

Principle 1: Customer Focus

Organizations depend on their customers and therefore should understand current and future customer needs, should meet customer requirements and strive to exceed customer expectations.

Key Benefits:

- Increased revenue and market share obtained through flexible and fast responses to market opportunities.
- Increased effectiveness in the use of the organization's resources to enhance customer satisfaction.
- Improved customer loyalty leading to repeat business.

Applying the principle of customer focus typically leads to:

- Researching and understanding customer needs and expectations.
- Ensuring that the objectives of the organization are linked to customer needs and expectations.
- Communicating customer needs and expectations throughout the organization.
- Measuring customer satisfaction and acting on the results.
- Systematically managing customer relationships.
- Ensuring a balanced approach between satisfying customers and other interested parties (such as owners, employees, suppliers, financiers, local communities and society as a whole).

Principle 2: Leadership

Leaders establish unity of purpose and direction of the organization. They should create and maintain the internal environment in which people can become fully involved in achieving the organization's objectives.

Key Benefits:

- People will understand and be motivated towards the organization's goals and objectives.
- Activities are evaluated, aligned and implemented in a unified way.

- Miscommunication between levels of an organization will be minimized.

Applying the principle of leadership typically leads to:

- Considering the needs of all interested parties including customers, owners, employees, suppliers, financiers, local communities and society as a whole.
- Establishing a clear vision of the organization's future.
- Setting challenging goals and targets.
- Creating and sustaining shared values, fairness and ethical role models at all levels of the organization.
- Establishing trust and eliminating fear.
- Providing people with the required resources, training and freedom to act with responsibility and accountability.
- Inspiring, encouraging and recognizing people's contributions.

Principle 3: Involvement of People

People at all levels are the essence of an organization and their full involvement enables their abilities to be used for the organization's benefit.

Key Benefits:

- Motivated, committed and involved people within the organization.
- Innovation and creativity in furthering the organization's objectives.
- People being accountable for their own performance.
- People eager to participate in and contribute to continual improvement.

Applying the principle of involvement of people typically leads to:

- People understanding the importance of their contribution and role in the organization.
- People identifying constraints to their performance.
- People accepting ownership of problems and their responsibility for solving them.
- People evaluating their performance against their personal goals and objectives.

- People actively seeking opportunities to enhance their competence, knowledge and experience.
- People freely sharing knowledge and experience.
- People openly discussing problems and issues.

Principle 4: Process Approach

A desired result is achieved more efficiently when activities and related resources are managed as a process.

Key Benefits:

- Lower costs and shorter cycle times through effective use of resources.
- Improved, consistent and predictable results.
- Focused and prioritized improvement opportunities.

Applying the principle of process approach typically leads to:

- Systematically defining the activities necessary to obtain a desired result.
- Establishing clear responsibility and accountability for managing key activities.
- Analyzing and measuring of the capability of key activities.
- Identifying the interfaces of key activities within and between the functions of the organization.
- Focusing on the factors such as resources, methods, and materials that will improve key activities of the organization.
- Evaluating risks, consequences and impacts of activities on customers, suppliers and other interested parties.

Principle 5: System Approach to Management

Identifying, understanding and managing interrelated processes as a system contributes to the organization's effectiveness and efficiency in achieving its objectives.

Key Benefits:

- Integration and alignment of the processes that will best achieve the desired results.
- Ability to focus effort on the key processes.
- Providing confidence to interested parties as to the consistency, effectiveness and efficiency of the organization.

Applying the principle of system approach to management typically leads to:

- Structuring a system to achieve the organization's objectives in the most effective and efficient way.
- Understanding the inter-dependencies between the processes of the system.
- Structured approaches that harmonize and integrate processes.
- Providing a better understanding of the roles and responsibilities necessary for achieving common objectives and thereby reducing cross-functional barriers.
- Understanding organizational capabilities and establishing resource constraints prior to action.
- Targeting and defining how specific activities within a system should operate.
- Continually improving the system through measurement and evaluation.

Principle 6: Continual Improvement

Continual improvement of the organization's overall performance should be a permanent objective of the organization.

Key Benefits:

- Performance advantage through improved organizational capabilities.
- Alignment of improvement activities at all levels to an organization's strategic intent.
- Flexibility to react quickly to opportunities.

Applying the principle of continual improvement typically leads to:

- Employing a consistent organization-wide approach to continual improvement of the organization's performance.
- Providing people with training in the methods and tools of continual improvement.
- Making continual improvement of products, processes and systems an objective for every individual in the organization.
- Establishing goals to guide, and measures to track, continual improvement.

- Recognizing and acknowledging improvements.

Principle 7: Factual Approach to Decision-making

Effective decisions are based on the analysis of data and information.

Key Benefits:

- Informed decisions.
- An increased ability to demonstrate the effectiveness of past decisions through reference to factual records.
- Increased ability to review, challenge and change opinions and decisions.

Applying the principle of factual approach to decision-making typically leads to:

- Ensuring that data and information are sufficiently accurate and reliable.
- Making data accessible to those who need it.
- Analyzing data and information using valid methods.
- Making decisions and taking action based on factual analysis, balanced with experience and intuition.

Principle 8: Mutually Beneficial Supplier Relationships

An organization and its suppliers are inter-dependent and a mutually beneficial relationship enhances the ability of both to create value.

Key Benefits:

- Increased ability to create value for both parties.
- Flexibility and speed of joint responses to changing market or customer needs and expectations.
- Optimization of costs and resources.

Applying the principles of mutually beneficial supplier relationships typically leads to:

- Establishing relationships that balance short-term gains with long-term considerations.
- Pooling of expertize and resources with partners.
- Identifying and selecting key suppliers.
- Clear and open communication.
- Sharing information and future plans.

- Establishing joint development and improvement activities.
- Inspiring, encouraging and recognizing improvements and achievements by suppliers.

The Next Step

This document provides a general perspective on the quality management principles underlying the ISO 9000: 2000 series. It gives an overview of these principles and shows how, collectively, they can form a basis for performance improvement and organizational excellence.

There are many different ways of applying these quality management principles. The nature of the organization and the specific challenges it faces will determine how to implement them. Many organizations will find it beneficial to set-up quality management systems based on these principles.

The requirements of quality management systems and supporting guidelines are given in the ISO 9000—Selection and use.

Further information on the ISO 9000 standards is available from ISO's national member institutes or from the ISO Central Secretariat ISO 9000 enquiry service. Sales enquiries should also be directed to the ISO members or to the ISO Central Secretariat sales department.

ISO publishes the bimonthly *ISO Management Systems*, which provides updates on these families of standards and news on their implementation around the world. A Spanish-language edition is published by the Spanish national standards institute, AENOR.

ISO 9000 : 2005—THE 'A TO Z' OF QUALITY MANAGEMENT SYSTEMS

ISO has published a new edition of the standard in the ISO 9000 family that defines the vocabulary and describes the fundamentals of quality management systems.

ISO 9000: 2005, *Quality Management Systems—Fundamentals and Vocabulary*, introduces no changes to the descriptions of the fundamentals of Quality Management Systems (QMS), as presented in the previous edition published in 2000. However, some definitions have been added and explanatory notes expanded or added to take account of more recent documents in the ISO

9000 family and to align ISO 9000 with these. Examples include the following: technical expert, requirement, competence, contract, auditor, audit team, audit plan and audit scope.

Youssef El Gamal, Chair of Subcommittee 1, *Concepts and terminology*, of ISO Technical Committee ISO/TC 176, *Quality management and quality assurance*, which is responsible for ISO 9000, explained: "The primary reason for this new edition is to provide a single unambiguous meaning of key words used in various management systems standards, in particular, ISO 9001: 2000, *Quality management systems—Requirements* and ISO 19011: 2002, *Guidelines for quality and/or environmental management systems auditing."*

The revised ISO 9000 also takes account of joint work by ISO and the IEC (International Electro-technical Commission) on dependability.

To reflect these changes, a number of the diagrams appearing in ISO 9000 have been enhanced for the 2005 version.

ISO 9000: 2005 will be useful for all users of standards in the ISO 9000 family, in particular for the following:

- suppliers, customers and regulators in providing them with a common understanding of the terminology of quality management,
- people who assess QMS, or audit them for conformity to ISO 9001: 2000—such as internal auditors, external auditors of certification bodies, and regulators, and
- providers of consultancy or training on QMS.

ISO 9000: 2005, *Quality management systems—Fundamentals and vocabulary*, costs 118 Swiss francs and is available from ISO national member institutes and from ISO Central Secretariat. It was developed by Subcommittee 1, *Concepts and terminology* of ISO Technical Committee ISO/TC 176, *Quality management and quality assurance.*

ISO Store: to order ISO 9000:2005, *Quality management systems Fundamentals and vocabulary.*

NEW MANAGEMENT SYSTEMS STANDARDS

The tremendous impact of ISO 9001 and ISO 14001 on organizational practices and on trade has stimulated the development of other ISO standards and deliverables that adapt the generic management system to specific sectors or aspects. The articles below on these new developments are drawn from ISO *Management Systems* magazine.

- Food safety
- Information security
- Supply chain security.

Food Safety Management Systems

ISO 22000 is First in Family of Food Safety Management System Standards

ISO 22000: 2005, published on 1 September 2005, is a new International Standard designed to ensure safe food supply chains worldwide and the first of a family on food safety management systems.

How to Implement a Food Safety Management System

ISO followed up its publication of ISO 22000: 2005, the International Standard for food safety management systems, with ISO/TS 22004: 2005, which gives implementation guidance.

Early Adopters Underline Benefits of New ISO Standard for Safe Food Supply Chains

Companies among the first in the world to implement ISO 22000: 2005 are underlining the benefits of the new International Standard for ensuring safe food supply chains.

ISO 22000: 2005, *Food safety management systems—Requirements for any organization in the food chain.*

ISO/TS 22004: 2005, *Food safety management systems—Guidance on the application of ISO 22000: 2005.*

Information Security Management Systems

State-of-the-art Information Security Management Systems with ISO/IEC 27001: 2005

The publication of ISO/IEC 27001: 2005 is a big event in the world of information security and one that has been eagerly awaited.

Improved ISO/IEC 17799 Heralds New Series on Information Security Management Systems

ISO/IEC 17799: 2005 is the international code of good practice for information security management.

ISO/IEC 27001: 2005, *Information Technology—Security techniques—Information Security Management Systems—Requirements.*

Supply Chain Security Management Systems

ISO/PAS 28000 Applies Management System Approach to Security of Global Supply Chains

With billions of dollars worth of goods moving at any given time along global supply chains, ISO/PAS 28000: 2005 for supply chain security management systems will help combat threats to the safe and smooth flow of international trade.

We have devoted an entire section on this site to help answer your questions about ISO 14000. It tells you what this family of environmental management standards is all about and what ISO 14000 will do for your business. It includes a list of the entire ISO 14000 family of standards and related publications by ISO which will help you in your implementation and certification programmes. The site is also linked to the site of the ISO technical committee responsible for ISO 14000, ISO/TC 207. You will also find information on our bimonthly publication, *ISO Management Systems,* which reports on developments and includes many case studies of implementation programmes from around the world.

The ISO Member in your Country

The special ISO 14000 section on this site will give you a basic understanding and list of ISO 14000 standards and other publications that will help you.

The ISO Survey, which you can access on this site, gives the latest available worldwide certification picture. It includes country-by-country breakdowns and comparisons with previous years.

ISO develops and maintains the ISO 14000 standards, but it does not itself issue ISO 14001: 2004 certificates. Certificates are issued independently of ISO by the various national and international certification or registration bodies operating around the world. Each certification or registration body has a list of its clients, but there is no central database of all these certifications/ registrations. The CD-ROM version of *The ISO Survey* includes a breakdown of certifications by business sector.

None. The term "certification body" is used in some countries because these bodies issue certificates. Elsewhere, they prefer to say that they "register" organizations complying with ISO 14000.

This information is compiled within the *ISO Directory of ISO 9001: 2000 and ISO 14001: 2004 accreditation and certification bodies.*

Contact the ISO member for your country, which may be able to point you in the direction of a relevant training scheme. Any certification or registration bodies operating in your country should also be able to advise you.

For Small and Medium-sized Enterprises (SME's)

Small and medium-sized enterprises (SME's) can achieve substantial benefits by implementing *quality management* and *environmental management systems.*

Taking the First Steps Towards a Quality Management System

Having taken the decision to implement a quality management system, SME's in particular are often unsure just how to get started. This article, which first appeared in *ISO Management Systems* magazine takes SME managers through the first steps.

ISO 9001 for Small Businesses

Taking the First Steps in Environmental Management

This article from *ISO Management Systems* magazine explains clearly how an SME can implement an environmental management system so that the process is not a series of hurdles, but rather a set of practical steps towards raising environmental and business performance.

Quality Management Consultants: Instructions for Use

A decision to implement a quality management system may be the organization's first real contact with the world of ISO 9000—especially if it is an SME—and many turn to an external consultant for help. This article from *ISO Management Systems* magazine gives some helpful pointers.

ISO 10019: 2005, *Guidelines for the Selection of Quality Management System Consultants and use of their Services*

Implementing ISO 14001: do you hire a consultant, or Do-It-Yourself?

This article from *ISO Management Systems* magazine helps SME managers answer some essential questions. Should you hire a consultant to help with environmental management system implementation, or go it alone? What are the advantages and potential pitfalls? How can you get best value for money if you hire a consultant and what are the criteria you should use for choosing one?

ISO 14001: 2004 and ISO14004: 2004 revisions were released for publication on November 15, 2004. ISO (International Organization for Standardization) and the IAF (International Accreditation Forum) have agreed to jointly develop the transition plan and have announced the period of making the transition from certificates of conformity to the ISO 14001: 2004 version to 18 months from the revision publication date. Beyond this period, the IAF will recognize only certificates to ISO 14001: 2004.

ISO 14001: 2004, What Changed?

ISO 14001: 2004	*Overview of Change*
4.1General Requirements 4.3.1 Environmental Aspects	Rearticulated for clearer meaning, with enhanced terminology.
4.2 Environmental Policy 4.4.6 Operational Control 4.4.7 Emergency Preparedness and Response	Updated to reflect terminology enhancements and clarification of the requirements.
4.3.2 Legal and Other Requirements	Provides clarification to the requirements and divides the requirement into sub-paragraphs, allowing for ease of understanding.
4.3.3 Objectives, Targets and Programme(s)	The addition of Programme(s), is an instinctive addition to the specification, bringing together the key activities of the system.
4.4.1 Resources, Roles, Responsibility and Authority	The title is updated and includes terminology enhancement for clarification of the requirements.
4.4.2 Competence, Training and Awareness	The title is updated and includes an emphasis on demonstrating competence and training documentation.
4.4.3 Communication	This section includes the addition of "internal" communication in addition to external communication (similar to OSHAS 18001 Health and Safety Management System or HSMS standard).
4.4.4 Documentation	The "Environmental Management System Documentation" has been updated and re-titled to "Documentation" and includes a clearer intent of the significant environmental aspects documentation.
4.4.5 Control of Documents	The title is updated and includes enhanced clarity to the requirement, allowing for ease of understanding.

(Contd.)

ISO 14001: 2004	Overview of Change
4.5.1 Monitoring and Measurement	A re-write of the paragraph for clearer meaning and the addition of calibration.
4.5.2 Evaluation of Compliance	The revision adds "Evaluation of Compliance" as a separate requirement within the Environmental Management System. The emphasis on compliance requires developing a documented process that includes evaluating and maintaining the results of periodic evaluations of compliance with applicable legal requirements.
4.5.3 Non-conformity, Corrective Action and Preventive Action	Provides clarification and restructures the requirement into subparagraphs, allowing for ease of understanding.
4.5.4 Control of Records	Updated title, with a restructure of the paragraph and terminology for ease of understanding with an emphasis on control of conformity records.
4.5.5 Internal Audit	Updated title and an emphasis on independent auditors.
4.6 Management Review	Management Review process is updated to include the identification of inputs and outputs. The addition of identifying inputs and outputs aligns ISO 14001: 2004 to ISO 9000: 2000, moreover, the revision clarifies the description of the information that needs to be collected and reviewed by top management.

ISO Releases new CD-ROM of ISO 14000 Environmental Management Standards

The collection on one *CD-ROM of the ISO 14000 standards for environmental management* is a practical tool that ISO has developed to meet the needs of businesses for a strategic approach addressing all aspects of the environmental challenges they face.

The CD-ROM contains 20 published standards of the ISO 14000 family, plus drafts nearing completion, and ISO Guide 64: 1997, which deals with the inclusion of environmental aspects in product standards.

The CD-ROM includes:

- ISO 14001: 2004 and ISO 14004: 2004 on, respectively, environmental management system requirements and general guidelines, principles and system support techniques;
- ISO 14050: 2002 on the vocabulary used in environmental management;

- ISO 14015: 2001 on the environmental assessment of sites and organizations.

The new drafts include (ISO 14064 parts 1, 2 and 3) on greenhouse gases (GHG). The underlying objective and principles for the development of these standards are to support market development by providing an auditable credible, standardized process for faster, better, cheaper quantification and verification while maintaining:

- Neutrality towards specific policies and programmes;
- Compatibility with the UNFCCC Kyoto Protocol rules and provisions; and
- Compatibility with the WRI/WBCSD GHG Protocol (Corporate and Project).

ISO Secretary-General Alan Bryden commented: "The ISO 14000 series of standards offers a complete tool box to address the various aspects of environmental management. The new CD-ROM contains its latest developments in a user friendly configuration, including those related to the accounting and verification of GHG emissions. It is a timely contribution to assisting in meeting the challenges of sustainable development."

Other new drafts included are:

- ISO 14025 on environmental labels and declarations;
- ISO 14040 dealing with principles and requirements for conducting and reporting lifecycle assessment studies;
- ISO 14044 specifies requirements and guidelines on life cycle assessment of environmental aspects and their potential impacts throughout a product's life cycle;
- ISO 14063, which gives organizations guidance on general policies and strategies with examples, to help improve internal and external environmental communication.

Today, the management of environmental aspects and impacts is a top priority and has established itself as a cornerstone of effective organizational practice alongside the management of quality, security, and health and safety issues. ISO/TC 207 was established in 1993 and is the committee responsible for developing the ISO 14000 series of environmental management standards.

Table 4.1: Application of the ISO 1400 Family

At the Organization Level

Implementing Environmental Management System (EMS)	*ISO 14001: 1996* *ISO 14004: 1996* Help an organization to establish a new or improve an existing EMS	*ISO 14001: 1996* Specifies the requirements for an EMS that may be objectively audited for self-declaration, second or third-party certification/registration purposes	*ISO 14004: 1996* Provides guidance to help an organisation establish and implement an EMS, including guidance that goes beyond the requirements of ISO 14001	*ISO/TR 14061: 1998* Contains information that assists in the implementation of ISO 14001 and ISO 14004 by forest management organizations and the forest products industry		
Conducting Environmental Audits and Other Related Investigations	*ISO 14010: 1996* Provides guidance on the general principles common to the conduct of any environmental audit	*ISO 14011: 1996* Provides guidance on the procedures for the conduct of EMS audits, including the criteria for selection and composition of audit teams	*ISO 14012: 1996* Provides guidance on the qualifications of internal or external environmental auditors and lead auditors	*ISO 14015: 2001* Helps an organization to identify and assess the environmental aspects and associated business consequences of sites and organizations to support the transfer of properties, responsibilities and obligations from one party to another	*ISO 19011: 2002* (replaces ISO 14010,14011 and 14012) Provides guidance on the principles of auditing; the management of audit programmes; the conduct of management system audits as well as on the competence of auditors	
Evaluating Environmental Performance	*ISO 14031: 1999* Provides guidance on the selection and use of indicators to evaluate an organization's environmental performance	*ISO/TR 14032: 1999* Provides examples from real organizations to illustrate the use of the guidance in ISO 14031	*Communicating Results*	*ISO/WD 14063* Will provide guidance on environmental communication related to an organization's environmental aspects and performance	*Understanding Terms and Definitions*	*ISO 14050: 2002* Helps an organization to understand the terms used in the ISO 14000 series standards

(*Contd.*)

Using Environmental Declarations and Claims	*ISO 14020: 2000* Provides general principles which serve as a basis for the development of ISO guidelines and standards on environmental claims and declarations	*ISO 14021: 1999* Provides guidance on the terminology, symbols and testing and verification methodologies an organization should use for self-declaration of the environmental aspects of its products and services (Type II Environmental Labelling)	*ISO 14024: 1999* Provides the guiding principles and procedures for third-party environmental labelling certification programmes (Type I Environmental Labelling)	*ISO/TR 14025: 2000* Identifies and describes elements and issues for consideration when making declarations of quantified product information based on Life Cycle Inventory data (Type III Environmental declarations)		
Conducting Life Cycle Assessment (LCA)	*ISO 14040: 1999* Provides the general principles, framework and methodological requirements for the LCA of products and services	*ISO 14041: 1998* Provides guidance for determining the goal and scope of an LCA study, and for conducting a life cycle inventory	*ISO 14042: 2000* Provides guidance for conducting the life cycle impact assessment phase of an LCA study	*ISO/TR 14043: 2000* Provides guidance for the interpretation of results from an LCA study	*ISO/TS 14048: 2002* Provides information regarding the formatting of data to support life cycle assessment	*ISO/TR 14049/14047* Provide examples that illustrate how to apply the guidance in ISO 14041 and ISO 14042
Addressing Environmental Aspects in Products and Product Standards	*ISO Guide 64: 1997* Helps the writers of product standards address environmental aspects in those standards	*ISO/TR 14062: 2002* Provides concepts and current practices relating to integration of environmental aspects into product design and development		*Understanding Terms and Definitions*	*ISO 14050: 2002* Helps an organization to understand the terms used in the ISO 14000 series standards	

Products and Sources of Information on ISO 14000

As the products may be updated regularly, ISBN numbers and details of pagination and pricing are liable to change and therefore have not been included here. Information, including these details, on the latest editions can be obtained from ISO's Web site (www.iso.org), or by contacting sales@iso.org.

ISO Standards Compendium

ISO 14000—Environmental management—brings together in one volume all published International Standards developed by ISO Technical Committee 207, *Environmental Management*. It also includes Draft International Standards.

ISO 14000—Environmental Management on CD-ROM—the entire ISO 14000 family—standards, drafts and technical reports on CD-ROM, featuring easy access, navigation and retrieval.

Manual 10, Environmental Management and ISO 14000—introduces the ISO 14000 family to readers who wish to obtain an overall idea of the published standards as well as those still in preparation and how they were developed. It is of interest to any reader who wants to gain insight into those aspects of environmental management dealt with by ISO/TC 207, Environmental management, and its sub-committees.

The ISO Survey of ISO 9000 and ISO 14000 Certificates—a worldwide survey of certifications to ISO's two families of management system standards, including country-by-country breakdowns.

Publicizing your ISO 9000 or ISO 14000 certification—advice to help ISO 9000 and ISO 14000 certificate holders avoid the pitfalls of false, misleading or confusing claims in advertisements or other promotional material.

ISO Management Systems (full colour magazine, six issues a year)—provides comprehensive coverage of international developments relating to the ISO 9000 family of quality management standards and to the ISO 14000 environmental management standards, including news on their implementation around the world. ISO Management Systems (available in English, French and Spanish editions) is the premier platform for exchange and dialogue among the worldwide community of ISO 9000 and ISO 14000 users.

Web Sites

www.iso.org

The ISO Web site, like that of many of its national standards institute members around the world, includes information on ISO 14000 and related products. A full list of ISO's members with contact details and hyperlinks is posted on the ISO site. Enquiries for information about ISO 14000 or sales enquiries should be directed to the national members institutes or to ISO Central Secretariat. The ISO Web site itself has a special section on ISO 14000 and ISO 9000 which includes both specifically prepared online material and free, downloadable copies of a number of the documents mentioned above. Latest ISO 14000-related developments are often the subject of press releases which are also posted on the site. Lastly, all ISO 14000 and related standards and publications are catalogued on the site and they can be ordered online.

www.tc207.org

The Web site of ISO/TC 207, Environmental management, responsible for the ISO 14000 family of standards presents the committee, its membership, structure and work programme and includes a section devoted to Frequently Asked Questions.

Table 4.2: The ISO 14000 Family of Standards, Guides and Technical Reports—Including Drafts

The ISO 14000 Family of Standards

Designation	*Publication*	*Title*
ISO 14001: 1996	1996	Environmental management systems—Specification with guidance for use
ISO 14004: 1996	1996	Environmental management systems—General guidelines on principles, systems and supporting techniques
ISO 14010: 1996	1996	Guidelines for environmental auditing—General principles
ISO 14011: 1996	1996	Guidelines for environmental auditing—Audit procedures—Auditing of environmental management systems
ISO 14012: 1996	1996	Guidelines for environmental auditing—Qualification criteria for environmental auditors
ISO 14015: 2001	2001	Environmental management—Environmental Assessment of Sites and Organizations (EASO)
ISO 14020: 2000	2000	Environmental labels and declarations—General principles
ISO 14021: 1999	1999	Environmental labels and declarations—Self-declared environmental claims (Type II environmental labelling)

(Contd.)

Designation	Publication	Title
ISO 14024: 1999	1999	Environmental labels and declarations—Type I environmental labelling—Principles and procedures
ISO/TR 14025: 2000	2000	Environmental labels and declarations—Type III environmental declarations
ISO 14031: 1999	1999	Environmental management—Environmental performance evaluation—Guidelines
ISO/TR 14032: 1999	1999	Environmental management—Examples of Environmental Performance Evaluation (EPE)
ISO 14040: 1997	1997	Environmental management—Life cycle assessment—Principles and framework
ISO 14041: 1998	1998	Environmental management—Lifecycle assessment—Goal and scope definition and inventory analysis
ISO 14042: 2000	2000	Environmental management—Lifecycle assessment—Lifecycle impact assessment
ISO 14043: 2000	2000	Environmental management—Lifecycle assessment—Life cycle interpretation
ISO/TR 14047	To be determined	Environmental management—Lifecycle assessment—Examples of application of ISO 14042
ISO/TS 14048: 2002	2002	Environmental management—Lifecycle assessment—Data documentation format
ISO/TR 14049: 2000	2000	Environmental management—Lifecycle assessment—Examples of application of ISO 14041 to goal and scope definition and inventory analysis
ISO 14050: 2002	2002	Environmental management—Vocabulary
ISO/TR 14061: 1998	1998	Information to assist forestry organizations in the use of the Environmental Management System standards ISO 14001 and ISO 14004
ISO/TR 14062: 2002	2002	Environmental management—Integrating environmental aspects into product design and development
ISO/WD 14063	To be determined	Environmental management—Environmental communications—Guidelines and examples
ISO/AWI 14064	To be determined	Guidelines for measuring, reporting and verifying entity and project-level greenhouse gas emissions
ISO 19011: 2002	2002	Guidelines for quality and/or environmental management systems auditing (This standard replaces ISO 14010, 14011 and 14012)
ISO Guide 64: 1997	1997	Guide for the inclusion of environmental aspects in product standards
ISO/IEC Guide 66*	1999	General requirements for bodies operating assessment and certification/registration of Environmental Management Systems (EMS)

Notes: AWI = Approved Work Item
WD = Working Draft
CD = Committee Draft
DIS = Draft International Standard
FDIS = Final Draft International Standard
DTR = Draft Technical Report
TR = Technical Report
* ISO/IEC Guide 66 was developed by the ISO Policy Development Committee on conformity assessment (ISO/CASCO)

DRAFTING PROGRESSES OF FUTURE ISO 26000 STANDARD ON SOCIAL RESPONSIBILITY

The building of international consensus on voluntary guidance to help organizations operate in a socially responsible way made progress at the recent meeting of the ISO group that is developing the future ISO 26000 standard on social responsibility.

Some 320 people from 55 countries and 26 international organizations attended the third plenary meeting of the ISO Working Group on Social Responsibility (WG SR) on 15-19 May, 2006 in Lisbon, Portugal.

ISO 26000 is intended for use by organizations of all types, in both public and private sectors, in developed and developing countries. ISO 26000 will contain guidelines, not requirements. It is not a management system standard and will not be for use as a certification standard like ISO 9001: 2000 and ISO 14001: 2004. It is now expected to be published in the first quarter of 2009.

Drafting of the content of the standard is in progress and at Lisbon, one of the main tasks was to review some 2100 comments from WG SR members on the first working draft. This work will continue in order to produce a second working draft for circulation and comment before the next WG SR meeting in early 2007.

ISO 26000 is being developed by representatives of the six main stakeholder groups: industry; government: labour; consumers; non-governmental organizations; and service, support, research and others. In addition, efforts are made to maintain a geographical and gender-based balance of participants.

The guidance in ISO 26000 will draw on best practices developed by existing public and private sector SR initiatives. It will be consistent with and complement relevant declarations and conventions by the United Nations and its constituents, notably the International Labour Organization (ILO), with whom ISO has established a Memorandum of Understanding to ensure consistency with ILO labour standards.

In addition to the work on the content of the standard, the Lisbon meeting further defined the WG SR's operating framework in order to strengthen participation and accountability. The WG SR also continues to develop communication tools for promoting SR awareness throughout the world, the significance of the ISO standard, and how diverse interests may most effectively contribute to the shaping of the ISO 26000 standard and to other social responsibility activities.

Figure 4.1: The ISO 14000 Model

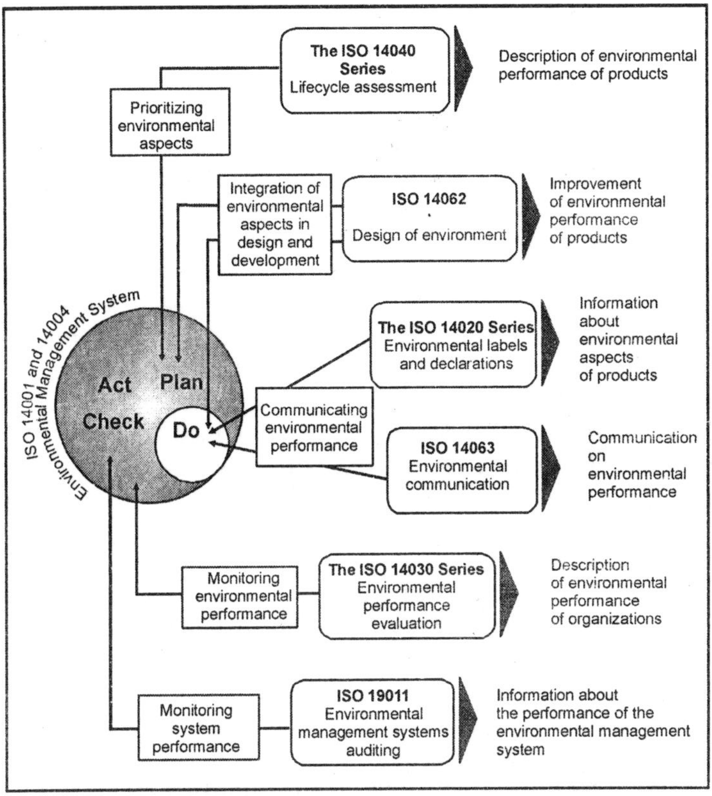

ISO AND THE ENVIRONMENTAL MANAGEMENT SYSTEMS

" Think globally, act locally"—the well-known credo for addressing environmental issues—also expresses the objective of ISO's many environmental standards. These standards reflect global consensus on good environmental practice in the international context that can be applied pragmatically by organizations all over the world in their particular situation.

ISO has a two-pronged approach to meeting the needs of all stakeholders from business, industry, governmental authorities and non-governmental organizations, as well as consumers, in the field of the environment.

Firstly, ISO offers a wide-ranging portfolio of standards for sampling and test methods to deal with specific environmental challenges. It has developed more than 350 International Standards for the monitoring of such aspects as the quality of air, water and soil, as well as noise and radiation. They also serve in a number of countries as the technical basis for environmental regulations.

Secondly, ISO has developed standards that help organizations to take a more pro-active approach to managing environmental issues. These environmental management standards can be implemented in any type of organizations in either public or private sectors (from companies to administrations to public utilities).

To spearhead this strategic approach, ISO established a new technical committee, ISO/TC 207 in 1993, *Environmental management*. This move was a concrete manifestation of ISO's commitment to respond to the complex challenge of "sustainable development" articulated at the 1992 United Nations Conference on Environment and Development in Rio de Janeiro. It also stemmed from an intensive consultation process, carried out within the framework of the Strategic Advisory Group on Environment (SAGE). SAGE was set-up in 1991 and brought together representatives of a variety of countries and international organizations—a total of more than 100 environmental experts—who helped to define how International Standards could support better environmental management.

As a result, the ISO 14000 family of standards on environmental management was developed to provide a practical toolbox to assist in the implementation of actions supportive to sustainable development.

Today, national delegations of environmental experts from 66 countries participate within ISO/TC 207, including 27 developing countries. In addition, 35 international non-governmental and business organizations participate as liaison organizations. The national delegations are chosen by the national standards institute concerned and they are required to bring to ISO/TC 207 a national consensus on issues being addressed by the technical committee. This national consensus is derived from a process of consultation with interested parties in each country.

From its beginning, it was recognized that ISO/TC 207 should cooperate closely with ISO/TC 176, *Quality Management* and *Quality Assurance*—the ISO technical committee responsible for the ISO 9000 family of quality management standards—in the areas of management systems, auditing and related terminology. Successful steps have been taken to ensure compatibility of ISO environmental management and quality management standards. These include a common standard giving guidelines for environmental and/or quality auditing.

BENEFITS OF THE ISO 14000 FAMILY OF INTERNATIONAL STANDARDS

In today's global economy, organizations are increasingly called upon to demonstrate sound management of economic, social and environmental issues. Evidence suggests that a focus on this "triple bottom line" results in advantages in financing, insurance, marketing, regulatory treatment and other areas.

An Environmental Management System (EMS) is a structured approach to addressing the environmental bottom line. ISO 14001 is the world's most recognized EMS framework—accepted from Argentina to Zimbabwe—that helps organizations both to manage better the impact of their activities on the environment and to demonstrate sound environmental management.

Since the publication of ISO 14001, many companies have implemented the standard and, by the end of 2001, nearly 37000 organizations in 112 countries had their EMS certified as conforming to its requirements. ISO 14001 is designed to be flexible enough to be applied to any sized organization in both the private and public sectors. The bottom line is that certification to ISO 14001 can improve environmental management and enables equal access to a growing "green" market place.

ISO 14001 is also the starting point for companies that want to use other environmental management tools developed by ISO/TC 207. For example, ISO 14004 provides additional guidance and useful explanations and complements ISO 14001.

Of course, an EMS will only be of maximum benefit if it is properly implemented. Environmental audits are important tools for assessing whether an EMS is properly implemented and maintained. The new auditing standard, ISO 19011, is equally useful for EMS and quality management system audits. It provides guidance on principles of auditing, managing audit programmes, the conduct of audits and on the competence of auditors. ISO 19011 replaces the ISO 14010, ISO 14011 and ISO 14012 first generation of environmental auditing standards in the ISO 14000 family.

Organizations implementing ISO 14001 can expect to improve their environmental performance. ISO 14031 provides guidance on how an organization can evaluate its environmental performance. The standard also addresses the selection of suitable performance indicators, so that performance can be assessed against criteria set by management. This sort of information can be used as a basis for internal and external reporting on environmental performance.

Communication on the environmental aspects of products and services is an important way to use market forces to influence environmental improvement. Truthful and accurate information provides the basis on which consumers can make informed purchasing decisions. The ISO 14020 series of standards address a range of different approaches to environmental labels and declarations, including self-declared environmental claims, eco-labels (seals of approval) and quantified environmental information about products and services.

ISO 14001 addresses not only the environmental aspects of an organization's processes, but also those of its products and services. Therefore, ISO/TC 207 developed additional tools to assist in addressing such aspects. Lifecycle Assessment (LCA) is a tool for identifying and evaluating the environmental aspects of products and services from the "cradle to the grave" from the extraction of resource inputs to the eventual disposal of the product or its waste. The ISO 14040 standards give guidelines on the principles and conduct of LCA studies that provide an organization with information on how to reduce the overall environmental impact of its products and services.

ISO/TR 14064 is another tool; it allows environmental aspects to be taken in account in the design and development of products.

Although the ISO 14000 standards are designed to be mutually supportive, they can also be used independently of each other to achieve environmental goals.

The whole ISO 14000 family provides management tools for organizations to control their environmental aspects and to improve their environmental performance. Together, these tools can provide significant tangible economic benefits, including:

- reduced raw material/resource use;
- reduced energy consumption;
- improved process efficiency;
- reduced waste generation and disposal costs; and
- utilization of recoverable resources.

Of course, associated with each of these economic benefits are distinct environmental benefits too. This is the contribution that the ISO 14000 series makes to the environmental and economic components of sustainable development and the triple bottom line.

FUTURE OF THE ISO 14000 FAMILY

Sustainable development policy and practice has attracted considerable attention and debate in the past 15 years. Our understanding of and concerns about environmental and sustainable development issues has evolved over time too. Just as the existing ISO 14000 standards play an important role in helping organizations to address today's priorities, so too can future standards help to address future priorities.

An integral part of an organization's EMS is the commitment to continual improvement. ISO/TC 207 takes this principle to heart and is constantly improving its process to identify and respond to new standardization needs. ISO/TC 207's success in continuing to work on relevant standards is evidenced by two new work items:

- ISO 14063 on environmental communication guidelines and examples, will help companies to make the important link to external stakeholders.
- ISO/TC 207 has responded to the challenge of climate change by agreeing to start work on standards on measuring, reporting and verification of entity and project level *Greenhouse Gas emissions*.

We hope that this information helps you to understand how your organization can obtain the maximum benefit from the ISO 14000 family. ISO/TC 207 is proud of its contributions to sustainable development since its inception in 1993. We are dedicated to ensuring, on an ongoing basis, that the ISO 14000 family meets the needs of the international user community and the concerns of those interested in the environment and sustainable development. You can help us to continue to evolve by contacting us and submitting your input and comments, either through your national standards institute (a complete list is posted on the ISO Web site: www.iso.org), directly to our ISO/TC 207 Secretariat, or through any of our sub-committees.

BUSINESS BENEFITS OF ISO 14001

Business today is not just about selling a product or service to a customer around the corner. In the rapid evolution to a global market-place, having a set of common rules is critical to facilitating trade. At the same time, these rules have to be flexible enough to be as applicable to a company in Hokkaido, Japan or Salvador, Brazil, as they are for one in San Francisco, USA, or Reykjavik, Iceland.

Increasingly in this single world market, an organization needs to be able to demonstrate sound business management that includes concern for the environment. There is growing evidence that this results in advantages in financing, insurance, marketing, regulatory, and other areas of operations. An Environmental Management System (EMS) provides a solid framework for meeting environmental challenges and realizing the above benefits. The International Standard ISO 14001 is used as a model for implementing an EMS by nearly 37000 organizations in 112 countries at the end of 2001.

There are many reasons for implementing an EMS. Businesses recognize that a focus on "command and control" by itself does not provide the bottom line results desired. ISO 14001 has proven to be a useful tool to evolve from maintaining regulatory compliance to a position of improved productivity and enhanced competitive advantage.

There is mounting evidence that companies which manage not only the standard economic factors but also the environmental and social factors affecting their business show financial performance superior to those which fail to manage all three.

Furthermore, experience has shown that ISO 14001 is a framework that inspires and channels the creativity of all members of an organisation, making them active agents of change promoting environmental protection, resource conservation and improved efficiencies. When all members in an organisation are challenged to think differently, it leads to the creation of innovative products and services. Innovation is a primary economic driver of economic growth. This makes ISO 14001 a powerful tool in which to invest.

How quickly and how effective the return for investment by an organisation in ISO 14001 occurs is a function of a variety of conditions that include:

- the status and level of sophistication of its existing management system;
- the degree of environmental challenge it faces, including the past, present and future situations;
- the amount and quality of resources it has access to, both internally or externally;

- its state of preparedness—such as existing environmental management practices;
- the knowledge, skill and ability of its staff with responsibilities relating to environmental management and their relationship with those in other departments;
- the expectations that stakeholders have in relation to the EMS;
- the current status of compliance with legal requirements;
- other requirements to which the organization may have made a commitment; and
- the level of verification required by the organization to meet market requirements or the expectations of stakeholders.

By design, ISO 14001 is flexible: it is as applicable to the small business as it is to the multi-national organization, enabling access to a global market-place where business and environmental performance go hand in hand.

STEPS TO ECO-EFFICIENCY

Description

This tool was developed to assist small and medium-sized manufacturers in Canada to develop an eco-efficiency programme that is custom tailored to their business needs. The process involves the following three steps:

1. Self-Assessment: Determines the current level of eco-efficiency activities in your company.
2. Strategic Planning: Provides a framework to develop a customized eco-efficiency programme.
3. Benefit-Cost Analysis: Helps you to get the biggest bang for your eco-efficiency buck.

This three-step process is available as a package of user-friendly work-sheets which can be downloaded or completed on-line using an automated version of the tool.

THE ECO-EFFICIENCY BUSINESS ASSISTANCE PROGRAMME

What is the Eco-Efficiency Business Assistance Programme?

It is an initiative to encourage eco-efficiency and pollution prevention in industry in the province. The programme is available to eligible small and medium-sized companies to assist them in identifying cost effective opportunities for improving their environmental performance and their bottom line. The programme has several components to help the companies identify opportunities and assess their viability. These involve centre staff and independent consultants.

There are four components to the Eco-Efficiency Business Assistance Programme.

Eco-Efficiency Review: No Charge

Eco-Efficiency Centre staff will visit your business and walk through your premises to gain an understanding of how eco-efficiency and pollution prevention may benefit your business.

Eco-Efficiency Opportunity Assessment: Value up to $2,000 (Your cost-up to $500, Programme Contribution-up to $1,500).

A qualified consultant (chosen by your company) will undertake a thorough assessment and prepare a report. This exercise will include an overview of your operations, identification of eco-efficiency and pollution prevention opportunities and explain their implementation. The report will provide you with an estimate of potential savings possible from implementing various pollution prevention opportunities. Priorities will also be recommended.

Eco-Efficiency Implementation Assessment: Value up to $6,000 (Your Cost-up to $1,500, Programme Contribution—up to $4,500).

Your consultant will prepare a comprehensive implementation plan which will include a detailed assessment of selected options and their technical, environmental and financial impacts and benefits. This report will provide you with a detailed action plan which includes cost-benefit analysis, projected savings, capital cost considerations, and overall pros and cons of eco-efficiency activities.

The in-depth assessment may include reviews of you energy, water, and material use, capital equipment, process operations, management practices, opportunities for improved public image, and environmental policy and plans for spill prevention and toxic material use. Recommendations will be mindful of your interest of improving your business performance and will be compatible with our mutual objective of eco-efficiency and pollution prevention.

Pollution Prevention Workshop: No Charge

This one-day workshop is conducted by EEC and programme staff. It is designed to help companies establish a pollution prevention/ green team and provide guidance and tools to make it work.

Quantified Eco-Efficiency Analysis for Sustainability

Preliminary Programme

- Eco-Efficiency Analysis: Philosophy, concepts and quantified tools.
- Methods Framework.
- Modelling and Operational Methods for Eco-Efficiency Analysis.
- Motives and Drivers for Eco-Efficiency.
- Applications of Eco-Efficiency Analysis and Users Contacts.
- Consensus and standardization.
- Suggestions for further subjects are welcomed and can be sent to the conference secretariat.

5

Sustainable Tourism Certification and Training: An Overview

SUSTAINABLE TOURISM CERTIFICATION

A growing number of tourism businesses are voluntarily participating in certification systems that grant a seal of approval to companies or destinations that demonstrate environmentally or socially sound practices. Not only do these labels serve as useful marketing tools, but they can motivate the industry to develop more environmentally-friendly products. They can also provide consumers with valuable information on sustainable tourism products, helping them to make more informed travel choices. The ultimate success of tourism certification as a conservation tool rests on whether or not it can set a trusted, reliable standard, and on the degree to which the industry and consumers worldwide demonstrate their support.

Tourism is a private sector activity, driven in large part by international hotel chains, tour companies and other businesses. The process of making tourism more sustainable requires careful planning at many levels and the participation of all potential stakeholders, particularly of local communities directly affected by tourism's presence. While the drive to adopt more sustainable practices is inherently complex, many in the tourism industry have already taken a number of positive steps toward becoming more environmentally and socially responsible. A number of the world's larger tourism companies, from hotels to tour operators, are in the throes of restructuring their management and operations to reduce the consumption of water, energy and other resources, and to improve the management, handling and disposal of waste.

Some companies are adopting the environmental management standard set out by the International Standards

Organization, ISO 140001. In addition to saving money, these operational shifts are key to sustainability. Agenda 21 ranks the incorporation of environmental management principles as "among the highest corporate priorities and as a key determinant to sustainability."

SUSTAINABILITY CERTIFICATION OF TOURISM ACTIVITIES

Kuala Lumpur, Malaysia, 11-13 December, 2003

Final Report

The need for greater sustainability in tourism services and activities is already widely recognized at all levels. Moreover, there are many and varied planning and development methodologies, as well as tourism management techniques that make it possible to attain higher levels of sustainability and to increase them gradually. Such methodologies and techniques can be complemented by voluntary certification systems for tourism services. The companies and organizations that provide them began appearing on the international tourism market in 1990 and have proliferated over the past few years.

Certifications and eco-labels basically serve three purposes, namely:

1. To stimulate tourism service providers to introduce improvements in their operations, aimed at greater environmental, economic and social sustainability, by providing incentives and technical assistance to do so;
2. To differentiate and distinguish tourism products and services that meet environmental, social and economic standards beyond the level required by the legislation in force;
3. To orient consumers with regard to the sustainability characteristics of the tourism services available on the market.

Additionally, certifications and eco-labels serve to promote and stimulate higher levels of sustainability and quality throughout the tourism sector, aside from enhancing the image of certified companies, with the commercial benefits that such enhancement brings.

Despite their recent proliferation, and partly because of it, certification systems have not managed to establish themselves among tourism enterprises in Asia or among tourists. There is also a lack of unanimity and homogeneity among the different systems that exist, resulting in confusion among users.

As a result of its participation in various United Nations forums on sustainability, the World Tourism Organization embarked upon an analysis of the effectiveness of certifications and eco-labels in the different branches of tourism activity in 1999. The WTO published the results of this study in a publication released in 2002, and its Sustainable Development of Tourism Committee analyzed these results at its third meeting, held in Costa Rica in September 2002. It also requested the General Secretariat of the WTO to prepare recommendations aimed at orienting governments in the field of certification for the purpose of setting up such systems, choosing from among existing ones, or supporting more widespread use of such systems. These recommendations were transmitted to the Member States in May 2003.

In this context, the Asia-Pacific Conference on Sustainability Certification of Tourism Activities was organized with the following objectives:

1. To disseminate the recommendations drawn up by the WTO on the subject of certification;
2. To foster permanent dialogue and cooperation among national tourism authorities, officials responsible for certification systems, and tourism service providers and their trade associations, to enable them to act in a coordinated manner in this area;
3. To move towards the harmonization of existing certification systems in Asia, at least in terms of basic procedures and criteria;
4. To contribute to the joint promotion of the concept and the practice of certification in tourism;
5. To consider the possibility of supporting a regional network of certifications and eco-labels for tourism sustainability in Asia;
6. To evaluate the advisability and need of establishing an accreditation system for certification bodies in tourism.

The Conference was convened by the World Tourism Organization, and hosted by the Ministry of Culture, Arts and Tourism of Malaysia. 107 participants from 12 countries in the region, as well as from international organizations took part in this Conference. Participants represented national tourism and environmental administrations, regional and local authorities, tourism trade associations and private companies, as well as NGOs and academic institutions.

Conference Programme

Thursday, 11 December, 2003

9.30–9.45—Opening Remarks by Mr. Eugenio Yunis, Chief, Sustainable Development of Tourism, World Tourism Organization.

9.45–10.30—Opening Address by Hon. Dato'Paduka Abdul Kadir Bin Haji Sheikh Fadzir, Minister of Culture, Arts and Tourism Malaysia.

10.30-11.15—First Plenary Session: Introductory Presentations:

- Sustainability of Tourism and the Role of Certification
  Mr. Eugenio Yunis, Chief, Sustainable Development of Tourism,
  World Tourism Organization
  (PowerPoint Presentation)
- An Introduction to Certification: A Tool to Support Voluntary Changes towards Sustainability
  Mr. Ronald Sanabria, Director, Sustainable Tourism, Rainforest Alliance
- Main Issues and Challenges about Certification
  Ms. Alice Crabtree, Research Associate on Certification: Asia Pacific Region,
  The International Ecotourism Society.

11.15–11.30—Coffee break

11.30–13.00—Second Plenary Session:
Case study Presentations of Certification Systems

- An ICT Approach Towards Ecotourism Rating
  Mr. Mohamed Daud, Professor in Knowledge Engineering, University Putra Malaysia, Selangor, Malaysia
- Green Leaf Programme

Mr. Pradech Phayakvichien, Advisor, Tourism Authority of Thailand, Thailand
(PowerPoint Presentation)

- Certification System for Sustainable Tourism in Nepal
Mr. Subash Nirola, Director, Tourism Products and Resources Development,
Nepal Tourism Board, Nepal
- VISIT—A Common Initiative of European Tourism Eco-labels
Mr. Naut Kusters, European Centre for Eco- and Agro-Tourism (ECEAT), The Netherlands
(Summary)
(PowerPoint Presentation)

Questions and Answers.

13.00–14.30—Lunch

14.30–15.30—Third Plenary Session:
Case study Presentations of Certification Systems

- The Role of Certification Schemes in Tourism
Mr. Stan Rodgers, Principal Green Globe Trainer, AVTEQ Consulting Services, Australia, SHEMSI Sdn Bhd, Malaysia
- Green Globe 21: A Global Sustainable Tourism Benchmarking and Certification Programme for China's Tourism Industry
- Dr. Zhuge Ren, Chief Representative, Green Globe 21 China
(PowerPoint Presentation)
- Ecotourism Certification—Australia and Green Globe
Mr. Guy Chester, Director, Eco-Sustainability (Ecotourism Australia), Australia

Questions and Answers.

15.30–15.45—Coffee break

15.45–18.00—Working Groups

Four parallel working groups debating on the topics of collaboration with other stakeholders, financing, facilitation of small and medium enterprises (SMEs) and marketing

20:00—Dinner hosted by Hon. Secretary-General, Ministry of Culture, Arts and Tourism Malaysia at Bistro Saloma.

Friday, 12 December, 2003

Plenary Sessions to present conclusions of the working groups and to discuss on the following issues:

8.30–9.30	Certification financing
9.30–10.30	Recommendations to facilitate the access of SMEs and community organizations to certification
10.30–11.00—	Coffee Break
11.00–12.00	Certification and Marketing: Providing market advantage to companies and reaching out to consumers
12.00–13.00	Collaboration among governments, private sector and certifiers
13.00–14.30—	Lunch
14.30–15.00	The Sustainable Tourism Stewardship Council and the Sustainable Tourism Certification Network of the Americas: Moving from Fragmentation to Consolidation Mr. Ronald Sanabria, Director, Sustainable Tourism, Rainforest Alliance
15.00–16.00	Coordination of Certification Systems in the Asia-Pacific Region (Plenary debate)
16.00–16.30	Coffee break
16.30–17.00	Closing Session.

Closing Remarks

Mr. Eugenio Yunis, Chief, Sustainable Development of Tourism, World Tourism Organization

Representative of Ministry of Culture, Arts and Tourism Malaysia.

Summary of Working Group Discussions and Plenary Debates

Problems, challenges, solutions and recommendations for certification were discussed in four working groups according to the following four themes:

1. The scope of certification—What should be certified?
2. Certification financing
3. Certification and Marketing
4. Collaboration among governments, private sector, NGOs, communities, academic institutions and certifiers.

The working groups results were presented and further debated in plenary. The following list contains the main points resulting from the working groups and the plenary debate.

Theme 1

The Scope of Certification—What should be Certified?

- Certification of products, businesses, guides, individuals, destinations.
- Sustainability criteria and indicators (environmental, social, economic).

Problems, Challenges

- Which type of organization(s) should perform the certification and by which criteria?
- How to choose among the variety of certification offers in Asia-Pacific? Which one is really credible?—There is a lack of international standards and recognition behind them.
- Tourism products represent a huge variety of products and a large spectrum, which makes difficult to create common standards.
- The cost of certification can be relatively high for many companies.
- There can be various barriers for companies to entry.
- There is lack of incentives for companies to participate in certification.
- It is difficult to produce immediate benefits of certification.
- How to define the standards that are both specific to a region or country and internationally recognized at the same time?
- How to ensure that other players in the commercialization chain also conform to sustainability standards?
- International standards have specific challenges as developed and developing countries have different performance levels.
- What should be the government's involvement and role in certification?
- Market players have different levels of understanding about certification.
- Who should participate? How to involve local communities in setting up a certification system?

- How to define the target market of the certification programme.
- What should be the marketing level—domestic or international?
- Ensure enough benefits are attached to the programme.
- The certification programme should be voluntary or mandatory?
- There is a need to provide training in the certification process.
- Convince industry to get on board and maintain compliance with the requirements.
- Should certification be used as defect regulation?
- Currently there are fragmented and isolated initiatives in the region, therefore there is a need for co-operation and networking.

Solutions, Recommendations

Scope of certification, what to certify:

- Certify the products and services as one company can run different kind of businesses.
- Destinations are also relevant to certify.
- Certification should be applied in a similar way for local businesses or international chains operating in a destination.
- Certification programmes could begin with hotels, but there is a need to consider the entire supply chain (life cycle) of tourism products. e.g., tour operators should ensure that the entire package (not just the hotels) be certified.
- Certification of guides can enhance the quality and professionalism in guiding services. Highly qualified and sensitized tour guides are especially important in fragile natural and cultural sites and ethnic villages.
- Certified businesses should provide a code of conduct to the tourists (e.g., on socio-cultural issues considering local communities), along with good information on the certified products and services that will foster responsible behaviour of consumers.

Criteria, Standards and Indicators

- Development of criteria should be done through a bottom up approach with community involvement.

- In addition to the WTO recommendations for certification systems (see Annex 1), it was suggested to include criteria in relation with:
  - Provision of proper wages for local employees.
  - Harmony of the establishments with their surrounding.
  - The need for the company to provide a code of conduct for tourists.
  - The consumers' point of view, such as safety and security, health, interpretation (tourist satisfaction).
- When consulting with communities it is also necessary to ask them to set up the maximum number of tourists that they are willing to receive at a time. This carrying capacity limit should be based on both cultural and environmental factors.
- Evaluate economic sustainability to ensure that tourism provides income for local communities instead of leaking to non-local investors. Include in the certification criteria how much of the economic benefits are redistributed among the local communities.
- There is a need to restructure traditional tourism indicators to reflect sustainability (e.g., tourism expenditure and how much of the benefits remains in the local communities).
- Set criteria and corresponding benefits for certified companies at different levels (the higher the level of criteria the bigger the benefit received).
- Include environmental issues into conventional quality schemes.
- It is necessary to define specialized standards for different tourism products and for countries or regions.
- Consider local culture in criteria of international labels.
- Create a minimum/basic regional standard for Asia-Pacific and define additional specific standards considering the specific characteristics of the individual countries and their internal regions.

Development of Certification Systems

- Make strong endorsement for certification as a definite value-adding element to tourism supply.
- Use sampling or pilot project to develop the programme.

- Create incentives for companies.
- Offer certification services to those sites that are considered a priority from an environmental and social point of view. It is necessary that the certification programmes proactively promote its services in such sites.
- Create/use an independent body to perform certification. If government is involved in certification processes, it should avoid political influence and rather play a facilitator and technical role.
- Government to play a role in providing incentives.
- Use hotels as pilot projects—e.g., use energy-saving as a theme to get started.
- Include both, process and performance-based criteria.
- Use regional platforms and structures (such as ASEAN) to create certification systems and connect with international organizations to help create international recognition. Existing regional structures could be also used for benchmark and marketing.
- There is a need to create regional and sub-regional alliances because there are differences in cultural and environmental matters. Standards should be established from the bottom, up to the local and then regional levels, building on the local/regional realities, before they are brought to the international level.
- Provide training programmes as part of the certification process.
- Start the certification process with self-declaration by parties to be certified as a step stone.
- Certification systems should sensitize entrepreneurs to develop a long-term sustainability perspective and considering the wider environment, instead of looking for short-term profits only.
- If used as de-facto regulation or policing of standards, the cost saved by government should be passed onto encouraging development of best practice and certification training and development.

Theme 2

Certification Financing

- Financing of certification programmes

- Supporting of participating enterprises
- Facilitation of SMEs and community organizations to access certification (financial support and incentives, technical assistance).

Problems, Challenges

- Certification programmes should become self-sufficient in financial terms.
- How to avoid creating dependency on outside resources to cover the needs of SMEs?
- Political dimensions of financing: funding of certification systems should be such that it does not influence the neutrality of the certification process, i.e., should be independent.
- Social responsibility of governments.
- Access for SMEs and micro-enterprises does not mean just covering cost of certification procedure but also training requirements and implementation costs to meet certification criteria.

Solutions, Recommendations

Financing certification programmes

- Aim at a mix of funding sources: governmental support, fees, donations, cash, in-kind.
- Utilize various resources i.e., universities to guide hotels and other market players and to do research and help with monitoring to ensure continuation of conformity of the certified parties.
- Seek funds from international bodies, including international financial institutions (e.g. World Bank, regional development banks, such as the Asia Development Bank or Islamic Bank and other international organizations like WWF, IUCN, etc.).
- Governments to provide infrastructure support (e.g. secretariat—office, personnel, equipment).
- Government to provide seed money and create a revolving fund to cover basic operational costs.
- Engage tourism industry to finance certification programme (contribution from those who benefit, i.e. airlines).
- Working with voluntary services (volunteers).

- Co-operation to avoid duplication of efforts.
- Involve academic institutions and students for research projects.

Support of Participating Enterprises

- There are financing needs for two main purposes:
  - for the process of applying for certification,
  - additional source of funding that help companies comply with certification criteria: capacity building and financing the technology that needs to be purchased to raise sustainability levels.
- Funding needs to be allocated for training with an emphasis on best practices but also include basic information on certification.
- Reinvest a percentage of tax from the tourism industry in local capacity development.
- Need to sell in innovative manner. Micro businesses will not buy into certification on the basis of saving the environment, but will adopt certification on the expectation of saving money (through implementing sustainable practices).
- Create incentives for certified products and companies, e.g.:
  - tax reduction
  - licensing advantages, longer permits
  - better credit conditions (preferential interest rates, soft loans, state guarantee)
  - government to channel funds through commercial banks by creating special credit packages
  - marketing advantages with local and national tourism boards
  - government grants, reimbursement of certification costs
  - publicize awarding ceremonies
  - link awards for economical performance (e.g. best company of the year) with sustainability certification achievements.
- Reduce cost of auditing by concentrating high-rigour on-site assessment on products that potentially can have a high negative impact on nature and/or culture.

- Preferential access to funding is already often available to operators and communities that are indigenous people or located in protected areas. These funds could be considered also for certification purposes.
- In case companies internalize costs of sustainability improvements through a certification programme, it should be reflected in the price to the consumer. In order to increase willingness to pay by consumers, it is important to provide information for tourists on sustainability issues and certification.
- There can be a levy established on service prices and user fees, to finance sustainable management of areas and projects (e.g. in Nepal), but it is important to explain clearly to tourists how that money is used.

SME Support

- Group companies for certification to bring the cost down.
- SMEs to form alliances for joint certification.
- Larger businesses support smaller ones.
- Create a foundation to support micro businesses.
- Undertake awareness raising and capacity building programmes especially designed for different types of SMEs.
- Create special financial packages for SMEs and local communities.

Theme 3

Certification and Marketing

— Providing market advantage to companies
— Reaching out to consumers.

Problems, Challenges

- Create a package of incentives and benefits to market the programmes.
- How to create a system that is recognized by the consumers?
- How the certification programme should be marketed?
- Multiplicity of logos confuses consumers.
- How can the community help in the promotion and marketing of certification programmes?

Solutions, recommendations:

- Awareness raising on the benefits of certification, like improved company image.
- Use relevant indicators that will help demonstrating the benefits of the programme, and thus promoting it.
- Develop regional cooperation to avoid proliferation of logos.
- Develop media support and publicity.
- Sell services locally.
- Marketing through tourism boards and trade missions (esp. overseas).
- Include information on certified products in official tourism promotion and information publications, as well as in web sites and link web sites of certified companies to them. For example, in Fiji, the Tourism Board has agreed to use images of certified products in promotional materials.
- Give priority to certified companies to participate in international tourism fairs. For example, in Australia, the Australian Tourism Exchange will have a large booth area for certified products, with preferential access for small ecotourism businesses.
- Government agencies to use preferentially certified products and services for public functions (e.g. meetings, trips).
- Companies to include logo and information on their certified products in their promotional materials.
- Providing information to schools.
- Official endorsement by international organizations, such as WTO, or others, that will help create recognition of the programme.
- Create one global logo.
- One global web site with all certified products.
- Provide incentives to consumers using certified products, e.g. free bicycle or public transport.
- Reach out to consumers through the involvement of consumer associations.
- Ensure that communities participate in the development of the certification programme, and then they can help also promoting it directly to tourists. Promotion can come through word of mouth, raise the community voice to

promote certified companies and, by default, certification systems will get more clients.

- Business to business recognition (Companies managing certified product uses/buys other certified products and services).
- If there is a country that has a sufficient number of certified businesses, it is recommended to convene meetings with foreign tour operators for them to learn about certified products. (For example, WTO has been promoting this with the Tour Operators Initiative. Workshops were organized in Turkey, Dominican Republic where foreign tour operators and local providers were brought together to define how could sustainability principles be implemented.) This type of workshops could be used to promote existing certification programmes, in order to convince tour operators to give preferential treatment to certified operations at destinations.

Theme 4

Collaboration among Governments, Private Sector, NGOs, Communities, Academic Institutions and Certifiers

- Areas of collaboration
- Mechanisms of collaboration
- Communication and networking.

Challenges

- What kind of collaboration mechanism and institutional framework could be set-up at the national level (national council, steering committee, forum)?
- Which organizations should participate, who should regulate the process, handle the funds?
- How to create a regional network for the Asia-Pacific and how to link regional networks?

Solutions, Recommendations

- Create political will in government and clear policy for certification.
- The process should not be solely top-down. It is necessary to develop participatory processes with involvement of government, private sector, NGOs (international and

local ones), academic institutions, experts, local communities.

- Include stakeholders from sectors other than tourism, not treating tourism in isolation, integrating with more global sustainable strategies (e.g. health, safety issues).
- Involve national standards and quality organizations.
- Coordinate at different levels (national-regional-local).
- Reach out to local communities through workshops, foray, awareness raising, training and capacity building programmes.
- Involve the local context in international certification systems, collaborate with traditional leaders.
- Create a regional network of certification programmes for Asia-Pacific, similarly to the Network in the Americas and the VISIT programme in Europe. The network should serve for sharing information and experiences in the first place.
- Create partnerships for coordination, communication, cooperation and transparency.
- Collaborate on branding and marketing (public-private partnership).
- Partnership with educational institutes for awareness raising and training.
- Create networking and easy-access information sharing mechanisms (e.g. database of good practices, certified products and companies—Internet based mechanisms).

NATIONAL CERTIFICATION SYSTEMS FOR SUSTAINABLE TOURISM & WTO RECOMMENDATIONS

Introduction

Certification systems for sustainable tourism play an increasing role in regulating tourism operations as voluntary instruments above legal frameworks. They usually address three main aspects, namely: (*i*) environmental performance of companies, operations and destinations; (*ii*) product quality; and (*iii*) corporate social responsibility of operations. They normally target tourism suppliers, such as accommodation, restaurants, sport and leisure facilities, tourist attractions, destinations, tour operators (tourist) transport companies, tourist associations, etc.

Considering the growing number and importance of certification systems and other voluntary initiatives in tourism, and based on a recommendation made by the UN Commission on Sustainable Development, WTO undertook a comprehensive worldwide study on this topic. The results of this study were published in 2002, under the title "Voluntary Initiatives for Sustainable Tourism: Worldwide Inventory and Comparative Analysis of 104 Eco-labels, Awards and Self-commitments."

The WTO Committee on Sustainable Development of Tourism, at its 3rd Session held in Costa Rica, 25-26 September, 2002 recommended the preparation of a set of guidelines for Governments on certification systems for sustainable tourism. Acting on this decision of the Committee, the present document aims at enhancing awareness among governments about the opportunities certification systems may provide as part of their sustainable development policy goals, and provides basic recommendations for supporting and/or establishing such systems at the national level. It is primarily based on the WTO study mentioned above. It also draws on the survey conducted among WTO Member States in November 2001–January 2002, considering the feasibility of a Sustainable Tourism Stewardship Council, on the experience gained in the area of certification through the International Year of Eco-tourism 2002, on comments received from the Committee members, and on other relevant documents.

The Role of Governments in Present Certification Systems

The WTO study on voluntary initiatives for sustainable tourism revealed that governments have an important role in many of the certification systems presently operating. Twenty of the 59 certification schemes investigated are lead by government agencies. A further 18 have government involvement, either through direct financial support, marketing support, expert know-how in criteria setting, verification procedures, or surveillance of procedures followed by the certification body. Government financial support is crucial to half the schemes for which data is available. Government agencies involved generally include either environment ministries, national tourism authorities and tourist boards, and in fewer cases, standards institutes.

Certification systems can bring benefits to society, the environment, governments, private companies and consumers as well.

Potential benefits for society:

- Generally speaking, societies will benefit from certification systems that cover the three aspects of sustainability: social, environmental and economic. Certified companies are supposed to generate benefits in these three areas, while reducing their negative impacts. Therefore, the contribution of tourism activities to the sustainable development of host societies will be more evident, more measurable and more accountable.
- Furthermore, the level of awareness on sustainability issues will be stronger in the host society if the large majority of tourism companies and/or destinations are certified.

Potential benefits for the environment:

- It is evident that certification systems and eco-labels that include strict environmental criteria result in benefits for the local environment and, to the extent that some mass tourism activities can impact biodiversity and climate change, also the global environment.
- Furthermore, the widespread use of eco-labels and certification systems in the tourism industry helps to generate increased environmental awareness among both, tourists and host societies and should result in more caring attitudes with respect to the natural and built environments.

Potential benefits for governments:

- Providing an effective alternative to direct regulation, which could prove more difficult and time-consuming to implement;
- Enabling governments to adopt a flexible approach to monitoring the tourism industry, permitting organizations to proceed at the pace they feel most comfortable with, while encouraging them to develop innovative approaches to environmental and socio-cultural improvements;
- Giving tourism companies greater scope for making environmental and social improvements by exploiting

opportunities specific to their individual circumstances, rather than governments having to control and inspect companies in order to check that they comply with general, industry-wide regulations;

- Allowing part of the costs of implementing and monitoring environmental protection measures to be transferred to the industry itself, thereby reducing the financial burden of regulation on the taxpayer;
- National programmes of tourism certification can enhance tourism's recognition in the country, national competitiveness and image in international markets.

Potential benefits for companies:

- Adherence to voluntary environmental initiatives can enable the company to market its products more effectively, and to improve their public image among consumers, business partners and with the host communities;
- Engaging in voluntary certification can help companies to signal their specific commitment to environmental, social and even economic improvements, which may in turn help to defer the need for further direct regulation by governments;
- Pursuing sound environmental management strategies can generate substantial cost savings for the company;
- Participation in a certification programme can provide better access to modern techniques, technology and know-how;
- Applying effective environmental management can help to protect the environmental and cultural assets upon which the tourism industry depends for its continued prosperity.

Finally, certification and eco-labels can of course benefit consumers by providing them with more information and guidance for their decisions on travel choices, as well as assurances for product and service quality.

Recommendations

Certification systems for sustainable tourism need to be developed and operated to fit geographical, political, socio-economic and sectoral characteristics of each country. For this reason, the following recommendations serve as general orientation and they need to be adapted to the economic, institutional, social and environmental conditions prevailing in each country.

1. Development of the Certification System

Governments can play a key role in the initiation and development of certification systems for sustainable tourism by creating the supportive legal and institutional structures. The following general recommendations can be made:

1. Consider a national certification system as an integral part of sustainable tourism development policies, strategies and objectives, and an effective tool to implement them.
2. Identify key stakeholders and potential target groups relevant to and interested in certification programmes.
3. Develop the certification system through multi-stakeholder consultation processes, involving all relevant interest groups, such us different government authorities (tourism, environment, transportation, finance, education, etc); tourism trade associations and other private groups; academic, education and research institutions; NGOs; consumer associations; etc. The development and the operation of a successful certification programme in many cases lays in the multi-stakeholder representation of the team awarding certificates and supporting the programme.
4. Coordinate an in-depth research on the conditions and feasibility of a certification system, including aspects such as:

   - Existing legal and voluntary instruments affecting the tourism sector (e.g. laws, regulations, taxes, subsidies, local certification systems, codes of conduct, environmental awards, etc.);
   - Experience of certification systems applied in other sectors in the country, like agriculture, forestry, and draw lessons from them for the tourism sector;
   - Certification criteria;
   - Operational mechanisms: application, verification, awarding, revision and inspection procedures; consulting and technical assistance for participants,

marketing and communication; funding (see section 3 below).

5. Provide finance and/or seek partners for co-financing and providing technical contributions for the research, development and operational costs of certification programmes (e.g. different government departments, NGOs, academic institutions, international finance and development agencies, private foundations, etc).
6. Ensure transparency throughout all the stages of the development and operation of the certification system and establish an appeals process.
7. Make clear to the private sector the benefits, costs and other implications of certification systems.
8. Develop incentives to motivate and encourage tourism companies to become certified, e.g. marketing incentives by giving priority in trade shows and nationally sponsored publicity, or ensuring access to environmental technologies, etc.
9. Consider issues affecting the sustainability of destinations as a whole, involving all tourism product and service providers.
10. Pay special attention to equitable access to certification, especially by small and medium size firms, as they can have more difficulties in meeting the costs and technical requirements than bigger companies.
11. Conduct pilot projects for testing and demonstration of the certification system.
12. Prepare the market for certification, in order to reach a good demand level from tourism companies, and a critical mass at the initial phase to get the system running.

2. Certification Criteria

Developing certification criteria is a critical part of the certification system development process. The following general recommendations need to be considered:

1. Base criteria on existing legal standards and instruments and set them well above legal compliance.
2. Include the pre-condition of compliance by the applicant with these legislations.

3. Address the three dimensions of sustainability: environmental, socio-cultural and economic issues.
4. Define core criteria and supplementary criteria specific for different tourism product and service groups (e.g. hotels and other accommodations, transportation services, restaurants, tour operators and travel agents, attractions, etc.). By this way consider the implications to destinations as a whole, and not just certain tourism product and service groups.
5. In bigger countries, criteria can be adjusted to specific regional and local environmental and socio-economic conditions.
6. For each criterion, define indicators that are measurable and easy to understand by the different type of stakeholders involved in the certification process.
7. Base criteria and indicators on scientific research that evaluates the key environmental and socio-economic impacts of the sector.
8. Criteria should refer to attainable and realistic goals for private sector participants.
9. Criteria can be set in different levels of requirements: from more easily achievable to very demanding criteria. Thus, the certification system sets a framework for continuous improvement whereby applicants can achieve higher performance levels step by step.
10. Compliance with criteria can be measured through process and performance-based assessments. Indicators are essential tools for measuring environmental, social and economic impacts of tourism operations:

    Environmental indicators can relate to the following factors, among others:

    - Environmental impact assessment conducted for setting up the operation or construction of establishments;
    - Environmental management practices, company policies and technical measures (e.g. energy, water saving and waste treatment devices, environmental friendly transportation, etc.) in place;
    - Land use and property issues in destinations;
    - Health and safety;

- Use of natural resources:
  - Energy (consumption, reduction, efficiency)
  - Water (consumption, reduction, quality)
  - Solid and liquid waste (reduction, reuse, recycling, treatment, disposal)
  - Appropriate building materials
  - Hazardous substances (reduction, handling, use of nature friendly cleaning products)
  - Noise (reduction)
  - Air quality (quality, improvement)
  - Habitat/eco-system/wildlife maintenance and enhancement.
- Environmental information/interpretation/education for customers;
- Transportation services (public transport, environmental friendly alternatives);
- Indicators and standards on the impacts at specific tourist use areas (e.g. beaches) and on the impacts caused by specific tourism activities and facilities (e.g. diving, golf, marinas etc.); and
- Visual impacts of establishments and infrastructure; etc.

Social indicators can relate to the following factors, among others:

- Social impact assessment conducted for setting up the operation and the establishments;
- Staff policies and management (information, education, training, incentives, health, safety, etc.);
- Relationships with local communities (local employees, outreach and education programmes);
- Emphasis on, and conservation of local/regional culture, heritage and authenticity;
- Maintaining aesthetics of physical development/ architecture;
- Community feedback systems, satisfaction of local population;
- Contribution to community development purposes (infrastructure improvement; social services, etc.);

- Information provided to guests on sustainability aspects;
- Guest feedback systems in place, customer satisfaction, etc.

Economic indicators can relate to the following factors, among others:

- Creation of local employment (number of employees from local communities and their level of skills);
- Supply chain management through green and sustainable purchasing policies;
- Creation of networks of environmentally friendly businesses within a given destination;
- Responsible marketing;
- Use of locally sourced and produced materials and food, etc.

In addition, certification criteria for eco-tourism should specifically address the elements below, besides the general sustainability criteria:

- Financial and in-kind contributions to conservation of eco-tourism sites by companies;
- Level of involvement of local communities and benefits accruing to them;
- Use of specialized guides and other interpretation techniques, information provided to tourists through eco-tourism operations;
- Environmental education activities provided for tourists and local populations;
- Locally appropriate scale and design for lodging, infrastructure and tours;
- Minimal impact on and the appropriate presentation of local and indigenous culture.

11. Indicators to measure the success of certification systems can address:

    - The number of applications and certified companies (i.e. increase over time of the number of companies registered in a certain certification system);
    - The percentage of certified companies in the different tourism product and service groups;

- Improvement in environmental and social performance in certified companies (e.g. changes in water and energy consumption, resource savings, etc.);
- Environmental and social performance of certified companies as compared to non-certified ones (e.g., a current estimate is that environmental performance per certified accommodation enterprises can be taken as about 20 per cent better than the average performance at accommodation facilities in Europe).

12. Consider the whole product life cycle when setting product environmental criteria (from the manufacturing, transporting, through purchasing, consumption, to recycling, disposal, etc.).
13. Undertake periodic revision and update of criteria (e.g. every 2-3 years).

3. Operation of Certification Systems

The procedure is normally composed of the application, verification and certification processes. The funding mechanism for the above services and procedures is a crucial and critical element for the success of certification systems. Normally there is a funding, verification and certification body interacting in these processes. In many cases, the funding and certification bodies coincide. Fundamental components of any certification system are the facilitation of consulting, advisory and technical assistance and marketing services. The following general recommendations can be made in relation to the operational processes:

3.1 Application

1. The system should be open to all potential applicants.
2. Provide clear and easily accessible information on the criteria, costs and benefits and other conditions of certification (e.g. through Internet, email, telephone, information kit).
3. Offer immediate sources for consultation services.
4. Show tangible benefits for applicants (e.g. costs savings, marketing advantage, access to technical assistance and modern technology and financial possibilities, etc.) and explain clearly the commitments and costs.
5. Application documents should be clear, easy to understand and fill in.

6. Conduct a pre-evaluation/assessment of the applicant in order to identify technical and technological aspects that need to be improved to meet the criteria. Provide assistance and financial incentives for these improvements.

3.2 Verification

7. Verification of compliance with criteria should be done by an independent or third-party organization. In other words by a body which is independent from the parties being certified and of technical assessment or funding.
8. Verification is normally done through a combination of different activities: review of application documents and references, self-assessment by the operation through questionnaire, on-site visit, fees to be paid by the applicant.
9. Verification audits should be conducted by suitably trained auditors.
10. The verification process can be also used to give recommendations to the applicants on how to improve their performance and achieve further progress.

3.3 Certification (Awarding of Certification)

The certification is basically the awarding of the certification to the applicant, granting a permit for using the logo, marketing and other services of the system.

11. Certification bodies can be composed of representatives of the mayor stakeholder groups participating in the development and operation of the system. Governments have a key role in certification bodies, by giving credibility and recognition of the system.
12. As it was also mentioned among the recommendations for criteria development, awarding of certification can be done at single-level or at multi-level. The latter one occurs if criteria are set on different scales with a view to ensure a framework of continuous improvement.
13. The certification, the use of a logo and related benefits should be granted for a pre-determined period, after which re-assessment and verification should be conducted to ensure continuous compliance with the same or higher criteria.

14. Follow up control can be conducted after certification. For example, the WTO study on voluntary initiatives demonstrated that more than 50 per cent of the certification systems currently operating undertake some control visits after certification: 38 per cent are announced, and 17 per cent are surprise visits. Some eco-labels either do phone checks, stimulating guests' feedback or sending "mystery guests" to the certified tourism service.
15. Procedures have to be in place for the cancellation and withdrawal of certification and the use of the corresponding logo in case of non-compliance.
16. The certification system can also include consumer and local community feedback mechanisms.

3.4 Consulting, Advisory and Technical Assistance Services

The facilitation of the following services represents important added value for tourism companies and can be decisive factors for joining the certification system.

17. Provide technical consultancy options from the initial expression of interest and through the application phases onward, and give guidance to the applicant at every stage of the process.
18. Facilitate technical assistance for applicants so that they can introduce advanced management techniques and technology to meet the certification criteria. Provide access to environmental technologies, equipment and techniques by creating alliances with other organizations that can provide assistance for this purpose.
19. Develop training and capacity building programmes in form of courses, workshops, distance learning, etc.
20. Organize regular meetings for certified companies to promote the exchange of experiences and the sense of group.
21. Constant assistance and advisory is especially important in certification systems where the criteria and awarding are set on different scales.

3.5 Marketing and Communication

Marketing is another fundamental element of certification programmes, representing perhaps the biggest attraction and the most tangible benefits for private companies. The following general recommendations can be made:

22. Develop a precise marketing strategy for the certification system targeting three groups in principle:
    - Potential candidates: aiming at attracting companies to join the programme.
    - Applicants and certified companies: providing marketing and promotional support and market advantages for them.
    - Consumers: reaching recognition of the certification programmes, fostering responsible travel choices, and make effective the marketing advantage for certified companies.
23. Develop a well-distinguished and unequivocal logo design for the system. The logo can be accompanied by a motto, or slogan. Ensure legal protection of the logo.
24. The presentation of the system in media and communication should reflect a well-recognized corporate image in the market for businesses and consumers as well. The system can represent a sort of brand.
25. Use all available forms and channels to publicize and provide information on the certification programme for companies and consumers (e.g. brochures, flyers, guide books, printed and electronic media, Internet, conferences, seminars, tourism and trade fairs, etc.).
26. Give good media coverage to the awarding ceremonies.
27. Provide marketing support and promotion for certified companies through national tourist boards or national tourism marketing organizations, e.g. presentation of these companies in national brochures, catalogues, listings, web sites, support for presence at national stands at tourism fairs and exhibition, etc.
28. Give recommendations and examples to applicants and certified companies on how to include the certificate in their own marketing activities.
29. Demonstrate the distinction on environmental performance, economic and socio-cultural effects between certified and non-certified products/companies.
30. Communicate on a regular basis with certified members (e.g. through periodic meetings and events,

newsletters, emails, exclusive access to information on Internet, etc.).

31. Provide clear and easily understandable information to consumers on the characteristics and added value that certification represents.
32. Develop consumer awareness raising and education campaigns on the certification system and certified products.
33. Involve consumer associations in these efforts.

3.6 Fees and Funding

Governments have a key role in providing funding themselves, and/or in conceiving and developing alternative funding mechanisms with other partners for the operation of the certification system.

34. Establish the right balance between financial contributions of the public and private sectors.
35. Ensure that the sources of funding do not create a conflict of interest, since undue influence by funding organizations should be avoided in the certification procedure.
36. Establish fees for participants to cover (at least part of) application and verification costs. Fees should be kept as low as possible in order to encourage participation.
37. Fees should be calculated proportionally to size of businesses (e.g. by number of beds or visitors, turnover, etc.).
38. Provide incentive measures and support the application of companies, especially of small and medium size enterprises that would otherwise be left out (e.g. by soft loans and subsidies to make the necessary improvements to meet the criteria).
39. Consider in-kind contributions by governments for the operation, e.g. providing facilities, office space and equipment.

Final Note: Governments are encouraged to convey to the World Tourism Organization their experience in connection with certification systems related to sustainability in tourism. This will allow WTO to periodically revise these guidelines, introduce any additional guidelines or modify those recommended above.

Madrid, March 2003

Dialogue on "Tourism, Cultural Diversity and Sustainable Development" a Success

Madrid, 27 July, 2004: The Universal Forum of Cultures Barcelona 2004 successfully held a Dialogue on "Tourism, Cultural Diversity and Sustainable Development", which took place on 14-16 July.

The Dialogue was organized by the *Instituto de Turism Responsable* (Institute for Responsible Tourism) with the active participation of the World Tourism Organization, which collaborated in its preparation and in the selection of speakers.

The Dialogue was opened by Prince Sultan bin Salman bin Abd al-Aziz al-Saud, President of the Supreme Commission for Tourism of Saudi Arabia and the President of the Dialogue. Among the speakers at the opening ceremony were the Secretary-General of the World Tourism Organization, Mr. Francesco Frangialli, and the Mayor of Barcelona and President of the Forum, Mr. Joan Clos.

Hundreds of tourism professionals from over 50 countries participated in the Dialogue, which was also attended by the Ministers of Tourism of Ecuador, Ethiopia, and Mexico, the Minister of Economy, Growth and Competitiveness of Cape Verde, and the Deputy Minister of Tourism of Indonesia. Among the speakers and participants were numerous entrepreneurs, local authorities and representatives of NGOs and the academic sector.

DEPARTMENT OF ECONOMIC AND SOCIAL AFFAIRS COMMISSION

Seventh Session 19-30 April, 1999, New York

A. Introduction

Tourism is a rapidly growing phenomenon and has become one of the largest industries in the world. The impact of tourism is extremely varied. On one hand, it plays an important and certainly positive role in the socio-economic and political development in destination countries by, for instance, offering new employment opportunities. Also, in certain instances, it may contribute to a broader cultural understanding by creating awareness, respecting the diversity of cultures and ways of life. On the other hand, as a tool to create jobs, it has not fulfilled its expectations. At the same time, complaints from tourist destinations concerning massive negative impacts upon environment, culture and residents' ways of life have given rise to a demand for a more sustainable development in tourism. Different parties will have to be involved in the process of developing sustainable tourism. This section focuses on what the tourism industry itself can do in order to increase its sustainability, defines three major problems, and suggests possible tourism initiatives to help solve these problems. Other problems should also be included in the discussion for it to become exhaustive.

B. Industry Initiatives for Sustainable Tourism

Problems

Decreased access to natural resources for the local communities and environmental degradation

Tourism is not, as many people assert, a clean and non-polluting industry. A major problem is the lack of a common understanding of what sustainable tourism or "eco-tourism" means. This ambiguity leads to violations of environmental regulations and standards. Hence, the environmental problems evolving from tourism are manifold. First of all, the tourism industry is very resource and land intensive. Consequently, the interest of the tourism sector will often be in conflict with local resource and land use practices. The introduction of tourism will imply an increased stress on resources available. An influx of tourists into the area will lead to a competition for resources. Employees working at the tourist sites compound this competition. Almost as a rule, tourists are supplied at the expense of the local population.

Tourist activities imply an intensified utilization of vulnerable habitats. Investors and tourists do not necessarily possess awareness on how to use natural resources sustainably, and subsequently this utilization often leads to a degradation of resources. Tourism is also a major generator of wastes. In most tourist regions of developing countries, sewage, wastewater and solid waste disposal are not properly managed or planned. Lastly, tourism is also responsible for a considerable proportion of increased volumes and mileage in global transport and hence the associated environmentally damaging pollutant emissions. The tourism industry has not shown sufficient willingness to (internalize or) compensate the cost of conservation of bio-diversity in, for instance, protected areas, even though they can profit from it.

Increasing Cultural Erosion and Disrespect for Human Rights

Tourism is a powerful agent of change. International tourism acts as a catalyst for the transition from traditional ways of life to so-called modern, Western forms of society. Accordingly, tourism often brings with it the introduction of new behaviour trends and norms. Very often, these are contrary to traditional norms existing in the host community, and can come into conflict with its cultural identity and threaten the traditional value systems there. The problem is that the investors seem to have a lack of cultural understanding of the invested society. There is a need for an increased awareness that establishment of new hotels etc. will have its consequences on the society and the people who live in it.

Tourism has become associated with violation of human rights. Many destination countries have experienced an increase in criminality, prostitution, alcohol and drug abuse as a consequence of tourism. Furthermore, child labour is commonplace in the tourism industry (particularly in the informal sector). According to estimates made by ILO (International Labour Organization), between 3 and 19 million children and teenagers work in the tourism sector. A particularly abominable form of violation of human rights is child slavery and despicable abuse of children taking place in the booming sex industry in many countries. In these countries, tourism has led to an incredible increase in prostitution and also in the exploitation of children. The tourism industry has not yet come up with a general condemnation of these violations of human rights.

Unqualified Jobs and Foreign Exchange Leakage

The tourism industry is characterized by a high degree of monopoly, which implies a concentration of services and profits into very few big transnational corporations. In many countries, tourism facilities mostly belong to foreigners. Furthermore, in local host communities in many countries a relatively small number of people are involved in the tourism industry in host communities in many developing countries. Very often, there is a lack of qualified manpower in the locality. Hence, most employees are recruited form the big cities, neighbouring countries or even from the country of origin of the investors.

Multiplier effects from tourism are less significant than is often assumed. One reason is that tourism industries purchase most of their inputs (materials, products or services) in their country of origin. As a result, a considerable amount of foreign exchange revenues leaks from the destination countries. The more goods, services, physical capital and human capital a country must import for its tourism services, the higher the leakage. Very often the investors are not approaching the local community to see what it actually can provide. In addition to this, the General Agreement on Trade in Services (GATS), with its liberalization of global trade and services, is increasingly undermining the possibilities of individual countries and regions to control their tourism industries and the possible economic gains from tourism.

Solutions

Decreased Access to Natural Resources for the Local Communities and Environmental Degradation

In general, the tourism industry should engage in promoting sustainability as a hallmark for investors. More specifically, investors in tourism should strive to adopt environmentally sound technologies or other measures to minimize the consumption of local ground water. In the case of water utilization, such measures might be water saving equipment, desalination systems and collecting and utilizing rainwater. Using other types of resources in a sustainable manner is, of course, also crucial. There is a need to use ecological materials and installation of renewable sources of energy systems (solar energy) in all new buildings and new construction. Furthermore there should be an acceleration of installation or solar/wind power in all public work projects of communities where tourism will be introduced. To prevent or minimise the impact of chemical inputs in soil, water and health, one should start utilizing sound ecological methods, including IPM (Integrated Pest Management). Ecological methods need to be applied in all areas utilized for tourism, including in the maintenance of golf courts, gardens and recreational facilities.

Pollution of ground and coastal waters must be prevented, and recommendations must be made (perhaps even legislation) for tourism investors to invest in proper sewage treatment facilities. Appropriate waste disposal systems and ways to separate garbage into organic and non-organic waste should be developed. Organic waste can be composted and possibly reused on hotel gardens or even for local farming. This could be done through collaboration with local residents. Residents could organize themselves and manage the allocated dumping sites, and hence benefit from the system in receiving payment from the hotel for services rendered. A system to separate the different materials, and recycle some should be in place at the landfill site, thus reducing the waste even further.

To avoid degradation of the natural environment, tourism projects can help finance protected areas and safeguard ecologically sensitive regions against further environmental deterioration. By empowering local populations and have them participating in the entire process, sustainability will be ensured as it becomes accepted by and adjusted to the local communities. Also, a protected area might certainly be a suitable tourist-attraction, where tourists can experience amazing nature and learn about conservation and traditional uses of natural resources in the area.

Investors in tourism should always respect the traditional land tenure system in the area and the traditional user-right systems of resources. In regard to this, the communication and consultation with the local communities about resource-use is important. Tourism investors should not exclude local people from using local resources, and thus take away what they depend on for maintaining their well-being. The tourism industry can and must take initiatives to implement that polluter(s) pay a principle (or other forms of internalization of externalities) for pollution related to tourism operations. This may be organized and carried out through local tax systems or through funds established by the tourism industry for local community development. However, the paid principle should be applied for minor pollution only and should not be developed into a possibility for investors to pay a symbolic fine for imposed irreversible negative impacts on the local environment.

Inaccurate and/or mild environmental legislation in destination countries may possibly attract more foreign investors contributing to fast economic growth and development, but with environmental damage as a consequence. To avoid the dilemma, destination countries will have to choose between economic development and environmental protection international. Multi-national enterprises must be committed to follow the environmental standards of their home country should these be stricter than those at the destinations.

Increasing Cultural Erosion and Disrespect for Human Rights

The tourism industry should promote projects, which are compatible with the cultural identity of the local population's way of life. Furthermore, the tourism sector should always make sure it acts in accordance with the cultural heritage, and respect the cultural integrity of tourism destinations. This might be accomplished by defining codes of conduct for the industry and hence providing investors with a checklist for sustainable tourism projects.

Establishing and developing tourist training programmes could be one way of managing codes of conducts for the tourists. Here, tourists can be informed and educated about the destination for their travel both before and after their arrival at the site. At the site, tourist information centres can be established through funding from the investor. The information given to tourists should include codes of conduct regarding appropriate behaviour and clothing. It is reasonable to assume that people's offending behaviour is largely a consequence of ignorance rather than intention. Consequently, information and facts about the destination, ways of life, history, cultural heritage is crucial to help tourists get along.

It is an absolute must that tourism investors do not engage in or promote child labour and prostitution. Moreover, it is appropriate that the industry commit themselves to a global campaign against such and any other violation of human rights. Evaluating the sustainability of the tourism development, in regards to cultural and human rights aspects, is highly recommended for those responsible for the tourism projects. As with the case mentioned earlier of preventing environmental degradation, this must be carried out through communication and consultation with the local communities.

Unqualified Jobs and Foreign Exchange Leakage

By devising local training programmes and establishing educational projects, the tourism industry can ensure that qualified local people are employed in their projects. One should train the local people instead of foreigners to become guides due to their knowledge of the area and resources. The investors should be responsive to the kind of knowledge, abilities and skills found in the local communities. Very often such knowledge and skills are well fitted to be used in tourist activities be it fishing trips, nature trails, souvenir sales or dancing courses for tourists etc.

To constrain foreign exchange leakage, those responsible for the tourism projects should ensure that local inputs are purchased for their projects. A proper examination of local resources available will be beneficial for both the industry and the local residents. Usually, there is considerable local willingness to start producing new products if a market for these products exists. The tourism sector should also adopt measures to prevent foreign exchange leakage by a commitment to re-investment of a fair share of the locally accrued profit. We have already mentioned protected areas, training programmes on codes of conduct for tourists, or possible training of local employees, as projects in need of funds. Initiatives towards more local community development projects should also be appropriate.

The tourism industry should promote the establishment of small and medium-sized tourism enterprises which, compared to large-scale hotels etc., have far more moderate impacts on the environment. It is the industry's responsibility to act as a model for communities to show that it is possible to do business whilst protecting natural resources. The industry should also promote and support local communities to start tourism-related businesses and grant access to low interest loans. It is the responsibility of the tourism sector to ensure total transparency in all transactions, and to prevent tourism projects from being used as projects for laundering illicit money, as well as to refuse using bribes as a means to obfuscate or avoid government rules and regulations. There should be a global boycott against those investors involved in such or other types of illegal activities.

General Recommendations and Possible Solutions which Concern all three Problem Areas

Empowerment of residents at tourist destinations, through local participation, may be facilitated by providing written and legally binding contracts between local people and tourism investors. The contracts will help to avoid broken promises, which too many examples and previous experience prove to be a huge problem. In addition to the mentioned examples (providing proper information for tourists and establishing training programmes for residents), the tourism industry, through for instance the WTTC or the WTO with NGOs in the selection panels, could issue awards especially for sustainable tourism projects as an encouragement for investors.

Agents and Partnerships for Change

In this section, the focus has been on what the tourism industry itself can do in order to augment and improve its environmental, cultural, social and economic profile and make sure this is sustainable. However, the industry's effort cannot be successful without a profound collaboration with all stakeholders.

Within the industry, it is important that both small and large-scale tourism operators are included in the collaboration and that they participate in solving problems related to tourism development. As mentioned, a sustainable development of the tourism industry can only be ensured through participation of all local residents in the destination countries. There is a need for a willingness and ability for the partners to work with this kind of bottom-up approach. In this context, both environment and social NGOs have an important role to play, putting pressure on the industry and facilitating contracts and local participation for community development. Governments in both destination and countries of origin of tourists and investors are responsible for providing appropriate legislation for sustainable tourism development, and to follow-up the tourism projects with sufficient monitoring and appropriate sanctioning. Exchange of successful experiences of sustainable tourism projects is an important factor in this connection. Lastly, an interdisciplinary approach to the problem is necessary: using local, regional and/or international consultative forums.

C. Influencing Consumer Behaviour to Promote Sustainable Tourism

Problems

International tourism plays an ambivalent role in contributing to cultural exchange and sustainable development. On the one hand, it involves a highly buffered, short-term consumer experience of other locales. Tourists can pay and leave, remaining isolated from negative impacts at the local level. On the other hand, tourism may increase recognition of the importance of respecting cultural diversity and developing an identity as a world citizen. It offers opportunities to educate consumers regarding responsible tourism and sustainable development. Consumers can play a major role in the transformation of societies towards sustainability. While mass tourism in the past was rather producer-driven, the industry today is becoming increasingly consumer-driven. In highly competitive tourism markets, well informed, responsible consumers can put increasing pressure on the industry to behave more responsibly.

A number of official proclamations have affirmed every individual's right to rest and leisure including tourism. However, tourism remains an unobtainable luxury for the majority of the world's population. Tourists primarily originate from affluent industrialized societies where tourism has become a mass phenomenon. Tourists' values, attitudes and behaviour are determined by their social environment, cultural identity and way of life which may be in conflict with local customs. Tourism is heterogeneous in nature, made up of many different types of traveller, seeking a wide range of tourism products. Demand is influenced by irrational factors, e.g. fashion and trends. Demand depends on the availability of time and money, on images, perceptions and attitudes. Tourists have various needs, desires and motivations, both of a 'push' and 'pull' nature. While household incomes in major tourist—sending countries are declining, industry sales projections continue to grow, indicating increasing competition. The consumer mind is set on discount prices and "buy now/pay later" options. This poses serious threats, as prices already lag far behind any realistic accounting of tourism costs and impacts.

Many of the demand patterns in tourism reflect the unsustainable lifestyles of industrialized consumer societies. Tourism acts as an agent in exporting these life-styles and consumerist attitudes to less industrialized societies via demonstration effects and modelling. Tourism increases demand for imported consumer goods in the destinations, with detrimental effects on the environment, due to the ecological costs of transport and the high amount of waste generated. Increasing imports also reduce local/national economic gains, due to foreign exchange leakage.

The over-consumption of resources by tourists and tourism infrastructure (e.g. the excessive use of water, firewood or food) is incompatible with sustainable development. The carrying capacity of natural environments is often exceeded with the addition of tourism demands. Tourist demand for resources (land, water, energy, food) may also compete with the needs of local people and may increase social inequality, gender inequality and injustice. Tourist transport, especially air travel, is highly energy intensive and causes pollutant emissions. Many tourism activities such as skiing, boating, mountain hiking, motorized water-sports (e.g. jet skies), and trekking represent stress for fragile ecosystems. Tourists often lack information and awareness about their impact in a different culture and environment, about their impacts on socio-economic and socio-cultural development, and about the environmental costs of tourism. While tourists may be open to learning, they are often unaware of inappropriate behaviour and have little guidance on how to improve them. Others may refuse to adapt to local life-styles (even when informed) insisting on their freedom to behave as they want.

While the tourism industry may be willing to improve their products and services, there is a conflict between the industry's pursuit of economic gains and social and environmental responsibility. The industry lacks information on the requirements of sustainable tourism and on how to integrate economic forces with environmental and social requirements. Tourists shopping for escapism generally abide by one fundamental consumer ethic: receipt upon payment. Consumer advocates may intervene where inferior customer service is delivered. However, the sustainability of corporate practices is self-regulated. This conflict of interest within the industry, and consumers' low awareness of tourism impacts, have led to a widespread abuse of 'green' labelling.

The mass media, especially television through films and reports about events, sights, etc. in other parts of the world, are increasingly influential on travel decisions and consumer behaviour in the destinations. However, these programmes often serve primarily as advertisements, painting images of destinations, rather than providing relevant information for potential travellers.

There is a lack of reliable and appropriate (e.g. age and gender segregated) research data on the determinants of tourist demand, motivation and behaviour. Few countries, whether tourist-sending or tourist-receiving, collect such data that are helpful under sustainable development criteria. Most studies of tourist behaviour focus on mainstream markets or market segments, rather than assessing or modelling sustainable alternatives. Governments in many tourist destinations and local communities have little or no information on what to expect from tourism and the incoming tourists, and how to influence and control tourism and guide tourist behaviour. They are controlled by international/global institutions, the industry and the consumers. Governments of the affluent countries are only beginning to look at the issues of outgoing tourism. They are not yet sufficiently aware of their responsibility and methods to influence tourist behaviour by political and legal guidelines/criteria and appropriate planning and policies. Trade unions have fought successfully for shorter working hours and more vacation. However, they need to take more responsibility for helping to create a leisure industry that is more sustainable.

Solutions

Consumer behaviour can and must be influenced by:

- Fighting unsustainable forms and aspects of tourism, at the various levels, by sanctioning unacceptable behaviour and discouraging inappropriate consumer behaviour;
- Promoting responsible and sustainable patterns of behaviour, at the various levels, by promoting best practises and encouraging responsible consumer behaviour. There are different types of instruments and remedial measures available;
- Legal measures (rules, regulations, sanctions);
- Market based instruments, such as taxes to influence market prices;
- Promotion of and (financial) support for best practice;
- Industry self-monitoring/codes of conduct;
- Information, education and research.

Agents and Partnerships for Changes

Institutional Action and Possible Partnerships

Consumer behaviour in tourism is both a product and cause of policies by government and industry. Therefore, a comprehensive approach is required to solve the problems associated with market-driven tourism. Tourism should be viewed as a major development issue that all stakeholders need to be actively engaged with. To develop effective partnerships, the imbalance of power between the different stakeholders needs to be addressed.

UN Action:

- Establish an NGO tourism advisory group for UN to provide technical support, analysis, and strategic advice;

- Create a 'best practices' information clearing-house, in order to collect consumer information useful to understanding and positively influencing consumer behaviour and to make documentation accessible on an equitable basis;
- Initiate a broad information and awareness campaign to highlight damaging forms of tourism and impacts, providing tools for informed decision-making. Initially, target participants in the CSD and CBD processes to clarify roles and responsibilities;
- Research and develop effective certification schemes, form a technical group under the CSD to assess how certification can be improved, e.g., through the review of voluntary codes set up by CSD1998;
- Designate an 'ombuds' office jointly between the CSD, CBD, and UN-CHR to encourage diligent self-regulation and compliance with international standards for sustainable tourism; and
- Develop guidance on tourism as an issue within Local Agenda 21 processes.

Governmental Action:

- Introduce and enforce legislation to abolish child prostitution, implement effective control mechanisms, conclude judicial assistance agreements;
- Regulate tourist access to ecologically fragile or stressed natural areas;
- Tourist-sending countries: develop policies on outgoing tourism from a development perspective;
- Provide frameworks for ecologically appropriate pricing by strictly applying the polluter-pays-principle to internalise external costs. This includes ecological tax reforms including the taxation of aviation gasoline and oil, removal of subsidies/other economic incentives with negative environmental impacts;
- Improve conditions for sustainable consumer behaviour by providing/promoting sustainable tourism facilities;
- Promote environmentally friendly modes of transport and transport concepts, reduce tourism-related traffic, shift demand to less environmentally damaging modes of transport;

- Promote renewable sources of energy (such as solar power), reduce the use of non-renewable energy and of limited local resources, through more sustainable practices/consumption patterns;
- Develop information and education programmes in co-operation with local stakeholders ensuring all stakeholders' involvement (e.g. women's); provide information to tourists on appropriate behaviour (sensitivity, respect for/adaptation to local culture), e.g. by establishing information centres in destinations, or by including briefing material for package tours;
- Take into account the specific information needs of various market segments, provide information to the local population on the opportunities and risks from tourism and on how to influence tourist behaviour;
- Adopt, observe, implement and promote codes of conduct, e.g. the planned WTO-OMT 'Global Code of Ethics for Tourism'; and
- Integrate sustainable development education including tourism in the curricula of schools at all levels, universities and training institutions, involving all stakeholder groups, create and promote open networks for information and research on sustainable tourism, disseminate and implement results.

Tourism Industry Action:

- Promote sustainable tourism products, using market related instruments and incentives, such as contests, awards, certification, model projects, culturally sensitive quality labels covering both environmental and social sustainability;
- Reduce inappropriate consumption, use local resources in preference to imports in a sustainable manner; reduce and recycle waste, ensure safe waste disposal, develop and implement sustainable transport policies and systems, e.g. efficient public transport, walking, cycling in destinations;
- Provide tourists with authentic information, enabling them to understand all environmental and related aspects (e.g. human rights situation) of tourism when selecting any destination or holiday package; educate visitors in advance of arrival and give guidance on 'dos' and 'don'ts';

make tourists aware of their potential impact on and their responsibilities towards host societies;

- Provide information on respecting the cultural and natural heritage of destination areas; employ tour guides who portray societies honestly and dispel stereotypes;
- Ensure that the marketing of 'green' tourism reflects sound environmental policy and practice; use non-exploitative marketing strategies that respect people, communities and environments of destinations, dismantle stereotyping, integrate sustainable tourism principles when creating new marketing strategies;
- Train staff to foster tourist responsibility towards the destinations, encourage multi-cultural education and exchange;
- Actively discourage exploitative sex tourism, particularly sexual exploitation of children, and tourism which causes or contributes to social problems; and
- Adopt, observe, implement and promote codes of conduct.

NGO Action:

- Disseminate information to a wide public about the complexity of tourism and about the objectives and criteria of sustainable tourism;
- Educate tourists to change consumption patterns and promote appropriate, environmentally and socially acceptable behaviour in the destinations;
- Launch broad awareness campaigns on the worst impacts of tourism, to be funded by international governmental and non-governmental agencies;
- Promote relevant research on tourism impacts, criteria for sustainable tourism and possibilities for implementation;
- Monitor tourism development, policy, industry initiatives, and local people's reaction to tourism development and policy, and implementation of stakeholder action.

D. Promoting Broad-based Sustainable Development through Tourism whilst Safeguarding the Integrity of Local Cultures and Protecting the Environment—Community Development Problems

Early tourism development has given little consideration to natural resource limitations, impacts on wildlife and indigenous cultures.

The human environment and development has been largely ignored. Within the process of globalization local communities' participation and nature conservation are threatened and often overlooked.

If tourism is to be sustainable, it must improve the lives of local people, protect their environment and health, and offer them a better future. In many instances, tourism can be seen as a vehicle to empower local communities and protect the environment through the development of new employment opportunities, the enhancement of local economies, preservation of indigenous knowledge and practices, public awareness and education. Sustainable tourism can create positive opportunities for community development in remote areas. The business sector can choose sustainable tourism over other more polluting ventures. Long and short-term development plans should be developed so that tourism and its benefits are spread within the area. To develop tourism in a sustainable manner, it is necessary to define optimal tourism destinations in local areas and regions, ensuring enjoyment for the tourist and minimum impact or disruption for the environment and local communities.

Complex and broad-based local communities' involvement in tourism development requires targeted investment strategies implemented by local decision-makers. Those strategies do not exist in many areas and the development of tourism is not planned. Often, tourism investments are imposed from the outside, and the potential for sustainable forms of tourism is weakened. Alternatives to mass tourism (e.g. cultural and ecotourism) can be influential in changing the nature of tourism. Tourism can benefit both tourists and local communities and allow for two-way interaction and education.

Solutions

In order for tourism to become a sustainable industry, countries, states, regions, and individuals must work with new technology, natural resource management and marketing concepts. Ideally, participatory planning and implementation will be a part of Local Agenda 21 processes. To ensure community involvement and to safeguard local cultures, sustainable tourism development should therefore involve all stakeholders in tourism development at all appropriate levels, facilitate the development of tourism services that are planned, managed and reviewed by the host community in Local Agenda 21 processes. This will also ensure that tourism revenue stays in the host communities to enhance livelihoods and generate a profitable source of income, empower and motivate local groups to direct cross-cultural exchange in the way they wish and adopt practices which conserve, protect and preserve the environment.

Local and regional Tourism Boards should be created, involving all stakeholders. These Boards should:

- promote sustainable tourism concepts in co-operation with local governments and all stakeholders, in line with Local Agenda 21 priorities;
- work systematically to attract investment in sustainable tourism;
- help other institutions in developing marketing strategies and training programmes and developing educational materials;
- work together with different public institutions to involve all stakeholder groups in tourism activities, and bring greater benefits to the entire community; and
- co-operate with grassroots organizations to develop employment strategies through sustainable tourism.

Agents and Partnerships for Change

Institutional Action:

The UN-CSD should:

- invite countries to integrate tourism into their sustainable development strategies for the 2002 review;
- ask the review progress in local communities involvement in tourism development in their country profiles to the preparatory meetings for Earth Summit III in 2002 as part of the review process;
- instruct DESA in co-operation with relevant UN agencies and convention secretariats, major groups and all stakeholders to develop indicators of sustainable tourism;
- invite convention secretariats and the Committee on the Environment of the WTO-OMC to report annually to the CSD;
- establish an international "ombuds" office to deal with human rights abuses and environmental destruction in tourism;

- ask UNEP, through their Technology Industry and Economics Division, to work with industry associations at all levels, trade unions, local authorities and NGOs to develop a framework for 'good practice' and to develop a database on good practice, criteria, examples and analysis which should be accessible to governments and stakeholders alike;
- ask UNEP together with UNCHS, the Sustainable Cities Programme and relevant stakeholders to develop guidance notes on tourism within Local Agenda 21;
- ask the UN Regional Commissions to prepare a report for the preparatory meetings for Earth Summit III in 2002 on sustainable and community-based tourism activities within their region and to work with UNEP/WTO to develop regional agreements to address sustainable tourism;
- invite UNDP to share its work on guidelines for "good practice" and to involve indigenous peoples and local communities this work;
- ask the UNDP country offices to bring together UN agencies, bilateral donors and other stakeholders to work together on sustainable tourism, as well as involve the gender development programme in this process;
- ask UNDP to include sustainable tourism into its poverty alleviation strategies and programmes;
- ask the United Nations Conference on Trade and Development to integrate tourism into their development strategies and include a progress review on the role of indigenous and local communities' involvement in tourism for the Earth Summit III (year 2002) review, and to support community-owned and controlled initiatives in tourism and bio-diversity through its BIOTRADE initiative;
- invite environmental conventions and treaties secretariats to include community-based tourism in their action plans and programmes, and to promote it as an incentive for the conservation and sustainable use of bio-diversity.

Multi-lateral financing and assistance agencies should:

- provide funds for applied research through pilot projects to determine optimal mechanisms for tourism development in a range of differing circumstances;

- create small-scale credit lines to assist small enterprises to invest in tourism without excessive risk on personal property;
- support community controlled tourism initiatives that are directed to poverty alleviation, bio-diversity conservation and promotion of human rights;
- assess their projects' effectiveness on local, sub-national and national levels involving all stakeholders, and publish the results by the Earth Summit III in 2002; and
- take part in a discussion forum on minimizing leakage, with findings to be brought back to the finance discussion at CSD-8 in 2000. Possible outcomes include the development of a purchasing/procurement strategy for the tourism industry, local/national investment strategies, improved mechanisms for informed choice by consumers, and a linking of aid with capacity building in tourism-dependent areas.

Governments should, at national level:

- establish/clarify institutional and departmental responsibility for developing outgoing tourism and harmonize institutional interventions;
- initiate the use of tourism for local economic development by involving all sectors alongside the tourist ministry; to build the capacity to work at the destination level, including product development and effective management of existing destinations;
- facilitate research grants on sustainable tourism, methodologies, impacts and analysis of good practice; finance pilot schemes to develop 'good practice' and establish systems for ongoing evaluation and monitoring;
- establish sustainable tourism policies and regulations, ensuring responsibly zoned development; natural and cultural heritage and resource conservation and protection;
- review land ownership in potential tourism areas and where possible transfer ownership to local communities and provide the necessary training for them;
- include the perspective of local and indigenous communities into local and national sustainable development strategies;

- increase funding for local NGOs to enable them to engage in a dialogue on tourism;
- support public education programmes which encourage responsible consumption, natural resource use, environmental protection and local culture conservation;
- give priority to the following investment suggestions: create funds to help tour operators improve their technical capacity for sustainable tourism development; create funds to develop recreational facilities for the public;
- encourage local banks and other lending institutions to set up regional investment funding programmes, including micro-credit programmes;
- create Regional Tourism Boards, fully staffed, to help in planning, promoting, regulating, and expanding sustainable tourism;
- initiate special marketing programmes by local governments and Tourism Boards, in which local tourism programmes will be advertised in the media;
- initiate programmes to improve the management of eco-tourism in protected areas; and
- set up training programmes for guides, tour operators, marketers, etc.

Governments should, at local level:

- harmonize laws on tourism including regulations, fee standards, licensing, etc. so that they will be more favourable to sustainable tourism in the region;
- ensure that tourism development is in line with Local Agenda 21 priorities and land-use plans and that the public can participate in local and regional decision-making;
- regulate tourism to ensure that profits benefit local people and conservation efforts;
- Develop and support programmes to revitalize the diverse aspects of local cultures.

The tourism industry should:

- reduce financial leakage and support local economies by buying food and resources locally, develop long-term partnerships with local operators, businesses and suppliers;

- train and hire local staff and contract with local businesses, promote management opportunities for women;
- prefer accommodations owned, built and staffed by local people, promote locally made handicrafts and traditional products;
- encourage clients to study and understand their destinations, respect local cultures and co-ordinate visits with local communities, authorities and women's organizations, being aware of and being sensitive to local customary laws, regulations and traditions, whilst respecting historical heritage and scientific sites; and
- educate staff to avoid negative environmental and cultural impacts and create incentive schemes to promote sustainable behaviour.

NGOs should:

- initiate stakeholder dialogue on community involvement in tourism development, recognizing social and gender divisions in communities;
- promote consultation processes in tourism planning, involving local communities;
- launch educational and awareness programmes on tourism for local communities, support and promote history research and museums;
- promote the respect for indigenous peoples and local communities' self-determination, autonomy and social and cultural integrity;
- strengthen their efforts to empower disenfranchized groups (in particular women) to become involved in local tourism planning and management;
- develop participatory programmes to support the integrity of local cultures and economies;
- support the sustainable resource use and initiate environmental actions on different levels to conserve the environment while the tourism is developing;
- analyze the experience with sustainable tourism in different parts of the world, in order to disseminate methodology/positive examples of community involvement in tourism;
- support the use of traditional knowledge, practices and innovation systems relevant for the conservation and

sustainable use of biological resources and promote actions on different levels to eradicate poverty, protect human rights and conserve the environment while working in tourism.

Possible Partnerships

There is an urgency to constructively shape tourism in order to support local development and conservation goals. UN bodies and institutions, governments, industry and civil society should co-operate to launch a dialogue process on sustainable tourism. This must be planned within the framework provided by the various UN treaties and declarations. All the stakeholders involved in and affected by tourism should be involved in the development of action plans for sustainable tourism. Identifying mechanisms to achieve sustainable development goals in tourism must be a priority for co-operation. 'Good practices' in conserving culture and nature while developing sustainable tourism should be collected worldwide, involving all stakeholders. This process should lead to a multi-stakeholder round-table on strategic planning of local community involvement in tourism to be organised by UNEP as a side event at the Preparatory meetings for Earth Summit III in 2002.

There is an urgent need to assess the impacts of globalization and the role of multilateral and bilateral development organizations in unsustainable tourism practices. An independent international assessment commission should be created under the CSD. NGOs, indigenous peoples, women's organizations and local communities should be involved in this assessment process together with all other stakeholders. The UN Working Group on Indigenous Peoples should be invited to monitor impacts of tourism on indigenous peoples and local communities. The assessment is to be completed and published by the year 2002.

E. Coastal Impact of Tourism

Problems

The United Nations Commission on Sustainable Development in 1999 will address both Oceans and Seas and the review of SIDS. Therefore, it is recognizing that: "The survival of small island developing States is firmly rooted in their human resources and cultural heritage, which are their most significant assets; those assets are under severe stress and all efforts must be taken to ensure the central position of people in the process of sustainable development." With these words, the Report of the Global Conference on the Sustainable Development of Small Island Developing States identifies the single most important issue to be borne in mind as we address the challenge of survival and development for our islands.

Article 25 of the Programme of Action from the United Nations Conference on the Sustainable Development of Small Island Developing States (SIDS) focuses our attention on another significant consideration: "Sustainable development in small island developing States depends largely on coastal and marine resources, because their small land area means that those States are effectively COASTAL ENTITIES".

Tourism is one of many anthropogenic activities with a special focus on coastal areas. The two most popular locations for holiday-makers are the mountains and the coast. The coastal area or zone (as it is often called) is hard to define as the area where fresh and salt waters mix, containing many complex, diverse and productive eco-systems on and offshore interacting with each other. New concepts including the whole watershed area seem to be the best approach, especially when aquatic pollution problems are considered. Most problems are related to conflicts between different uses and access restrictions. Tourism leads to increased traffic flow and overcrowding in already densely populated areas. Up to 130 tourists has been calculated per inhabitant in the most popular coastal regions. Therefore, tourism adds substantially to the following pressures:

- Pollution by waste water, garbage, heating, noise and traffic emissions;
- Encroachment of buildings, facilities and roads close to the coastline;
- Beach erosion due to building, dune removal and dredging;
- Excessive use of natural areas;
- Destruction of natural areas to accommodate tourism or other needs;
- Inter-sectorial competition and conflict over (marine and terrestrial) space;
- Exclusion of local communities from any role of significance in decision-making;

- The loss of natural and architectural heritage in the face of rapid expansion;
- Strain on public utilities and facilities;
- displacement of local population;
- Creation of restricted exclusive zones that are off-limits to the local people;
- Loss of business by local enterprises as all-inclusive resorts supplies all the needs of their guests.

Additional typical tourism impacts are socio-economic conflicts as property and general costs of living increases, and social structure can be changed significantly, when summer guests overrun small communities. Foreign customs and expectations can create conflicts and a deterioration of cultural and regional values.

Solutions

A major focus should be on the integration of tourism planning and operation of tourist facilities into local planning instruments. Local agenda 21 can play a key role here in ensuring the involvement of all stakeholders. Ideally, this would be done in the context of Integrated Coastal Area Management (ICAM). This instrument bridges sectorial approaches in order to avoid or mitigate user conflicts, and it ideally takes into account eco-system features and physical, not man-made borders. New tourism developments should be planned together with municipal, industrial, agri/aqua-cultural and nature protection activities, to allow for multiple complementary uses and to segregate conflicting activities. Area development plans should inform sector plans which should then be incorporated into a co-ordinated national development plan. All planning should be accompanied by widespread public information dissemination and provide opportunity for discussion leading to integrated coastal zone management. The tourism development strategy should protect local culture, respect local traditions and promote local ownership and management of programmes and projects, so as to foster community stewardship of the natural resource base. Environmental Impact Assessment (EIA) on a strategic level as well as for projects is an invaluable tool for this stage. Criteria for planning and EIA should be:

- Strict environmental standards for solid, liquid and gaseous waste emissions;

- Taking the integrity of coastal values and resources into account;
- Enhancement of public transport infrastructure (train, boat, bike, bus);
- Locally adapted styles and maximum height/size limit for facilities;
- Setting of local/regional carrying capacities on a case-by-case basis;
- Limits to sale of property to foreigners;
- Maintenance of public access to the coastal strip; and
- Safeguarding cultural values and customary uses.

During the operation of tourism facilities, several instruments can be applied to enable sustainable development. The details have to be developed according to the use, and together with the local community, the facility operator and local NGOs. Local Agenda 21 could play an important role here (They will be different for a diving site than for a big hotel complex). Modern instruments, which should be, and partly are, already applied in the tourism industry are:

- Introducing environmental management (according to ISO 14000 or the European EMAS Initiative);
- Increasing cultural and nature awareness of guests through interactions with local initiatives, guided nature walks, museums, etc.; and
- Integrating the local economy by giving priority to local produce (e.g. fish, fruit, vegetables, furniture and building materials).

However, all these efforts will be in vain, unless carrying capacity limits can be agreed upon in a dialogue and on a case-by-case basis. These limits have to follow sustainability criteria and have to come out of discussions on the development objectives and the natural and cultural values to be protected. They can be tiered in respect to nature used, number of beds and other facilities for guests, and amount of property to be sold to foreigners. (But management efforts for sustainable development cannot allow an ever increasing growth, which will destroy and, in fact already has, the resources the guests have come to see and experience.) To diminish conflicts a better use of facilities over the year, instead of only in a short season of two to three months should be aimed at. These limits probably have to be stricter for "nature use." Here the introduction and implementation of ranger and guide systems together with limits, regarding the number of visitors, can lead to increased awareness and control at the same time. A simple example is the different approaches to beach litter: Instead of excessive beach cleaning of all organic matter, a plastic litter clean-up by volunteers plus hands-on teaching on the originally inhabiting the beach and its natural detritus (like algae and wood) could reinstate and appreciation of nature.

We also believe that the recommendations for action at the national, regional and international levels have been detailed in the SIDS Programme of Action (1994), at the CTO Conference on Eco-tourism in Dominica (1997) and more recently in the CEP Technical Report No. 38 (1997) need to be implemented.

Agents and Partnership for Change

Institutional Actions

Actions on several levels are necessary. First and foremost, the historically grown sectorial approach to managing coastal issues, relating to tourism and other uses, has to be changed substantially. Under the lead of one coastal agency, all stakeholders, especially local people and NGOs, and also sectorial agencies, small and medium enterprises and industry representatives should meet regularly to promote sustainable development of their coastal area. The planning process and the operation of tourism developments should reflect the country's commitment to the guidelines set out in international accords such as Agenda 21 and the SIDS Programme of Action. Depending on the region, this could mean enhancing human resource development including public awareness building and training; institutional strengthening and networking. Lessons learned in one community should be accessible to others. This will start the ICAM process, which is a goal-directed planning and decision-making process. ICAM leads to inter-agency and inter-sectorial collaboration, resulting in operational decision-making with strong public participation and feedback mechanisms. ICAM could mean in practice:

- To start an environmental management initiative through an award scheme;
- To raise an environmental tax from visitors for small projects, e.g. for funding ranger;

- Training or environmental training for tourism staff;
- To start joint actions with local fishermen, farmers, hotels, or other local initiatives; and
- To develop a tourism master plan for the region.

In the long-term, a development plan should be devised and discussed thoroughly in order to achieve a common understanding on the objectives and necessary restrictions. As all coastal areas contain particularly sensitive sites, environmental protection has to feature strongly in this planning process, with representatives from government nature protection agencies and NGOs having an equal standing with all other participants. Depending on the nature of the coastline, regional and inter-governmental collaboration may be necessary in addition to local initiatives. For some issues, such as the reduction of pollution and especially "eutrophication", co-operation on a larger regional scale is necessary. Maybe the Baltic Sea States, consisting of very poor and rich states (can serve as example) are co-ordinating their fight against pollution under the Helsinki Convention, funding projects in neighbouring countries according to a list of hot spots. They have just finished the development of a joint Agenda 21 for the development of the Baltic region, including tourism. Generally, national plans should be converted into area development plans, which would provide the local context within which enterprise-level proposals can be evaluated. All these plans should inform and be incorporated into wider regional plans.

As integrated processes take time, tourism umbrella organizations should start with voluntary self-restraint, until locally adapted objectives have been reached. In the north, which bears the brunt of world-wide tourism, a development of quality tourism should be the focus for the future instead of an increase in quantity. The term quality should include ecological and social carrying capacities at the same time as being economically sustainable. In the south, tourism development objectives should be developed according to the local needs. A specially developed Code of Conduct, taking into account inter-area, the Coastal Code of Conduct by EUCC and the Berlin Declaration on Biological Diversity and Sustainable Tourism, could lead the way. Environmental management should become a standard of operation as well as social accountability thus leading to sustainable development.

Possible Partnerships

Additional to those partners mentioned above, there is a major role for environmental and social NGOs to play. The involvement of local initiatives, heritage and nature protection organizations and agencies can lead to a balanced ICAM process in the spirit of the Agenda 21.

Umbrella organizations, such as scuba diving, boating, and yachting associations should develop and promote the application of codes of conduct focussing on environmental and sustainability issues in their respective fields.

The Convention on Biological Diversity contains an eco-system approach, which is consistent with the ICAM logic. Its experts could sensibly focus on questions of nature use and ecological carrying capacities for sensitive sites in order to obtain harmonized world-wide standards with legal standing.

The instruments and strategies are all already developed, now is the time to utilize and combine them in local dialogue processes.

ENVIRONMENTAL CODES OF CONDUCT FOR TOURISM

The United Nations on Environment and Development, the Earth Summit held in Rio during 3-14 June, 1992, marked an important stage in the development of environmental concern among most of the world's industries. Agenda 21, the programme of action agreed upon at the Conference, established the development, adoption and implementation of Codes of Conduct by industries as a main priority for reaching the goals of sustainable development. Chapter 30, 'Strengthening the role of business and industry' states:

"Business and industry, including transnational corporations, should be encouraged to adopt and report on the implementation of codes of conduct promoting best environmental practice, such as the International Chamber of Commerce's Business Charter on Sustainable Development and the chemical industry's responsible care initiative."

The Development of Codes of Conduct

The International Chamber of Commerce (ICC) was one of the first international organizations to establish a general Code of Conduct for all industries and businesses. The ICC Business Charter was first published in April 1991. It has been widely, distributed, adopted by many organizations, large and small, and served as a basis for the preparation of codes specific to the travel and tourism industry, such as the one prepared by The World Travel and Tourism Council (WTTC).

Voluntary codes of conduct are sets of guidelines which industries draw up as a guide to how they should operate. They are not enforced, nor are they enforceable. However, experience shows that where such codes exist, it is important that steps be taken to implement them, and that attempts then be made to monitor the degree of implementation.

Industry finds voluntary codes to be an attractive alternative to enforced regulation, and indeed often proposes such codes in an effort to pre-empt regulation. Voluntary codes seem likely to play a particularly effective role in relation to the environment. Many voluntary codes of conduct from part of a larger package of plans and policies which detail a particular industry's environmental stance.

Voluntary codes have become important in the tourist industry. Not only have governments prepared codes for their tourism industry but the industry has prepared a number of codes for itself. In addition, codes now exist in many countries for both host communities and for tourists themselves.

Tourism and the Environment

Tourism is a major world industry. According to World Tourism Organization (WTO) statistics, international tourist arrivals reached 500 million for the first time in 1993, an increase of 3.8 per cent over 1992. In the same year, international tourism receipts totalled USS324 million (an increase of 9.3 per cent over 1992). Tourism makes an important contribution to gross national product in many countries and provides much needed foreign exchange. The World Travel and Tourism Council (WTTC) estimates that travel and tourism accounted for 10.1 per cent of global gross domestic product in 1994. It is also an industry with considerable growth potential. Furthermore, since the industry's core product is the environment, it is not surprising that the environmental impact of travel and tourism, underestimated in the past, is now receiving more and more serious attention from governments, industry and conservationists. Voluntary environmental codes of conduct appear increasingly to be a valuable tool for raising awareness in the tourism industry about environmental issues and for promoting self-regulation.

The 1980 Manila Declaration of the World Tourism Organization (WTO) challenged the industry with a concept of tourism that emphasizes the social, cultural, environmental, economics, educational and political values of tourism.

> "The protection, enhancement and improvement of various components of man's environment are among the fundamental conditions for the harmonious development of tourism. Similarly, rational management of tourism may contribute to a large extent to protecting and developing the physical environment and the cultural heritage as well as improving the quality of life.... tourism brings people closer together and creates an awareness of the diversity of ways of life, traditions and aspirations."
>
> *Manila Declaration*

INTERNATIONAL CHAMBER OF COMMERCE

Foreword

There is widespread recognition today that environmental protection must be among the highest priorities of every business.

In its milestone 1987 report *Our Common Future,* the World Commission on Environment and Development (Brundtland Commission) emphasized the importance of environmental protection in the pursuit of sustainable development.

To help business around the world improve its environmental performance, the International Chamber of Commerce established a task force of business representatives to create this Business Charter for Sustainable Development. It comprises 16 principles for environmental management which, for business, is a vitally important aspect of sustainable development.

This Charter will assist enterprises in fulfilling their commitment to environmental stewardship in a comprehensive fashion. It was formally launched in April 1991 at the Second World Industry Conference on Environment Management.

Introduction

Sustainable development involves meeting the needs of the present without comprising the ability of future generations to meet their own needs.

Economic growth provides the conditions in which protection of the environment can best be achieved, and environmental protection, in-balance with other human goals, is necessary to achieve growth that is sustainable.

In turn, versatile, dynamic, responsive and profitable businesses are required as the driving force for sustainable economic development and for providing managerial, technical and financial resources to contribute to the resolution of environmental challenges.

Market economies, characterized by entrepreneurial initiatives, are essential to achieving this.

Business thus shares the view that there should be a common goal, not a conflict, between economic development and environmental protection, both now and for future generations.

Making market forces work in this way to protect and improve the quality of the environment with the help of performance based standards and judicious use of economic instruments in a harmonious regulatory framework is one of the greatest challenges that the world faces in the next decade.

The 1987 report of the World Commission on Environment and Development, *Our Common Future,* expresses the same challenge and calls on the cooperation of business in tackling it. To this end, business leaders have launched actions in their individual enterprises as well as through sectoral and cross-sectoral associations.

In order that more businesses join this effort and that their environmental performance continues to improve, the International Chamber of Commerce hereby calls upon enterprises and their associations to use the following Principles as a basis for pursuing such Improvement and to express publicly their support for them.

Individual programmes developed to implement these Principles will reflect the wide diversity among enterprises in size and function.

The objective is that the widest range of enterprises commit themselves to improving their environmental performance in accordance with these principles, to having in place management practices to effect such improvement, to measuring their progress, and to reporting this progress as appropriate internally and externally.

Principles for Environmental Management

1. *Corporate Priority*: To recognized environmental management as among the highest corporate priorities and as a key determinant to sustainable development; to establish policies, programmes and practices for conducting operations in an environmentally sound manner.
2. *Integrated Management*: To continue to improve corporate policies, programmes and environmental performance taking into account technical developments, scientific understanding, consumer needs and community expectations, with legal regulations as a starting point and to apply the same environment criteria internationally.
3. *Employee Education*: To educate, train and motivate employees to conduct their activities in an environmentally responsible manner.
4. *Prior Assessment*: To assess environmental impacts before starting a new activity or project and before decommissioning facility or leaving a site.
5. *Products and Services*: To develop and provide products or services that have no undue environmental impact and are safe in their intended use, that are efficient in their consumption of energy and natural resources, and that can be recycles reused or disposed of safely.
6. *Customer Advice*: To advise and where relevant, educate customers distributors and the public in the safe use, transportation, storage, and disposal of products provided: and apply similar considerations to the provisions of services.
7. *Facilities and Operations*: To develop design and operate facilities and conduct activities taking into consideration the efficient use of energy and materials, the sustainable use of renewable resources, the minimization of adverse environmental impact and waste generation, and the safe and responsible disposal of residual wastes.
8. *Research*: To conduct of support research on the environmental impacts of raw materials, products, processes, emissions and wastes associated with the enterprise and on the means of minimizing such adverse impacts.

9. *Precautionary Approach*: To modify the manufacture, marketing of use of products or services or the conduct of activities, consistent with scientific and technical understanding, to prevent serious or irreversible environmental degradation.
10. *Contractors*: To promote the adoption of these principles by contractors acting on-behalf of the enterprise, encouraging and where appropriate, requiring improvements in their practices to make them consistent with those of the enterprise, and to encourage the wider adoption of these principles by suppliers.
11. *Emergency Preparedness*: To develop and maintain, where significant hazards exist, emergency preparedness plans in conjunction with the emergency services, relevant authorities and the local community, recognizing potential transboundary impacts.
12. *Transfer of Technology*: To contribute to the transfer of environmentally sound technology and management methods throughout the industrial and public sectors.
13. *Contributing to the Common Effort*: To contribute to the development of public policy and to business governmental, and inter-governmental programmes and educational initiatives that will enhance environmental awareness and protection.
14. *Openness to Concerns*: To foster openness and dialogue with employees and the public, anticipating and responding to their concerns about the potential hazards and impacts of operations, products wastes of services, including those of transboundary or global significance.
15. *Compliance and Reporting*: To measure environmental performance to conduct regular environmental audits and assessments of compliance with company requirements, legal requirements and these principles: and periodically, to provide appropriate information to the Board of Directors, shareholders, employees the authorities and the public.

In 1985, a Tourism Bill of Rights was adopted by WTO at its general assembly in Sofia, Bulgaria. It acknowledges the rights of individuals to rest and leisure. The rights of tourists and host populations are set out along with reciprocal obligations to respect each other in their enjoyment of these rights. The bill also addresses the obligations of states to develop policies aimed at promoting harmonious development of domestic and international tourism. This Bill of Rights was an historic voluntary code of conduct for the tourism industry and, although it is not specifically concerned with the environment, it is included as an appendix for this reason.

The industry itself has recognized and acknowledged the vital relationship between tourism and the environment for many years. The World Travel and Tourism Council, for example, has issued a set of definitive guidelines which stress a number of key issues such as the importance of self-regulation the need for monitoring, and the encouragement of education and research. It has also set up a research centre with a specific brief to examine the environmental practices of the travel and tourism industry in response to these guidelines. Similarly, the Pacific Asia Travel Association (PATA) has consistently supported the improvement of the natural, social and cultural environment since its inception more than 40 years ago through conferences such as PATA 73 in Kyoto, and PATA 91 in Bali.

Agenda 21 recognizes the considerable role that tourism can play in bringing about environmental improvement. Attempts have been made to use the tourism industry in this way. The Eco-tourism Society (TES), for example, an international, non-profit organization, was created specifically to find the resources and build up the expertise needed to make tourism a viable tool for conservation and sustainable development. It serves tour operators, conservation professionals, park managers, government officials, lodge owners, consultants and other professionals striving to implement eco-tourism projects worldwide, and has published *Eco-tourism Guidelines for Nature Tour Operators.*

THE WORLD TRAVEL AND TOURISM COUNCIL'S ENVIRONMENTAL GUIDELINES

Travel and Tourism is the world's largest industry. A clean, healthy environment is essential to further growth. The World Travel and Tourism Council (WTTC) is working with governments, industry and international organizations to promote environmentally compatible growth, improve industry practices through education and information, and tract Travel and Tourism environment implementation programmes. The WTTC commends these guidelines to companies and governments to take them into account in policy formulation.

Travel and tourism companies should state their commitment to environmentally compatible development: The WTTC recommends a proactive approach for Travel and Tourism companies. This includes conducting Environmental Impact Assessments for all new projects and conducting regular Environmental Audits for all on-going activities, leading to the development of environmental improvement of environmental improvement programmes.

Targets for improvements should be established and monitored: Wherever possible, specific goals should be developed and communicated for environmental improvement programmes, including cost, benefit assessments. Results should be reviewed and assessed regularly by senior management.

The environmental commitment should be company wide: These environment programmes should carry the full support of the Board of Directors, should be an integral part of management practices, and should be communicated to all personnel, who should be encouraged to participate in the process. Such programmes should also be communicated to the public.

Education and research into improved environmental programmes should be encouraged: Company training and research programmes should incorporate environmental issues.

Travel and tourism companies should seek to implement sound environment principles through self-regulation, recognizing that national and international regulation may be inevitable and that preparation is vital: Travel and Tourism companies should take a pro-active approach, by translating the conclusions of Environment Impact Assessment and Audits into management policies. They should co-operate with other companies and the public sector in the advancement of environmental improvement.

Environmental improvement programmes should be systematic and comprehensive: They should aim to:

- Identify and continue to reduce environmental impact, paying particular attention to new projects.
- Pay due regard to environmental concerns in design, planning, construction and implementation.
- Be sensitive to conservation of environmentally protected or threatened areas, species and scenic aesthetics, achieving landscape enhancement where possible.
- Practice energy conservation.
- Reduce and recycle waste.

- Practice fresh-water/management and control sewage disposal.
- Control and diminish air emissions and pollutants.
- Monitor, control and reduce noise levels.
- Control and reduce environmentally unfriendly products, such asbestos, CFSs pesticides and toxic, corrosive, infectious, explosive or flammable materials.
- Respect and support historic or religious objects and sites.
- Exercise due regard for the interests of local populations, including their history traditions and culture and future development.
- Consider environmental issues as a key factor in the overall development of Travel and Tourism destinations.

The UNEP Industry and Environment Survey

The United Nations Environment Programme's Industry and Environment Centre (UNEP/IE) conducted a survey on environmental codes of conduct for tourism among countries and international associations in late 1992. The purpose of the survey was to:

- identify existing codes of conduct at the national and international level, and activities being undertaken to implement them; and
- identify actions that can be taken at the international level in support of the development and implementation of voluntary codes of conduct.

The International Institute for Peace through Tourism (IIPT) assisted UNEP/IE in this initiative. The survey showed a growing interest among both countries and international associations in developing voluntary codes of conduct and a desire to learn more about existing codes and examples of good practice. It also showed that the development of environmental codes of conduct for tourism is still in its infancy, with most codes having been developed only within the past two years or so.

The survey enabled UNEP to identify the main codes produced to date. However, UNEP does not claim that its survey was exhaustive, and further codes have been developed since the survey was completed. The 30 or so codes reproduced here are only a sample of those in existence. They have been included to illustrate certain key points about the development of codes. Neither the order in which they appear, nor the exclusion of codes from this publication, should be interpreted as significant.

The survey showed that the one resource on which the tourism industry can thrive and grow is the environment—protecting the environment is thus essential to the survival of tourism in many regions of the world; as much is apparent from the decline of tourism in areas where the environment has already been damaged.

The survey also showed that consumers are increasingly looking for more environmentally responsible products and services. Governments, industry and individual firms are aware that improved practices have to be developed, and that codes of conduct are one of the best means of promoting such practices, particularly in an industry that is comprised mainly of a large number or small and medium sized firms. All these firms have to be involved if the industry as a whole is to move towards sustainable development, and codes of conduct are one of the best means of unifying the industry's efforts to protect the environment on which its future business largely depends.

ECO-TOURISM GUIDELINES AND CODES OF ETHICS: MULTIPLE INITIATIVES

For Nature Tour Operator

Predeparture Programmes

- *Visitor information and education*: Prepare travellers to minimize their negative impacts while visiting sensitive environments and cultures before departure.

Guiding Programmes

- *General principles of guiding tours*: Prepare travellers for each encounter with local cultures and; with native, animals and plants.
- *Prevention of environmental impacts*: Minimize visitor impacts on the environment by offering literature, briefings, leading by example, and taking corrective actions.
- *Prevention of cultural impacts*: Minimize traveller impacts on local cultures by offering literature, briefings, leading by example, and taking corrective actions.

Monitoring Programmes

- *Prevention of accumulated impacts of tourism*: Use adequate leadership, and maintain small enough groups to ensure minimum group impact on destinations. Avoid areas that are undermanaged and overvisited.

Management Programmes

- *Prevention of nature tour company impacts*: Ensure managers, staff and contract employees know and participate in all aspects of company policy to prevail impacts on the environment and local cultures.
- *Training*: Give managers, staff and contract employees access to programmes that will upgrade their ability to communicate with and manage clients in sensitive natural and cultural settings.
- *Conservation contribution programmes*: Be a contributor to the conservation of the regions being visited.
- *Local employment and jobs programmes*: Provide competitive, local employment in all aspects of business operations.

Local Accommodating Checklist

Offer site-sensitive accommodations that are not wasteful of local resources or destructive to the environment that provide ample opportunity for learning about the environment and sensitive interchange with local communities.

The Objectives of Voluntary Codes of Conduct for Tourism

The objectives of voluntary codes of conduct are to:

- serve as a catalyst for dialogue between government agencies, industry sectors, community interests, environmental and cultural NGOs and other stakeholders in tourism development;
- create and awareness within industry and governments of the importance of sound environmental policies and management, and encourage them to promote a quality environment and therefore a sustainable industry;
- heighten awareness among international and domestic visitors of the importance of appropriate behaviour with respect to both the natural and cultural environment they experience;
- to sensitize host populations to the importance of environmental protection and the host-guest relationship; and
- to encourage cooperation among industry sectors, government agencies, host communities and NGOs to achieve the goals listed above.

The Benefits of Voluntary Codes of Conduct for Tourism

The benefits of successfully implementing voluntary codes of conduct include:

- improvements in the natural environment and in the sustainability of the tourist industry, strengthening the industry's long-term future;
- an improved image for the tourist destinations covered by the code, giving them a competitive edge over other destinations;
- improvements in the quality of tourism products and services in both the short- and long-term;
- political support which help to extract funding and assistance for new tourism product;
- an ability to attract tourists who are seeking environmentally-responsible forms of tourism;
- improved motivation and team spirit for those working in the tourism industry;
- improved company image;
- reduced costs as a result of more efficient practices for energy conservation, water conservation and waste reduction;
- support for local economy and infrastructure which may catalyze—further tourism development; and
- improved quality on life for the host communities.

PREAMBLE TO THE CANADIAN CODE OF ETHICS AND GUIDELINES

The Tourism Industry Association of Canada (TIAC) recognizes that the conservation of our natural, cultural, historic and aesthetic resources, the protection of our environment; and a continued welcoming spirit among our enterprises, employees and within our host communities, are essential conditions for high quality tourism.

Accordingly, the Association has joined with the National Round Table of the Environment and the Economy to initiate a dialogue on 'Sustainable Tourism.' The dialogue has resulted in a Code of Ethics and a set of Recommended Guidelines for the industry.

We believe that a commitment to these principles and practices will achieve the following:

- enhance Canada's image as a destination and our ability to compete in the rapidly expanding world markets for tourism;
- ensure our capacity to provide quality tourism products and services in both the short- and long-term;
- attract tourists who increasingly are seeking environmentally responsible tourism experiences;
- provide a source of motivation, and team spirit for staff at all levels;
- improve the quality of life within our host communities; and
- reduce costs through more efficient practices for energy conservation, water conservation and waste reduction.

The tourism industry acknowledges its responsibility to help protect the environment and conserve resources, and will cooperate with other industry sectors and governments at all levels towards this end.

We ask for your support in achieving these objectives.

Tourism Industry Association of Canada
National Round Table on the
Environment and the Economy

The Purpose of this Document

This publication is produced in order to:

- review existing codes of conduct at the national and international level which relate to the industry as a whole and to key sectors of the industry;
- to review codes related to tourists and to host populations;
- suggest the main areas to be covered in developing codes of conduct for the industry and provide examples of clauses from existing codes which cover these areas; and
- provide examples of programmes and initiatives carried out by governments, industry associations, companies and NGOs in support of sustainable tourism practices.

UNEP/IE organized a workshop in Paris, in December 1993, as a follow-up to the survey on codes of conduct mentioned above. Senior representatives from governments, tourist boards, industry associations and NGOs participated.

The workshop reviewed an earlier draft of this documents, suggesting valuable ways of improving and adding to it which have been included in this version.

Environmental Codes of Conduct for the Tourism Industry

The UNEP/IE survey indicates that government organizations such as national tourist boards, industry associations and non-governmental organizations are the principle developers, of environmental codes for the, tourism industry. However, the codes vary greatly in coverage and content: there are national, regional and international industry codes, as well as codes that focus on specific sectors of the industry and on specific sites. The codes tend also to focus on a few specific themes that are common to many of them. There is also considerable variation in the status, responsibility and resources of the organizations that have developed codes.

A discussion of industry codes therefore needs to consider both the origin and the scope of codes. This chapter deals in turn with:

- government organizations such as national tourist boards;
- industry association codes, at national, regional and international levels;
- sector-specific codes;
- site-specific codes; and
- codes by Non-Governmental Organizations (NGOs).

This is followed by a discussion of the contents of the code, which deals with the themes found in many of the codes:

- overall environmental commitment;
- recognizing overall responsibility;
- taking the environment into account in planning and development;
- environmentally sound management practices;
- cooperation with other sectors; and
- public awareness.

The Origin of the Codes

Government Organizations

Government organization codes have a national focus, and address the development and management of sustainable tourism without specific relevance to the different sectors that comprise the industry.

With the primary intention of initiating a nation-wide dialogue on sustainable tourism for example, the Tourism Industry Association of Canada joined forces with the National Round Table of the Environment and Economy to produce a Code of Ethics and Guidelines for the Tourism Industry. The guidelines were then formulated in greater detail for five key sectors of the tourism industry, one of which was for ministries of tourism at national and provincial level.

The English Tourist Board has published *Principles for Balanced Development,* which has since been followed by a number of sustainable tourism development initiatives which are discussed later in this publication.

In cooperation with a number of government and non-government bodies, the Finnish Tourist Board developed and published *Sustainable Tourism—The Challenge for the 1990s* for Finnish Tourism. This contains an introduction to environmentally sustainable tourism, and outlines key principles together with information on practical measures on how they could be implemented.

In some cases, governments have worked together to frame codes for areas which lie outside strict national jurisdiction. Thus, the Antarctic Treaty Consultative Meetings, which are responsible for managing the 1961 Antarctic Treaty and implementing its Environmental Protocol, adopted in April 1994 a recommendation with two sets of guidelines for Antarctic tourism, one for the tourism industry and another for tourists.

Industry Associations

National Level

Most industry association codes are focused on cross-sectoral tourism development at the national level.

In Australia and New Zealand, national tourism industry associations have taken similar initiatives. In Australia, an industry association initiative led to the compilation of the *Code of Environmental Practice for the Australian Tourism Industry,* while *Principles for Environmentally Responsible Tourism* were developed and published in New Zealand.

CANADA'S CODE OF ETHICS AND GUIDELINES FOR THE INDUSTRY

Code of Ethics

The Canadian Tourism Industry recognizes that the long-term sustainability of tourism in Canada depends on delivering a high quality product and a continuing welcoming spirit among our employees and within our host communities. It depends as well on the wise use and conservation of our natural resources; the protection and enhancement of our environment; and the preservation our cultural, historic and aesthetic resources. Accordingly, in our policies, plans decisions and actions, we will:

1. Commit to excellence in the quality of tourism and hospitality experiences provided to our clients through a motivated and caring staff.
2. Encourage an appreciation of, and respect for, out natural, cultural and, aesthetic heritage among our clients, staff, and stakeholders, and within out communities.
3. Respect the values and aspirations of our host communities and strive to provide services and facilities in a manner which contributes to community identity, pride, aesthetics and the quality of life of residents.
4. Strive to achieve tourism development in a manner which harmonizes economic objectives with the protection and enhancement of our natural, cultural and aesthetic heritage.
5. Be efficient in the use of all natural resources, manage waste in an environmentally responsible manner, and strive to eliminate or minimize pollution in all its forms.
6. Cooperate with our colleagues within the tourism industry and other industries, towards the goal of sustainable development and an improved quality of life for all Canadians.
7. Support tourists in their quest for a greater understanding and appreciation of nature and their neighbours in the global village. Work with and through national and international organizations in helping to build as better world through tourism.

Guidelines

1. Bring economic objectives into harmony with conservation of resources and environmental, social, cultural and aesthetic values in the formulation of vision statements, mission statements, policies plans, and the decision-making process.
2. Provide tourists with a high quality experience which contributes to a heightened appreciation of our natural and cultural heritage. Facilitate as possible, meaningful contact between hosts and guests and respond to the special travel needs of diverse population segments including youth, mature citizens and the disabled.
3. Offer tourism products and services that are consistent with community values and the surrounding environment. Reinforce and enhance land-scape character, senses of place, community identity, and benefits flowing to the community as a result of tourism.
4. Design, develop and market tourism products, facilities and infrastructure in a manner which balances economic objectives with the maintenance and enhancement of ecological systems, cultural resources and aesthetic resources. Achieve tourism development and marketing within a context of integrated planning.
5. Protect and enhance our natural, historic, cultural and aesthetic resources as a legacy for present and future generations. Encourage the establishment of parks, wilderness reserves and protected areas.
6. Practice and encourage the conservation and efficient use of natural resources including energy and water.
7. Practice and encourage environmentally sound waste and materials management including reduction, reuse and recycling. Minimize and strive to eliminate release of any pollutant which causes environmental damage to air water, land, flora and wildlife.
8. Reinforce environmental and cultural awareness through marketing initiatives.
9. Encourage tourism research and education which gives emphasis to ethics, heritage, preservation and the host community; and the necessary knowledge base to ensure

the economic, social, cultural and environmental sustainability of tourism.

10. Foster greater public awareness of the economic, social, cultural and environmental significance of tourism.
11. Act with a spirit of cooperation within the industry and related sectors to protect and enhance the environment conserve resources, achieve balanced development and improve the quality of life in host communities.
12. Embrace the concept of 'One World' and collaborate with other nations and international bodies in the development of a socially, environmentally, and economically responsible tourism industry.

A different approach has been taken, however, by the Travel Industry Association of America. This has addressed environment issues not through a code but through a publication called *Tourism and the Environment.* In the sub-section entitled. 'Things businesses can do', travel and tourism companies are told how they can develop and maintain environmentally responsible operations. Information and practical advice are provided on the greening of corporate philosophies and internal management strategies, compliance with legislation, communication with grassroots groups and environmental organizations, and operational guidelines on waste management, the improvement and protection of air quality, and energy conservation are provided.

Regional Level

Regional codes developed by industry associations outline principles for sustainable tourism development, applicable to the all sectors of the industry. The codes tend also to serve as a tool to guide the activities of the organization itself, as well as its members.

Industry association codes on a regional basis are best exemplified by PATAs *Code of Environmental Responsible Tourism in the Pacific Asian Region.* This code included environmental guidelines and addresses the education of tourists and the establishment of environmental policies and guidelines for various sectors of the industry. The FATA code has served as a basis for many sustainable development efforts in the Asia Pacific region. The Tourism Authority of Thailand, for example, has launched a country-wide tourism development programme based on this Code.

Still on a regional level, the *eco-tourism Manifesto* of the Africa Travel Association and the European Tourism Action Group's Policy

Statement are of interest. Though these are not codes of conduct in a traditional sense, they serve as guidelines on environmentally responsible tourism to the organization and to its members.

CHARTER FOR ENVIRONMENTAL ACTION IN THE INTERNATIONAL HOTEL AND CATERING INDUSTRY (INTERNATIONAL HOTELS ENVIRONMENT INITIATIVE)

Recognizing the urgent need to support moral and ethical conviction with practical action, we in the hotel industry have established the international Hotel Environment Initiative to foster the continual upgrading of environmental performance in the industry-worldwide.

With the co-operation and active participation of individual companies, hotels and related organizations the Initiative, which will be coordinated by "The Prince of Wales Business Leaders Forum," will endeavour to:

- provide practical guidance for the industry on how to improve environmental performance and how this contributes to successful business operations;
- develop practical environmental manuals and guidelines;
- recommend systems for monitoring improvements in environmental performance and for environmental audits;
- encourage the observance of the highest possible standards of environment, not only directly within the industry but also with suppliers and local authorities;
- promote the integration of training in environmental management among hotel and catering schools;
- collaborate with appropriate national and international organizations to ensure the widest possible awareness and observance of the initiative and the practice it promotes; and
- exchange information widely and highlight examples of good practice in the Industry.

The Prince of Wales
Business Leaders Forum

International Level

When considering internationally focused industry codes, the ICC's *Business Charter for Sustainable Development,* though not specifically concerned with tourism, has been widely accepted, and has been used as the basis for the development of many environment codes including the WTTC's environmental guidelines. Based upon the Charter, the Global Environmental Management Initiative (GEMI) has developed and Environmental Self-Assessment Programme which is being used to help enterprises improve their environmental performance.

More relevant to tourism, the WTTC's *Environmental Guidelines* are intended to help companies and governments engaged in policy formulation. These guidelines were used as a base for the development of the Green Globe environment management and awareness programme WTTC also asks member companies to 'sign up' for implementation of the guidelines.

The Charter of Ethics for Tourism and the Environment of the AIT/FIA is concerned mainly with the development of tourism in harmony with the natural and human environment of the host destination.

Sector Specific Codes

Sector-specific codes have been formulated by both industry organization and NGOs.

The International Hotels Environment Initiative (IHEI), for example, was founded in collaboration with 11 of the world's leading hotel chains and the Prince of Wales Business Leader's Forum. The Initiative's *Charter for Environmental Action in the International Hotel and Catering Industry* outlines a number of activities that are being implemented to promote environmental practices in the hotel industry.

SUSTAINABLE TOURISM: THE CHALLENGE OF THE 1990s FOR FINNISH TOURISM

Key Principles

The following is a brief summary of the key principles of sustainable tourism together with practical measures. An over all approach should be taken in this respect. Simply replacing disposable tooth, mugs with washable mugs, for instance, does not make an enterprise environmentally friendly. On the other hand, measures which may seem small can have a significant effect if they are wide-spread enough.

- In making new and additional investments in the tourism field, environmental viewpoints should be taken into consideration from the start. In determining the location of tourist spots, enterprises and authorities should cooperate to find alternatives which place the least possible burden on the environment. Thought should be given to the future, and solutions should be of a long-term nature.
- Local traditions should be taken into account in construction. Architecture should be in harmony with the environment and landscape. Tourist spots should be designed so that they follow local customs and support the preservation of local building culture. Construction materials and technical solutions should be environmentally friendly. This includes the use of wood as a building material, the avoidance of plastic, the proper disposal of wastewater and the use of ground filters and composing toilets.
- Attention should be paid to landscape management. Care should be taken to preserve nature blend in will with one another. In planning and taking care of yards and gardens, the aim should be a natural approach. Asphalt surfaces should be avoided and space should be saved for plants.
- Traffic noise and other problems caused by traffic should be reduced as much as possible. The distance from traffic arteries should be taken into account when tourist investments are planned.
- Tourist enterprises should make use of local products and services as much as possible. In addition to labour, they should use local agricultural and handicrafts products as well as guide and programme service. Naturally grown foodstuffs should be given preference.
- The attitudes of staff in the tourism field should be influenced through training and information. Personnel should act in accordance with the principles of sustainable tourism in every aspect of their work. They should also be trained to guide customers in this respect.
- Sustainable tourism includes the use of public transport as far as possible. Necessary transfers should be arranged in the form of group transport.

- Forms of exercise which are based on the use of muscle power should be given preference. Hiking, hiking and canoeing are examples of environmentally friendly exercise, as are horseback riding, carriage rides dog sledding and reindeer driving.
- In nature areas, visitors should stick to trails. Nature programmes should be designed so that they use existing trails and routes. The goal of guided nature trips should be to improve tourists knowledge of the environment and awareness of nature.
- In marketing tourist products, customers should be given correct information based on fact regarding their quality and environmental properties. Customers who appreciate sustainable tourist products are also an environmentally aware target group who expect the promised level in this respect as well.

Sustainable Measures on the Part of Tourist Enterprises

Water

- regular checks of, water consumption and use of regulating equipment on faucets and showers;
- regulation of toilet water consumption, use of composting toilets when possible;
- use of grey wastewater for watering and toilet rinsing;
- careful cleaning of wastewater, draining in the ground so as to avoid the pollution of waterways;
- changing of linen and towels only when necessary;
- use of environmentally friendly detergents; and
- discontinuation of the use of chemical disinfectants, chemical cleansing agents for pipes, softeners, toilet fresheners and other unnecessary chemicals.

Energy

- location and design of new buildings so as to save energy;
- experimental use of alternative forms of energy (sun, wind);
- constant checking of heating and improvement of heat insulation, including sealing of windows;
- use of equipment to regulate lighting and heating;
- use of thermostats in radiators;
- recovery of waste heat with the help of heat exchangers;

- avoidance of direct electric heating and electric sauna heaters;
- use of energy-saving electrical appliances, light bulbs etc.;
- use of wood heating where appropriate;
- avoidance of electric hand dryers etc;
- reduction of indirect energy consumption by offering locally raised natural products, especially vegetables.

Waste

- use of natural material;
- use of recycled paper (toilet paper, stationery, brochures etc.) and economy in the use of paper;
- avoidance of the use of environmentally harmful products in offices;
- use of bulk packages and refillable packages;
- avoidance of disposable plates, table cloths, toilet articles, tooth mugs, etc.;
- avoidance of canned drinks and drinks in unrecyclable plastic bottles in favour of refillable glass bottles;
- giving of preference to durable equipment which has a long service life and can be repaired;
- sorting of paper and board, glass, compostable waste and special waste;
- sending of lubricants, oil and other problem waste to enterprise qualified to dispose them;
- composing and utilization of organic waste; and
- removal of waste from nature.

In a related area, a survey conducted in 1989 revealed that hostellers have a keen interest in environmental issues. These results, together with the fact that educating youth about the environment is a part of Hostelling International's mission, prompted that International Youth Hostels Federation to develop and adopt an Environmental Charter in 1992. This was followed by the development of guidelines to help National Association to implement the Charter.

Recognizing the need for an integrated approach to environmental issues and the importance of maintaining the environment as an renewable resource, the European Tour Operators Association formed an environmental working group which led to its *Environmental Guidelines for Tour Operators*. These guidelines outline areas where both the tour operator and the visitor can help protect the environment and emphasize the need for increased cooperation between tour operators, visitors, local residents and local authorities.

Guidelines for eco-tourism and nature tourism are numerous and focus on specific destinations or activities, in the United States, for example, the Eco-tourism Society has formulated *Guidelines for Nature Tour Operators* which outline pre-departure, guiding, monitoring and management programmes aimed at minimizing the environmental impacts of the tour.

Site-Specific Guidelines

The UNEP survey revealed a number of site-specific industry codes. The National Parks Service of the United States, for example, sets out guidelines in regard to sustainable development and design, in a publication entitled 20-20 *Sustainable Design.* This publication stresses the importance of designing parks to reflect their environmental setting; to maintain and encourage biodiversity; to construct and retrofit facilities using energy efficient materials and building techniques; to operate and maintain facilities to promote their sustainability, and to illustrate and promote conservation principles and practices through sustainable design and ecologically-sensitive use.

The National Parks Board of South Africa addresses the question of responsible tourism in its mission statement and list of key objectives. Among other things, the Board

- endorses the principles of The World Conservation Union (IUCN), the World Wide Fund for Nature (WWF) and the United Nations Environment Programme (UNEP);
- commits itself to executing the resolutions that resulted from UNCED in 1992 in Rio de Janeiro;
- supports the guidelines of the World Conservation Strategy;
- commits itself to international, national and local co-operation;
- acknowledges the need for the use of natural resources in wilderness areas for the recreation and spiritual inspiration of South Africans;
- commits itself to the non-consumptive use and management of wilderness areas; and

- commits itself to the conservation and judicious usage of the natural, historical and cultural heritage of South Africa.

As already mentioned, the Antarctic Treaty Consultative Meetings have recently adopted a recommendation covering two aspects of tourism in the Antarctic. These are *Guidance for those Organizing and Conducting Tourism and Non-government Activities in the Antarctic and Guidance for Visitors to the Antarctic.* The International Association of Antarctic Tour Operators has also developed its own Guidelines of Conduct for Antarctic Tour Operators.

NEW ZEALAND: PRINCIPLES FOR THE TOURISM INDUSTRY

Protection and Development

1. To manage existing natural and cultural areas associated with tourist development and use in such as way that they are protected and enhanced;
2. To recognize that every environment has limits of acceptable change which in some areas may be considerable but which in other areas may be small or zero;
3. To encourage the relevant agencies to identify areas worthy of special protection and determine carrying capacities for sensitive areas;
4. To adopt general conservation policies and to minimize adverse environmental impacts.

Assessment and Monitoring

5. To ensure that environmental assessment becomes an integral step in the consideration of any site as a tourist development;
6. To ensure that community attitudes and feelings are incorporated from the earliest stages of planning for a tourist development;
7. To encourage the review of current environmental management practices throughout the tourist industry and the modification of these practices where necessary;
8. To ensure that an on-going responsibility for environmental care and protection and community concerns is adopted.

Liaison

9. To co-operate with relevant local, regional and national authorities and communities in order to integrate environmental requirements into resource management;
10. To ensure that those involved in the tourist industry contribute to discussions on environmental planning and management issues as they affect tourism;
11. To provide the opportunity for the wider community to be involved in discussions and consultations on tourism and environmental management issues.

Education and Information

12. To promote and to reward environmentally responsible tourist organizations and businesses;
13. To foster in both management and staff, environmental awareness and conservation principles;
14. To enhance visitor's appreciation and understanding of the natural environment through the provision of accurate interpretation and information;
15. To encourage an understanding of the Maori lifestyle, customs, beliefs and traditions as they relate to the environment.

Non-Government Organizations (NGOs)

Minimising the environmental impacts of tourism is increasingly considered a global priority. As a result, several NGOs have implemented green tourism programmes. For example, WWF and Tourism Concern have jointly published *Beyond the Green Horizon,* in which are included *Principles for Sustainable Tourism.* ICOMOS has adopted a *Charter for Cultural Tourism* which was followed by a further publication. *Basis for Action,* which calls for the integration of cultural assets in social and economic planning, and the joint efforts of tourism bodies and bodies concerned with natural and cultural heritage to protect the cultural patrimony which is the very basis of international tourism. IUCN has developed sustainable tourism strategies and The Eco-tourism Society has developed *Guidelines for Nature Tour Operators* as with codes, these aim to catalyze and strengthen efforts to promote environmentally responsible tourism.

PATA CODE FOR ENVIRONMENTALLY RESPONSIBLE TOURISM

The Pacific Asia Region's natural, social and cultural environment is a unique and finite resource. This environment is a key asset for the tourism industry. In order to plan for a sustainable future for the region and for the tourism industry, the Pacific Asia Travel Association recognizes the need for an environmental ethic amongst all those involved in tourism.

In this code environmentally responsible tourism means tourism which

- recognizes the necessity to ensure a sustainable future;
- meets the needs of the tourism industry today; and
- does not compromize the ability of this and future generations to conserve the environment.

The Pacific Asia Travel Association here-by ratifies the code and in so doing adopts the following philosophy and responsibilities as the environmental ethic guiding action by its members:

Philosophy

- Recognition that all forms and all aspects of tourism have an impact upon the environment.
- Acceptance that tourism should be environmentally responsible.
- Acknowledgement that to be environmentally responsible the tourism industry should ensure that the impact of tourism does not adversely affect the environment.
- Acceptance that both tourism and conservation can be valid and complementary uses of the environment.
- Recognition that every part of the environment has limits beyond which development should not take place.
- Recognition of the need to foster a greater understanding of the inter-relationship between tourism and the environment.

Definitions

Environment: Means that aspects of the surroundings of human beings both cultural, natural, and man-made, whether affecting human being as individuals or in social groupings. Environmental has the corresponding meaning.

Conservation: means the management of human use of the environment to yield the greatest sustainable benefit to present generations while maintaining its potential to meet the needs and aspirations of future generations.

Development: means the modification of the environment to whatever degree and the application of human, financial, living and non-living resources to satisfy human needs and improve the quality of human life.

The PATA Code urges Associations and Chapter Members and their industry partners to:

1. Adopt the necessary practices to conserve the environment, including the sue of renewable resources in a sustainable manner and the conservation of non-renewable resources.
2. Contribute to the conservation of any habitat of flora and fauna, and of any site whether natural or cultural, which may be affected by tourism.
3. Encourage relevant authorities to identify areas worthy of conservation and to determine the level of development if any which would ensure those areas are conserved.
4. Ensure that community attitudes, cultural values, and concerns, including local customs and beliefs, are taken into account in the planning of all tourism related projects.
5. Ensure that environmental assessment becomes an integral step in the consideration of any site for a tourism project.
6. Comply with all international conventions in relation to the environment.
7. Comply with all national, state and local laws in relation to the environment.
8. Encourage those involved in tourism to comply with local, regional and national planning policies and to participate in the planning process.
9. Provide the opportunity for the wider community to take part in discussions and consultations in tourism planning issues insofar as they affect the tourism industry and the community.
10. Acknowledge responsibility for the environmental impacts of all tourism related projects and activities and undertake all necessary responsible remedial and corrective actions.

11. Encourage regular environmental audits of practices throughout the tourism industry and to encourage necessary changes to those practices.
12. Foster environmentally responsible practices including waste management, recycling and energy use.
13. Foster in both management and staff of all tourism related projects and activities, an awareness of environmental and conservation principles.
14. Support the inclusion of professional conservation principles in tourism education, training and planning.
15. Encourage an understanding by all those involved in tourism of each community's customs, cultural values, beliefs and traditions and how they relate to the environment.
16. Enhance the appreciation and understanding by tourists of the environment through the provision of accurate information and appropriate interpretation.
17. Establish detailed environmental policies and/or guidelines for the various sectors of the tourism industry.

The Content of the Codes

The UNEP/IE survey identified several issues which are common to most industry codes:

- overall environmental commitment;
- recognizing overall responsibility;
- taking the environment into account in planning and development;
- environmentally sound management practices;
- cooperation with other sectors; and
- public awareness.

Overall Environmental Commitment

Most codes make an overall commitment to the environment. Some of the most common points made are:

- that tourism development must consider all aspects of the human and natural environment;
- that tourism development should be sustainable;
- that the industry should be supportive of local and national planning bodies;

- that environmentally responsible tourism organizations should be rewarded; and
- that the environment should be interpreted to include not only eco-systems but also people and their communities.

These points are stressed, for example, in the publications of AIT/FIA, FATA, the English Tourist Board, and the country codes of Australia, New Zealand, Canada and Finland.

The WTTC's *Environmental Guidelines* addressing both governments and travel and tourism companies, explicitly recommends that travel and tourism companies should state their commencement to environmentally compatible growth.

The ICOMOS *Charter on Cultural Tourism* declares that "its primary aim is to respect and protect the authenticity and diversity of cultural values."

The WWF and Tourism Concern *Principles for Sustainable Tourism* state that "conservation and sustainable use of resources-natural, social and cultural is crucial and makes long-term business sense."

Recognizing Overall Responsibility

Many codes stress that the industry should accept responsibility for the environmental impact of tourism development, and that it should undertake corrective action where necessary.

The ICC *Business Charter* advocates that environment management should be recognized as one of the highest corporate priorities and as a key determinant to sustainable tourism.

The country codes of Australia, Canada and New Zealand, as well as those of PATA and WTTC, remark that the industry as a whole should accept environmental responsibility, and PATA goes on to stress the importance of complying with local and international legislation because legislation is one of the fundamental starting points of environmentally responsible practices.

The WTTC guidelines also advocate self-regulation in environmental practices.

Taking the Environment and Account in Planning and Development

Since tourism should be developed as a self-sustaining activity, the industry must be integrated with other land-use policies. This may involve a number of activities, including:

- recognizing that every part of the environment has limits beyond which development should not take place, particularly in sensitive areas;
- taking into account land-use planning and environmental constraints for the siting of facilities;
- integrating tourism development with the human values of the host destination and encouraging the participation of host communities in decision-making processes;
- Incorporating sustainability concepts into design and construction; and
- integrating these considerations into a full environmental impact assessment, and monitoring implementation after development.

These issues are mentioned in the publication of the ICC, AIT/FIA, PATA, WTTC, ETB, and the country codes of Australia, Canada, Finland, Mauritius and New Zealand.

WWF/TOURISM CONCERN PRINCIPLES FOR SUSTAINABLE TOURISM

1. *Using Resources Sustainably*: The conservation and sustainable use of resources-natural, social and cultural—is crucial and makes long-term business sense.
2. *Reducing Over-Consumption and Waste*: Reduction of over-consumption and waste avoids the costs of restoring long-term environmental damage and contributes to the quality of tourism.
3. *Maintaining Diversity:* Maintaining and promoting natural, social and cultural diversity is essential for long-term sustainable tourism, and creates a resilient base for the industry.
4. *Integrating Tourism into Planning*: Tourism development which is integrated into a national and local strategic planning framework and which undertakes environmental impact assessments, increases the long-term viability of tourism.
5. *Supporting Local Economics*: Tourism that supports a wide range of local economic activities and which takes environmental costs and values into account, both protects those economies and avoids environmental damage.
6. *Involving Local Communities*: The full involvement of local communities in the tourism sector not only benefits them

and the environment in general but also improves the quality of tourism experience.

7. *Consulting Stakeholders and the Public*: Consultation between the tourism industry and local communities, organizations and institutions is essential if they are to work alongside each other and resolve potential conflicts of interest.
8. *Training Staff*: Staff training which integrates sustainable tourism into work practices, along with recruitment of local personnel at all levels, improves the quality of the tourism product.
9. *Marketing Tourism Responsibility*: Marketing that provides tourists with full and responsible information increases respect for the natural, social and cultural environments of destination areas and enhances customer satisfaction.
10. *Undertaking Research*: On-going research and monitoring by the industry using effective data collection and analysis is essential to help solve problems and to bring benefits to destinations, the industry and consumers.

Environmentally-Sound Management Practices

Management functions include:

- minimizing the negative impacts of tourism by carrying out environment audits or using other techniques to assess and improve on water and energy conservation, waste minimization and recycling (cited in the codes of WTTC, FATA, ETB, all country codes, the Eco-tourism Society Guidelines, the WWF/Tourism Concern principles, and the Travel Industry Association of America publication);
- ensuring positive visitor experience by effective visitor management, control and education, cited in the country codes of Australia, Canada, Finland and New Zealand, the TES guidelines, and the European Tour Operators guidelines;
- providing environmental training for staff, and motivating them effectively, cited in the country codes of Australia, Canada, Finland and New Zealand as well as in the codes of WTTC and IHEI, and in the WWF/Tourism Concern principles;
- monitoring and reporting of environmental performance, cited in the ICC charter, the guidelines of the WTTC and

TES, the IUCN's sustainable development strategies and the WWF/Tourism Concern principles;

- continuous improvement or environmental performance, cited in the ICC charter and the guidelines of the WTTC; and
- managing tourism enterprises so that they support the local economy (mentioned in the Finnish Code and the WWF/Tourism Concern principles).

Co-operation with other Sectors

Many codes, charters and strategies stress the importance of effective cooperation and communication between the public and private sectors as well as the need to exchange information and experience between and within sectors. These issues are cited in the country codes of Australia, Canada and Finland as well as the codes of WTTC, FATA, AIT/FIA, IIPT, ETAG and ETB, the cultural tourism charter of ICOMOS, the IUCN's sustainable development strategies, and the WWF/Tourism Concern principles.

The International Hotels Environment Initiative collaborates with appropriate national and international organizations to ensure the widest possible awareness and observance of the initiative and the practice is promotes.

AUSTRALIA: CODE OF ENVIRONMENTAL PRACTICE

Because Australia's unique resources are key assets to the tourism industry, the Australian Tourism Industry Association affirms the following code:

Philosophy

- To recognize tourism as a legitimate, and valuable resource utilization.
- To recognize both development and conservation as important and valuable expressions of.
- To recognize both development and conservation as important and valuable expressions human utilization of the environment.
- To work towards an improved understanding of the allocation process of land and other resources and establish uniform environmental policy guidelines for the tourism industry.

- To support local, regional and national planning concepts and participate in the associated processes.
- To work towards the highest level of professionalism in the industry.

Assessment

- To develop an appreciation of the land and an understanding of its capabilities to support alternative uses in order to establish a basis for environmentally sustainable activities.
- To ensure assessment processes recognize individual and cumulative implications of each activity.
- To establish and apply methods to enhance beneficial and minimize adverse effects on the environment.
- To assess from actual and potential effects on the environment from individual tourist development and use which may positively or negatively affect aspects of the environment.

Protection

In co-operation with relevant agencies help:

- To review private sector tourism infrastructure environmental management and modify such management where necessary.
- To contribute towards protection irreplaceable segments of the natural and created environment on which the industry relies and to review and modify protection management activities where necessary.
- To protect and preserve existing habitat flora and fauna and natural and cultural areas of local national or international significance directly related to and involved with tourism development and use.

Responsibility

- To accept responsibility for the enterprise related environmental impacts of tourism development, operation and use and to undertake responsible corrective and remedial action where necessary.
- To ensure that natural eco-systems are not used beyond their sustainable capability by the activities of the tourism industry.

- To take account, where appropriate of environmental policies and codes of environmental practice in developing tourism proposals, including the incorporation of such policies and codes in contract documents.
- To co-operate with relevant authorities and communities, in order to integrate environmental requirements into tourism management and land use processes.

Information

- To incorporate environmental policies and codes of environmental practice within tourism training programmes.
- To ensure all involved in tourism both directly and indirectly, have the opportunity to develop a sound knowledge of the natural resources and environmental principles associated with a sustainable tourism industry.
- To support the inclusion of conservation principles in education, training and planning for tourism.
- To enhance visitor's appreciation and understanding of their surroundings within the conservation objectives for the area.
- To consider the value of other legitimate developments and utilizations and respect those values in making decisions for tourism development and utilization.
- To participate in and facilitate positive discussions on tourism related land utilization issues.

Australian Tourism Industry Association

The European Tourism Action Group spells out the issues involved in some detail; Government and industry partnership is also required.

- Private sector investment is crucial, but successful action depends on a close partnership between the public and private sectors to meet market needs yet respect environment considerations.
- The industry in Europe is increasingly aware of the importance of such partnerships and has expressed willingness to play an active role, but the machinery for consultation and co-operation in the wide field of tourism is lacking too, and too often government policies are uncoordinated.

- Improved public/private sector co-operation, rather than regulatory measures are needed to ensure that environments programmes are effective and comprehensive, especially in developing new tourist regions.
- International co-operation may be necessary to preserve public health and safety and the conservation and preservation of natural resources.
- Where this is necessary it should be done-in consultation with industry.

ALLIANCE INTERNATIONALE DE TOURISME/ FEDERATION INTERNATIONALE DE L' AUTOMOBILE: CHARTER OF ETHICS FOR TOURISM AND THE ENVIRONMENT

Tourism and Human Values of the Host Country

Full respect must be paid to the cultural and spiritual environment of the hosts in the country visited, and all direct or indirect implications of the conservation of its heritage and traditions.

There are societies who do not want to be visited by tourists and others, where visits produce negative reactions, shock and disequilibrium. A list of such special cases should be drawn up, and international tourism should be strongly requested to respect these wished of these protected societies.

In any case, the host country is entitled to respect of its lifestyle, of its moral and psychological sensibilities. Any form of intrusion by tourists disturbing the local environment—such as noise, showy behaviour and pollution or destructive activities must be banned. Contrasts in economic status between tourism and hosts should not be emphasized by inappropriate behaviour.

Tourism and Health

Tourist organizations should advise their customers of any necessary health requirements prior to visiting a country, as well as any specific health risks in particular tourist destinations, illnesses can be brought back from foreign countries but can also be brought into the host country with tourism.

The precautions and rules of hygiene used in the host countries should be known to the visitor.

Tourism and Protection of Biological Environment (Fauna and Flora)

The environment of fauna or floral species which are locally fragile, rare or close to extinction should be the object of scrupulous respect, in order to save the existence of such populations and their habitats as much as possible, to inhibit damages and to allow a regeneration of territories and waters subtracted from them by tourism.

These precautions should also apply to animal life of all kinds and birds of all eco-systems in all continents, for animals in all waters and also for animals dwelling in caves. Forests, coastlines, fresh and brackish waters should be observed with special diligence.

It is urgent to carry out studies for the inventory of all fragile zones and to communicate the result to the organizations responsible for tourism.

Tourists should respect international rules established by treaties protecting fauna and flora such as:

- the Ramsar treaty (2.2.1971) about wetlands of international concern.
- the treaty of Washington (3 March, 1973) concerning the possession transport and trading of threatened species or part of their bodies.
- the treaty of Berne (19 September, 1979) about fauna, flora and natural environment in Europe.

These texts, as well as local regional regulations, should be made available to tourists.

Tourism and Protection of Cultural Heritage

Monuments and sites, protected or not by guards or fences, must be fully respected as well as the laws prohibiting illegal use of prospective or detecting devices, the trading of antiquities or their clandestine excavation:

Special attention should be paid to prevent inscriptions and graffiti on monuments, sites, trees, etc. Moreover, the aesthetic milieu of monuments and sites must be observed carefully and protected against advertising for tourists.

Tourism, Waste Disposal and Fires

Tourists must avoid leaving waste and litter or any refuse which cause a deterioration in the quality of the environment. They should be particularly careful to avoid any risk of forest fires.

Tourists should be educated to avoid the waste of objects of all kinds currently abandoned and scattered everywhere; they should be aware that beside the disfiguring the litter produces, it also contributes to pollute the environment and in certain cases, may also start fires. Pieces of broken glass may act as lenses, humid piles of organic matter left by tourists may ferment, produce heat and burn.

Tourism and Education

Mass media, schools and colleges should implement, appropriate educational programmes at all levels, supported by visits to sites in order to enforce this code for tourism and environment. Such programmes should encompass both scientific and humanistic matters related to tourism and the natural and cultural heritage.

At the level of higher education, professional schools and research departments in universities should unite their efforts to achieve a better understanding of the impact of tourism and a better grasp of improving the planning and behaviour of mass tourism.

Promoting Alternative Solutions and Careful Planning

Natural parks with marked itineraries should be promoted, as well as new resorts with planned capacity, as alternatives to unplanned careless and over-crowded invasion of tree nature, while the limits of carrying capacity require new ways of presentation and measures of conservation of sites and heritage without depriving the tourist public of its legitimate pleasures.

Alternative routes uniting less known sites and monuments are encouraged in many countries or tourists who wish a deeper and a more personal insight.

The responsible authorities have the obligation to organize carefully the quantity of visitors and schedules for fragile sites with limited capacity, they must clearly instruct the tourist in order to convey a proper cultural message and also to avoid damage to the natural and cultural heritage.

Public Awareness

Increasing public awareness of the importance of environmentally and culturally responsible tourism is cited as an important issue in many codes. PATA, for example, encourages its members to celebrate the UN Environment Day in June every year as means of increasing public awareness of the importance of environmentally sound forms of tourism. The AIT/FIA code is more specific:

- Mass media, schools and colleges should implement appropriate educational programmes at all levels, supported by visits to sites in order to enforce this code for tourism and environment. Such programmes should encompass both scientific and humanistic matters related to tourism and the natural and cultural heritage.
- At the level of higher education, professional schools and research departments in universities should unite their efforts to achieve a better understanding of the impact of tourism and a better grasp of improving the planning and behaviour of mass tourism.

Canada's *Guidelines for the Industry* stress that it should "Foster greater public awareness of the economic, social, cultural, and environmental significance of tourism." A public awareness programme is recognized as an important part of the Code of Conduct, and details are developed for five separate audiences. That for national and local Ministries of Tourism includes these points.

- Promote public and industry awareness of the economic, social, cultural and environmental significance of tourism.
- Encourage, efforts within schools and the community to bring increased awareness to the concept of sustainable development and the potential contribution of tourism towards this end.
- Include Codes of Ethics of Tourists and for Industry in literature.
- Collaborate with industry in identifying and publicizing success stories.

Some of the smaller but tourist-intensive countries also devote considerable effort to increasing public awareness of the issues involved. The Finnish code was given wide media attention in an effort to raise public awareness about the environmental impact of tourism and related environmental issues. Similarly, the Tourism Development Authority in Trinidad and Tobago works closely with all agencies and departments (especially the Forestry Department and the Institute of Marine Affairs) to create public awareness of and sensitivity to environmental matters. This is achieved through such activities as poster and essay competitions, seminars and workshops, and publishing articles in management and newspapers.

ADDITIONAL CODES OF CONDUCT FOR THE TOURISM INDUSTRY

ENGLAND: PRINCIPLES FOR BALANCED DEVELOPMENT

- The environment has an intrinsic value which outweighs its value as a tourism asset. Its enjoyment by future generations and its long-term survival must not be prejudiced by short-term considerations.
- Tourism should be recognized as a possible activity with the potential to benefit the community and the place as well as the visitor.
- The relationship between tourism and the environment must be managed so that it is sustainable in the long-term. Tourism must not be allowed to damage the resource, prejudice its future enjoyment or bring unacceptable impacts.
- Tourism activities and developments should respect the scale, nature and character of the place in which they are sited.
- In any location, harmony must be sought between the needs of the visitor, the place and the host community.
- In a dynamic world some change is inevitable and change can often be beneficial. Adaptation to change, however, should not be at the expense of any of these principles.
- The tourism industry, local authorities and environmental agencies all have a duty to respect the above principles and work together to achieve their practical realization.

THE AFRICA TRAVEL ASSOCIATION: ECO-TOURISM MANIFESTO

Our Member Countries Pledge

- *To Establish*: the machinery for protection of the ecology, natural resources and wildlife.
- *To Enhance*: the quality of the tourist visit by easing the entry and exit formalities.

- *To Create*: good infrastructure assuring easy access and to use trained personnel to highlight each country's unique appeal.
- *To Establish*: rigid codes of quality for accommodation and services, making sure the local tourist economy does not overshadow the attraction.
- *To Work*: with transportation companies to make travel safe, comfortable and convenient.

The Travel Industry Pledges

- *To prepare*: the visitor by providing detailed information on the future.
- *To provide*: clients with opportunities to participate in ecological and environmental programmes.
- *To adhere*: to a strict code of truth in advertising by accurately describing facilities and costs.
- *The visitors should be encouraged to respect*: the land and water, not only to avoid damaging, abusing or littering, but to contribute to the preservation and protection of these resources.
- *To enjoy*: the wildlife in its natural habitat and refrain from harassment of these magnificent creatures.
- *To honour*: the sensitivities, customs and culture of the people they are visiting and observe local rules of etiquette and behaviour.
- *To share*: and exchange cross-culture ideas and to keep an attitude to local values.
- *To continue*: this habit of caring and concern upon returning, home by not supporting industries that harm eco-systems and the environment.

THE INTERNATIONAL YOUTH HOSTELS FEDERATION ENVIRONMENTAL CHARTER

Hostelling International

Introductory Information

A survey conducted in 1989 revealed that hostellers have a keen interest in environmental issues. These results, together with the fact that educating youth about the environment is a part of hostelling International's mission, prompted the IYHF to develop and adopt an Environmental Charter in 1992. This was followed by the development of guidelines to help National Associations to implement the Charter. In July 1994, a work plan, based on the guidelines, was submitted to the IYHF International Conference for approval.

The Charter

The Charter encourages environmental awareness and good practice amongst its members, making specific reference to the following:

- the responsible consumption of resources;
- waste minimization;
- recycling;
- the control and reduction of pollution;
- energy conservation;
- encouraging the use of public transport;
- conservation and protection; and
- providing opportunities for environmental education.

The Work Plan

The work plan has been formulated to provide suggestions for the implementation of the Charter, and has been drawn up within a flexible framework that allows each national association to modify the plan to suit the needs of individual hostels.

Section 1: Implementation by National Associations

Practical guidelines and checklists are provided for the implementation and monitoring of the charter at the level of national associations. The main topics covered are:

- the incorporation of the charter into national governing policies;.
- assigning the responsibility for implementing the charter;
- developing a work plan;
- developing support for hostel managers; and
- monitoring and reporting.

Section 2: Implementation by Issues Area

This section lists minimum standards and advanced activities for each issue area in the charter.

The minimum standards establish basic levels of environmental practices which help the hostels to set achievable objectives and indicate which are or operation needs the most urgent attention.

The advanced standards are targeted at the facilities where minimum standards are already in operation. In this manner, recognition of the progress made, and incentives for further improvement are provided simultaneously.

Case studies demonstrating good environmental practices are provided for both the preliminary and advanced levels. These represent facilities of varying sizes in urban and rural locations. Information on the direct results of the activity with its cost affectiveness is also made available.

Section two deals mainly with consumption, recycling, pollution, energy conservation, transport and nature conservation, and protection.

Further Implementation

The IYHF plans to provide:

- advice on work plan development;
- training on implementing environment standards;
- promotional of environmental awareness through the youth hostel experience; and
- a case study library to facilitate the exchange of experiences.

It is the intention of the Federation that all hostels should be in a position to comply with the minimum standards of the Environment Charter implementation work plan before the end of 1998. At this point the Federation will encourage the publishing of environmental standards along with the IYHF Hostel Standards and Common Practices.

Additionally each association is to give detailed progress reports on compliance with environmental standards in their annual reports.

GUIDANCE FOR THOSE ORGANIZING AND CONDUCTING TOURISM AND NON-GOVERNMENTAL ACTIVITIES IN THE ANTARCTIC

Attachment to Recommendation XVIII-1 Adopted at the ATCM, Kyoto, Japan, April 1994

Antarctica is the largest wilderness area on earth, unaffected by large scale human activities. Accordingly, this unique and pristine environment has been afforded special protection. Furthermore, unpredictable and potentially dangerous. All activities in the Antarctic Treaty Area, therefore, should be planned and conducted with both environmental protection and safety in mind.

Activities in the Antarctic are subject to the Antarctic Treaty in 1959 and associated legal instruments, referred to collectively as the Antarctic Treaty system. These include the Convention for the Conservation of Antarctic Seals (CCAS) (1972), the Convention on the Conservation of Antarctic Marine Living Resources (CCAMLR) (1980) and the Recommendations and other measures adopted by the Antarctic Treaty Consultative Parties under the Antarctic Treaty.

In 1991, the Consultative Parties to the Antarctic Treaty adopted the Protocol on Environment Protection to the Antarctic Treaty. This Protocol sets out environmental principles, procedures and obligations for the comprehensive protection of the Antarctic environment, and its dependent and associated eco-systems. The Consultative parties have agreed that pending its entry into force, as far as possible and in accordance with their legal systems, that the provisions of the Protocol should be applied as appropriate.

The Environmental Protocol designates Antarctica as a natural reserve devoted to peace and science, and applies to both governmental and non-governmental activities in the Antarctic Treaty Area. The Protocol seeks to ensure that human activities, including tourism, do not have adverse impacts on the Antarctic environment nor on its scientific and aesthetic values.

The Protocol states, as a matter of principle, that all activities are to be planned and conducted on the basis of information sufficient to evaluate their possible impact on the Antarctic environment and its associated eco-systems, and on the value of Antarctica for the conduct of scientific research. Organizers should be aware that the Environmental Protocol requires that "activities shall be modified, suspended or cancelled if they result in or threaten to result in impacts upon the Antarctic environment or dependent or associated ecosystems."

Those responsible for organizing and conducting tourism and non-governmental activities must comply fully with national laws and regulations which implement the Antarctic Treaty system, as well as other national laws and regulations implementing international agreements on environmental protection, pollution, and safety that relate to the Antarctic Treaty Area. They should also abide by the requirements imposed on organizers and operators under the Protocol on Environmental Protection and its Annexes, insofar as they have not yet been implemented in national law.

Key Obligations on Organizers and Operators

1. Provide prior notification of and reports on, their activities to the competent authorities of the appropriate party or parties.
2. Conduct an assessment of the potential environmental impacts of their planned activities.
3. Provide for effective response to environmental emergencies, especially with regard to marine pollution.
4. Ensure self-sufficiency and safe operations.
5. Respect scientific research and the Antarctic environment, including restrictions regarding protected areas, and the protection of flora and fauna.
6. Prevent the disposal and discharge of prohibited waste.

Procedures to be Followed by Organizers and Operators

A. When Planning to Go to the Antarctica

Organizers and operators should:

1. Notify the competent national authorities of the appropriate Party or Parties of details of their planned activities with sufficient time to enable the Party(ies) to comply with their information exchange obligations under Article VII(5) of the Antarctic Treaty.
2. Conduct an environmental assessment in accordance with such procedures as may have been established in national law to give effect to Annex 1 of the Protocol, including if appropriate, how potential impacts will be monitored.
3. Obtain timely permission from the national authorities responsible for any stations they propose to visit.
4. Provide information to assist in the preparation of contingency response plans in accordance with Article 15 of the Protocol; waste management plans in accordance with Annex III of the Protocol; and marine pollution

contingency plans in accordance with Annex IV of the Protocol.

5. Ensure that expedition leaders and passengers are aware of the location and special regimes which apply to Specially Protected Areas and Sites of Special Scientific Interest (and on entry into force of the Protocol, Antarctic Specially protected Areas and Antarctic Specially Managed Areas) and of Historic Sites and Monuments and, in particular, relevant management plans.
6. Obtain a permit, where required by national law, from the competent national authority of the appropriate Party or Parties should they have a reason to enter such areas, or a monitoring site (CEM Site) designated under CCAMLR.
7. Ensure that activities are fully self-sufficient and do not require assistance from Parties unless arrangements for it have been agreed in advance.
8. Ensure that they employ experienced and trained personnel, including a sufficient number of guides.
9. Arrange to use equipment, vehicles, vassels, and aircraft appropriate to Antarctic operations.
10. Be fully conversant with applicable communications, navigation, air traffic control and emergency procedures.
11. Obtain the best available maps and hydrographic charts, recognizing that many areas are not fully or accurately surveyed.
12. Consider the question of insurance (subject to requirement of national law).
13. Design and conduct information and education programmes to ensure that all personnel and visitors are aware of relevant provisions of the Antarctic Treaty system.
14. Provide visitors with a copy of the Guidance for Visitors to the Antarctic.

B. When in the Antarctic Treaty Area

Organizers and operators should:

1. Comply with all requirements of the Antarctic Treaty system, and relevant national law, and ensure that visitors are aware of requirements that are relevant to them.
2. Reconfirm arrangements to visit stations 24-72 hours before their arrival and ensure that visitors are aware of any conditions for restrictions established by the station.

3. Ensure that visitors are supervised by a sufficient number of guides to have adequate experience and training in Antarctic conditions and knowledge of the Antarctic Treaty system requirements.
4. Monitor environment impacts of their activities. If appropriate, and advise the competent national authorities of the appropriate Party or Parties of any adverse or cumulative impacts resulting from an activity, but which were no foreseen by their environmental impact assessment.
5. Operate ships, yachts, small boats, aircraft, hovercraft, and all other means of transport safely and according to the appropriate procedures, including those set out in the Antarctic Flight Information Manual (AFIM).
6. Dispose of waste materials in accordance with Annex V of the Protocol. These annexes prohibit, among other things the discharge of plastics, oil and noxious substances into the Antarctic Treaty Area; regulate the discharge of sewage and food waste; and require the removal of most waste from the area.
7. Co-operate fully with observers designated by Consultative Parties to conduct inspections of stations, ships, aircraft and equipment under Article VII of the Antarctic Treaty, and those to be designated under Article 14 of the Environmental Protocol.
8. Co-operate in monitoring programmes undertaken in accordance with Article 3(2) of the Protocol.
9. Maintain a careful and complete record of their activities conducted.

C. On Completion of the Activities

Within three months of the end of the activity, organizers and operators should report on the conduct of it to the appropriate national authority in accordance with national laws and procedures. Reports should include the name details and state of legislation of each vessel or aircraft used and the name of their captain or commander; actual itinerary; the number of visitors engaged in the activity; places, dates and purposes of landings and the number of visitors landed on each occasion; an meteorological observations made, including those made as part of the World Meteorological Organization (WMO) Voluntary

Observing Ships Scheme; any significant changes in activities and their impacts from those predicted before the visit was conducted; and action taken in case of emergency.

Environmental Codes of Conduct for Host Communities

Host communities have a major role in play in the development and maintenance of sustainable tourism. Host-guest relationships and their associated conflicts are well documented but have received little practical attention. Codes for host communities, when thoughtfully developed and implemented can be a useful tool to address issues such as:

- the role of the local population in tourism development;
- safeguarding local cultures and tradition;
- educating the local population on the importance of maintaining a balance between conservation and preservation, and economic development; and
- providing quality tourist products and experiences.

Codes for host communities have not yet been extensively developed but address four major issues: (*i*) the social norms and practices of the host community, (*ii*) the cultural norms and practices of the host community, (*iii*) the economic development of the destination, and (*iv*) the protection and preservation of the environment.

The codes used to illustrate these issues in this chapter are the *Tourism Codes of Ethics for Mauritians* which was developed by the Bishops of Mauritius with the assistance of tourism professionals, and we, *the responsible host population* created by the working group Tourism with Insight and Understanding, based in Germany.

THE MAURITIAN CODE OF ETHICS FOR TOURISM: FOR MAURITIANS

- Open your door to the tourist who comes to visit you. He is different from your team to know him.
- Be open and generous. Bring the tourist things to discover, share the values of your country with him.
- Keep your houses, gardens, roads and footpaths tidy for the tourist.
- Respect property and orderliness wherever you go... the tourist will go there too.

- Have pride in the multi-cultural island in which we live; introduce visitors to your music, that of your heart and of your roots, your original and personal art and your family cooking, which comes from your customs.
- Be yourself and be simple; do not imitate other cultures and thus lose your identity.
- Do not regard tourists as people to be exploited, tourists do not visit us to suffer but to find joy.
- Do not allow our spiritual rituals to be regarded as folklore fit simply for filming. Teach our visitors respect for our sacred places.
- Whoever goes home with nostalgia for the smile of welcome, for kindness and sincerity, will come back with friends.

The Mauritian code tends to concentrate on the cultural and social aspects of the local population. It exhorts the local Mauritian population to greet tourists with a smile, to keep their roads and houses clean and orderly and to offer examples of their local music, art and cuisine. At the same time, it stresses, Mauritians should not forget their culture in an attempt to influence tourists. Do not allow our spiritual rituals to regarded as folklore fit simply for filming it says: "Teach our visitors respect for our sacred places."

The German example has been developed as a broader code which stresses the importance of community participation in the sustainable development of tourism. The full text of the German example is reproduced above. Our of our principles in tourism development says, We *the host population,* is to observe and foster the natural and cultural characteristics or our region. We expect our guests to be prepared to accept this principle. We want our local culture to remain independent and alive. We protect and promote our architecture, our handicrafts, our language, our customs and our cuisine.

The code is also careful to allot tourism its appropriate place in development priorities. We want to counter the danger of one-sided economy development and over-dependence on the tourist trade. We support the strengthening of agriculture and small-scale trade as well as their partnership with tourism. We strive for a qualitative improvement of jobs in tourism. We also continually explore all possibilities for the creation of new jobs outside the tourist trade.

'WE, THE RESPONSIBLE HOST POPULATION' GERMANY, TOURISM WITH INSIGHT AND UNDERSTANDING

1. Tourism should supplement our economy appropriately. We know however, that is also represents a danger to our culture and our environment. We therefore want to supervise and control its development so that our country may be preserved as a viable economic, social and natural environment.
2. By independent decision-making in tourism development we mean that the host population should decide on and participate in all matters relevant to the development of their region: tourist development by, with and for the local population. We encourage many forms of community participation in decision-making, without neglecting the interests of minorities.
3. The tourism development we aim for is economically productive, socially responsible and environment conscious. We are prepared to cease pursuing further development where it leads to an intolerable burden for our population and environment. We want to avoid the pitfalls of economic imperatives.
4. We determine the tourism development targets in our areas in a binding way, limiting them to what is desirable and not what is feasible. We adhere to this policy and are prepared to put up with the bottlenecks that may arise from doing so.
5. We want to keep control over our land. We pursue an active planning and land use policy. We limit our new construction by carefully considered zoning policies. We decline to sell land to non-locals. We promote and encourage the utilization the existing buildings and infrastructure.
6. Our infrastructure development policies are based on restraint. We are therefore careful in building new or extending the existing infrastructure (especially roads, parking lots, airports, water supply and sewage systems) and tourist transport facilities (aerial cableways, ski-lifts) and strictly observe the set development targets.
7. We want to protect nature and the landscape effectively. In addition to careful land management and conservative

infrastructure development, we create large nature reserves in order to preserve particularly valuable ecosystems. We ensure the participation of environmentalists and nature experts in all planning and construction activities.

8. We want to counter the danger of one-sided economic development and over-dependence on the tourist trade. We support the strengthening of agriculture and small-scale trade as well as their partnership with tourism. We strive for a qualitative improvement of jobs in tourism. We also continually explore all possibilities for the creation of new jobs outside the tourist trade.
9. One of our principles in tourism development is to observe and foster the natural and cultural characteristics of our region. We expect our guests to be prepared to accept this principle. We want our local culture to remain independent and alive. We protect and promote our architecture, our handicrafts, our language, or customs and our cuisine.
10. We shall provide information for all concerned; the local population, the tourist trade, politicians and tourists and try to win their support for socially responsible and environmentally conscious behaviour. We shall use all tourism marketing tools and general information channels to promote our concept.

Environmental Codes of Conduct for Tourists

The primary reason for producing tourist codes is to persuade tourists to play an active and positive role in helping protect the environment and engage sympathetically with their host communities. They also help promote the concept of sustainable consumption, as stressed in Agenda 21 Codes for tourists can also be used:

- as a means of informing tour operators and travel agents about the additional information on environmental issues that can be provided to tourists;
- as a means of highlighting to tour operators and travel agents the issues that need to be addressed when developing 'greener' tour packages; and
- as a valuable tool in the preparation of training programmes for tour guides.

Tourist codes are widely used and are often site-specific. They have been developed by many different institutions, including ministries of tourism, national tourist commission, tourist boards, industry associations, non-governmental organization, the management of tourist attractions, resorts and sites, and educational and community organizations.

The UNEP survey identified three different kinds of codes for tourists:

- codes which serve as general behaviour guidelines;
- codes which address specialist activities such as sports and other pastimes; and
- codes which deal with specific sites and cities.

AMERICAN SOCIETY OF TRAVEL AGENTS: TEN COMMANDMENTS ON ECO-TOURISM, IN ASSOCIATION WITH CLUB MED

Thank you for booking your travel with us. Whether you are travelling on business, pleasure or a bit of both, all the citizens of the world, current and future, would be grateful if you would respect the ten commandments of world travel:

1. Respect the frailty of earth. Realize that unless all are willing to help in its preservation, unique and beautiful destinations may not be here for future generations to enjoy.
2. Leave only footprints. Take only photographs. No graffiti No litter! Do no take away "souvenirs" from historical sites and natural areas.
3. To make your travels more meaningful educate yourself about the geography, customs, manners and cultures of the region you visit. Take time to listen to the people. Encourage local conservation efforts.
4. Respect the privacy and dignity of others. Inquire before photographing people.
5. Do not buy products made from endangered plants or animals, such as ivory, tortoise shell, animal skins and feathers. "Know Before you Go" the U.S. Customs list of products which cannot be imported.
6. Always follow designated traits. Do not disturb animals, plants or their natural habitats.

7. Learn about and support conservation-oriented programmes and organizations working to preserve the environment.
8. Whenever possible, walk or utilize environmentally-sound methods of transportation. Encourage drivers of public vehicles to stop engines when parked.
9. Patronize those (hotels, airlines, resorts, cruise lines, tour operators and suppliers) who, advance energy and environmental conservation; water and air quality/ recycling; safe management of waste and toxic materials; noise abatement; community involvement; and which provide experienced, well-trained staff dedicated to strong principles of conservation.
10. Ask your ASTA travel agent to identify those organizations which subscribe to ASTA Environmental Guidelines for air, land and sea travel. ASTA has recommended that these organizations adopt their own environmental codes to cover special sites and eco-systems.

THE HIMALAYAN TOURIST CODE

Prepared by Tourism Concern

By following these simple guidelines, you can help preserve the unique environment and ancient cultures of the Himalayas.

Protect the Natural Environment

- Limit deforestation—makes no open fires and discourage others from doing so on your behalf. Where water is heated by scarce firewood, use as little as possible. When possible choose accommodation that uses kerosene or fuel efficient wood stoves.
- Remove litter, burn or bury paper and carry cut all non-degradable litter. Graffiti are permanent examples of environmental pollution.
- Keep local water clean and avoid using pollutants such as detergents in streams or springs, if no toilet facilities are available, make sure you are at least 30 meters away from water sources, and bury or cover wastes.
- Plants should be left to flourish in their natural environment—taking cuttings, seeds and roots is illegal in many parts of the Himalaya.

- Help your guides and porters to follow conservation measures.

The Himalayas May Change You—Please do not Change Them

As a guest, respect local traditions, protect local cultures, maintain local pride.

- When taking photographs, respect privacy—ask permission and use restraint.
- Respect Holy places—preserve what you have come to see, never touch or remove religious objects. Shoes should be removed when visiting temples.
- Giving to children encourages begging. A donation to a project, health centre or school is a more constructive way to help.
- You will be accepted and welcome if you follow local customs. Use only your right hand for eating and greeting. Do not share cutlery or cups, etc. it is polite to use both hands when giving or receiving.
- Respect for local etiquette earns you respect—loose, light weight clothes are preferable to revealing shorts, skimpy tops and tight fitting action wear. Hand holding or kissing in public are disliked by local people.
- Observe standard food and bad charged but do not condone over charging. Remember when you are shopping that the bargains you boy may only be possible because of low income to others.
- Visitors who value local traditions encourage local pride and maintain local cultures, please help local—people gain a *realistic* view of life on Western Countries.

Be patient, friendly and sensitive. Remember—you are a guest.

General Behaviour Guidelines

General behaviour guidelines address body the planning of the trip, and issues which arise at the destination or site.

Planning advice includes:

- learn as much as possible about tour destination;
- patronize suppliers (such as airlines, tour operators, travel agents and hotels) which demonstrate a commitment to environmental practices;

- plan vacations and visits during the off-peak season;
- visit lesser-known destinations.

Destination advice includes:

- respect local cultures and traditions (many codes advise discretion when taking photographs and when making gifts;
- consider the privacy, culture, habits and traditions of host communities;
- support the local economy by buying local goods and services;
- contribute to local conservation efforts;
- conserve and preserve the natural environment, its ecosystems and its wildlife;
- do not disfigure cultural sites and monuments;
- use energy and water, and dispose of waste, efficiently;
- do not make unnecessary noise; and
- use only designated roads and paths.

Two example of general behaviour codes are shown here, one for ASTA'S 10 Commandments and one for the Himalayan region (above) produced by Tourism Concern in conjunction with people in the area and with the industry.

TRINIDAD AND TOBAGO GUIDE FOR TURTLE WATCHING

Introduction

The Leatherback Turtle (*Dermochelys coriacea*) is the largest species of marine turtle, with some individuals weighing up to 728 kilograms and with carapace lengths of approximately 125-185 cm.

These turtles prefer to nest on beaches with coarse sand and are generally found on the North and on the leeward side of Tobago.

The period between March and August (their nesting season) is the best time for Turtle Watching. In Trinidad, three of the more accessible beaches for viewing the Leatherback Turtle while nesting are Matura, Grand Riviere and Fishing Pond.

Generally nesting is observed between the hours of 7.00 p.m. and 5.00 a.m.

A female leatherback deposits between 80-125 white eggs in a nest which is excavated previously with the use of its flippers in the sand.

After an incubation period ranging between 55-70 days, another amazing sight can be witnessed when the hatchings emerge from the sand and each makes an instinctive dash towards the sea.

Of the sixty per cent that will emerge from the sandy nest, only one or two will ever reach maturity and return to our beaches, from which they originally hatched.

. , For more detailed information, kindly contact officers of the Wildlife Section, or you may wish to purchase our informative booklet and posters. Help us to protect our wildlife by educating at least one other person about the beautiful event you are about to witness.

Enjoy but do not destroy.

Precautions Observers should Note to Ensure that Turtles are not Hindered

Make a minimum of noise—speak softly, no radios.

Use only a minimum amount of artificial lights—only flashlights and turn on only as necessary. When turtles emerge from the sea, there should be absolute silence and no lights should be put on. Turtles turn back to the sea very easily if disturbed at this stage.

A distance of 15 metres should be kept until nest is prepared and the laying process has begun. This is the only time when photographs can be taken.

Observers should approach quietly, with a minimum of lights when laying is in progress. Care must be taken to prevent nests from caving in.

Do not handle turtle eggs.

Do not attempt to ride on turtle back.

Do not use lights when turtles are returning to the sea.

Law Enforcement

To give greater protection to these species the Matura Bay and Fishing Pond beaches have been declared as prohibited areas under Section 2 of the Forest Act—Chapter 66:01, and would take affect of 1st March to 31st August annually.

Persons desirous of visiting these beaches must obtain Permits to enter a Prohibited Area, from the Forestry Division offices San

Fernando between the hours of 9.33 a.m. and 3.00 p.m. at a cost of: $ 5.00 per adult and $ 2.00 per child (under 12) for single visits.

Seasonal permits can be obtained for the period of 1st March to 31st August at the cost of $50.00 per adult.

Read Conditions of All Permits Carefully and Uphold the Law to Aid in Conserving these Magnificent Wildlife Species.

The way in which guidelines are distributed affects their success. Visitor codes need to be frequently reiterated to be most effective. The most successful codes reach travellers before they leave home.

Specific Tourist Activities

These codes attempt to educate the tourist on the basic premise: enjoy but do not destroy.

The UNEP survey found that these codes are usually developed by the authority managing the site where the activity takes place. The Swiss Sports Federation, for example, has developed codes of behaviour for ramblers, skiers, water sports enthusiasts and mountain bikers. The Marine Parks Authority of the Cayman Islands has developed guidelines for divers on the prevention of damage. The Ministry of Environmental and Natural Services of Trinidad and Tobago has developed a guide on turtle watching.

EXTRACT FROM WELCOME TO HEIDELBERG

The Environmental Package

A package that benefits both the pocket and the environment has been put together by the Heidelberg Convention and Visitors Bureau for all convention visitors: the "Convention Environment Ticket", which includes:

- Rail journey to Heidelberg at substantially reduced fares (including seat reservation).
- Cut-rate ticket for use on all public transport in the Greater Heidelberg District (Rhine-Neckar transport network; DM 5 per day and person).
- Overnight accommodation in the hotel of your choice.

Enjoy Heidelberg and its surroundings in a relaxed mood and with no parking worries. You save money, there is no stress, and the city is spared the impact of even more traffic.

For more details on the "Convention Environment Ticket" please contact the Heidelberg Convention and Visitors Bureau.

A Welcome Guest

- When you leave your room please switch off the radio, the television and all the lights.
- During the heating period, you can save energy when ventilating your room by opening windows wide for a short time only.
- Take a shower instead of a both—it is good for your circulation and you use less water; and do not forget to turn off the water while brushing your teeth. Lower water consumption is good news for the hotel and is even better news for the environment.
- If you are staying for a longer period, a daily change of hand towels is not an absolute necessity. Many hoteliers already operate on this basis, and recognize these signals, if the towels are hanging on the rail, they will be used again. If they are lying on the floor or in the bathtub, they are to be changed. If this has not been suggested in the place you are staying at, mention it.
- Most hotels separate useful materials from trash. It is a good idea, therefore, for the guest to place glass, for example, in a separate bag.
- Incidentally, several hotels in Heidelberg already offer "environmental breakfast buffets" where everything is served fresh and no disposable packaging is used.

To Buy or Not to Buy...?

There is a very high value placed on protecting the environment in Heidelberg.

The city has an approach that concentrates primarily on the avoidance of waste, and then on recycling and disposal. This is the reason whey several things are no longer to be found in the shopping bags of environmentally-conscious consumers: elaborately packed products, non-returnable bottles, or Battery-driven devices. Alternatives abound-articles bearing the "blue angel", and thus identified as environmentally-compatible, returnable bottles and rechargeable batteries. And the plastic bag has now given way to the cloth bag or the traditional shopping basket.

You will take care that your camera always has fully charged batteries. But when they finally go flat, you should return them to a camera shop for recycling. There are containers located in all local state schools, by the way, offering a safe way to dispose of all your used batteries. And you will find special containers throughout the city for glass and for paper and in which no other waste is to be placed.

But "to buy or not to buy?" that is the question each of must ask when filling that shopping basket.

- avoid disturbing wildlife and damaging ecosystems;
- dispose of waste properly;
- respect the practices of the local community; and
- respect local legislation.

Site-Specific Codes

Site-specific codes address the behaviour of tourists at specific locations, for example the *Guidelines of Conduct for Antarctica Visitors,* developed by the International Association of Antarctic Tour Operators; the Anapurna Conservation Area (Nepal) Project's code of conduct, developed by the operators of the project; and the code for visitors developed by the Convention and Visitors Bureau and Environment Protection Office of the City of Heidelberg, Germany.

These codes combine guidelines which are location-oriented as well as those of a more general nature:

- dispose of waste carefully;
- protect the natural and cultural environment;
- use energy efficiently;
- pay a fair price for goods and services—haggling over tiny sums usually results in an unfair return and generates ill feeling; and
- do not give money, sweets or other items to begging children—there are other ways to help them.

Codes for cities, such as the Heidelberg visitors code/make special mention of the following elements:

- environmentally-sensitive means of transport;
- purchase eco-labelled products; and
- avoid buying elaborately packaged products, non-returnable bottles and battery-driven devices—use returnable bottles and rechargeable batteries.

Conclusions

Some codes of conduct have not been well received by tourists, and efforts should be made to ensure that codes of conduct create a positive impact on tourists. They should carry a positive message, and be precise and functional. It is vital that all codes are prepared in consultation with both potential tourists and with host populations.

Though most codes address international tourists, the importance of domestic tourists should not be over-looked. In most countries the volume and importance of domestic tourism heavily outweighs that of international tourism. It is thus of vital importance that codes address these visitors, especially young people. Finally, it should be stressed that a wide range of media be used to distribute codes.

Additional Codes of Conduct for Tourists

The following sections include a number of additional codes of conduct for tourists.

ENGLISH TOURIST BOARD: 20 TIPS FOR VISITORS

1. Always remember you are the guest: show consideration for residents and their environment. Respect local laws and customs.
2. Leave beaches, parks, and public places as you would like to find them.
3. Put litter in a bin or take it home: don't expect others to clean up after you.
4. Keep noise levels down, especially at night or in quiet places like in churches and the countryside.
5. Show respect for nature: keep to proper footpaths, don't feed wildlife and don't pick flowers or shrubs.
6. Remember that many people find smoking offensive, and careless smokers may cause countryside fires.
7. Don't carve your initials on trees and historic monuments or spoil them with graffiti.
8. Complain if you have just cause, but do it politely.
9. Don't argue with staff who seek to enforced rules: they are only doing their jobs.
10. Avoid the temptation to touch valuable objects such as paintings, tapestries and vases.
11. Keep an eye on your children to see they don't indulge in destructive or annoying behaviour.

12. If you want to photograph other people, ask them first.
13. Behave towards others as you would wish them to behave towards you: do not push or above or jump queues.
14. Good manners are always appreciated do not forget to say please and than you.
15. Dress properly to visit places of worship; remember they are not holiday playgrounds.
16. Wear suitable footwear to visit historic buildings: high-heeled shoes can cause a lot of damage.
17. Be enterprising: visit parts of the country off the usual tourist trail.
18. If you live in Britain, try to visit our popular attractions in off-peak periods; you will enjoy them much more.
19. Use public transport whenever possible. If you take your car, park in a designated space, not just where you please.
20. Help the local economy: buy locally grown or made goods wherever possible.

AMERICAN AUTOMOBILE ASSOCIATION: ENVIRONMENTAL TIPS FOR WORLD TRIPS

Every journey can widen your perception of the world... but every step leaves a footprint.

Wilderness preserves, city centres, ecologically sensitive areas, man-made historic sites—they are all part of our environment. And they are all endangered.

The care you take as a traveller will help determine that is left for future generations. Remember, our planet is fragile. And your actions have consequences.

How, then do you see the world yet care for the world? How do you balance the adventure of travel with a sense of obligation?

The travel tips in this brochure won't make a lot of difference in the way you live your life. But following them would have a positive impact on the environment and your quality of life:

- Experience the day-to-day life of the people around you. Visit a variety of public places, not just monuments and tourist spots.
- Practice a few phrases in the language of your host country. People will appreciate your efforts.
- Behave with respect if you visit a religious or holy place. Proper dress might mean removing your shoes or covering your head and shoulder.

- Respect the privacy of others. Not every person and event is a subject for your camera or recorder. Ask permission to photograph or videotape.
- Respect the rules. Do not insist on privileges or exceptions, such as special operating hours or across to restricted areas.

Sightsee and Shop with Sensitivity

- Be energy conscious. Turn off lights and adjust thermostats when you leave your hotel room.
- Schedule sightseeing with eye toward traffic congestion. Keep in mind some cities, such as Rome and Florence, ban private vehicles during peak traffic hours.
- Enjoy visits to monuments and natural points of interest, but leave them as you found them for future generations to enjoy.
- Seek out historical sites off the beater path, such as specialized museums and preserved homes.
- Use trash receptacles. It there is not one, carry litter until you can dispose of it properly.
- Help the local economy by shopping at small, private businesses as well as airport or hotel gift shops.
- Refuse to buy items made from an dangered animals or plants, including reptile skins and leathers, ivory, coral, furs of spotted cats or marine mammals, archids and cacti. Don't purchase exotic pets such as parrots or snakes.
- Bring a canvas tote bag with you when you shop to minimize the need for paper and plastic packaging.

Widen your Horizons Responsibly

Whatever mode of transportation you choose for side trips, travelling smart is a three-step process: prepare, take care and be aware.

- Fly into the best "pub" destination you can. Choosing the right home base will make day-tripping easier.
- Visit lesser known destinations travel off-season. Your "discoveries" will be less crowded and less expensive.
- Use mass transit when you tour urban centres. Train and bus travel reduce pollution and out travel costs.
- Take a walking tour or rent a bike. Some scenery is just too good to view through a windshield!

- Observe posted speed limits and local laws/when you do get behind the wheel.
- Stick it designated roads if you drive. Off-road monitoring is both risky and potentially damaging to the environment.
- Try not to travel during rush hour as stop-and-go traffic consumes more fuel and adds to air pollution.
- Visit environmentally fragile areas in groups of 10 or fewer and always with an experienced guide.

Keep Waterways and Beaches Sparkling

When you visit a beach or river, leave the smallest, possible footprint-environmentally speaking.

- Put safety first. Locate the lifeguard or ranger station.
- Study the site so you understand recreational opportunities and risks. Most public waterways and wetland areas offer educational pamphlets, tours or displays.
- Leave sea oats and wild flowers where they are growing to protect the eco-system, don't take other plants, rocks, fossils or artifacts as souvenirs.
- Enjoy wildlife and their habitate from a distance of at least 30 feet.
- Don't get between a marine mammal and the water's edge.
- Don't feed wildlife—it could endanger you both.
- Tread lightly near fragile nesting areas, plants and where erosion is a concern.
- Don't dump anything from a boat. Use marine and sewage pump-out stations.
- Dispose of fishing nets, rings from beverage six-packs and other plastics with special care. This debris can kill marine life and shore birds.
- Use biodegradable soap, shampoo and insect repellent. Check labels before you purchase.

Be Aware and Care

- Protect yourself and your belongings. Leave valuables at home, locked in the trunk of your car, or in the hotel's safe deposit box.
- Be flexible. Change the hours you eat and sleep to match the tempo of the place you are visiting.

- Be considerate about noise. Keep the volume down-on the radio, television and your voices.
- Support organizations that give something back to the area. Many nature preserves, botanical gardens and, wildlife watching organizations donate to conservation and preservation efforts.

Ethics Code for World Travellers

Whether your destination is a rational park or another continent, you can practice responsible world travel skill by:

- Learning the local language, geography and beliefs.
- Conserving resources, including clean air and water.
- Respecting local laws and customs.
- Treading lightly at ancient ruins and historical sites to preserve history for future generations.
- Protecting wildlife and plants, especially in parks, wilderness areas and reserves.

GUIDANCE FOR VISITORS TO THE ANTARCTIC

Attachment to Recommendation XVII-I adopted at the ATCM, Kyoto, Japan, April 1994

Activities in the Antarctic are governed by the Antarctic Treaty of 1959 and associated agreements, referred to collectively as the Antarctic Treaty system. The Treaty established Antarctica as a zone of peace and science.

In 1991, the Antarctic Treaty Consultative Parties adopted the Protocol on Environmental Protection to the Antarctic Treaty, which designates the Antarctic as a natural reserve. The Protocol sets out environmental principles, procedures and obligations for the comprehensive protection of the Antarctic environment, and its dependent and associated eco-systems. The Consultative parties have agreed that, pending its entry into force, as far as possible and in accordance with their legal system, the provisions of the Protocol should be applied as appropriate.

The Environmental Protocol applies to tourism and non-governmental activities as well as governmental activities in the Antarctic Treaty Area. It is intended to ensure that these activities do not have adverse impacts on the Antarctic environment, or on its scientific and aesthetic values.

This *Guidance for Visitors to the Antarctic* is intended to ensure that all visitors are aware of and are therefore able to comply with the Treaty and the Protocol. Visitors are of course bound by national laws and regulations applicable to activities in the Antarctic.

Protect Antarctic Wildlife

Taking or harmful interference with Antarctic wildlife is prohibited except in accordance with a permit issued by a national authority.

1. Do not use aircraft, vessels, small boats, or other means of transport in ways that disturb, wildlife, either at sea or on land.
2. Do not feed, touch, or handle birds or seals, or approach or photograph them in ways that cause them to alter their behaviour. Special care is needed when animals are breeding or moulting.
3. Do not damage plants, for example by walking, driving, or landing on extensive moss beds or lichen-covered screen slopes.
4. Do not use guns or explosives. Keep noise to the minimum to avoid frightening wildlife.
5. Do not bring non-native plants or animals into the Antarctic (e.g. live poultry, pet dogs and cats, house plants).

Respect Protected Areas

A variety of areas in the Antarctic have been afforded special protection because of their particular ecological, scientific, historic or other values. Entry into certain areas may be prohibited except in accordance with a permit issued by an appropriate national authority. Activities in and near designated Historic Sites and Monuments and certain other areas may be subject to special restrictions.

1. Know the locations of areas that have been afforded special protection and any restrictions regarding entry and activities that can be carried out in and near them.
2. Observe applicable restrictions.
3. Do not damage, remove or destroy Historic Sites or Monuments, or any artifacts associated with them.

Respect Scientific Research

Do not interfere with scientific research facilities or equipment.

1. Obtain permission before visiting Antarctic science and logistic support facilities; reconfirm arrangements 24-72 hours before arriving; and comply strictly with the rules regarding such visits.
2. Do not interfere with, or remove, scientific equipment or marker posts, and do not disturb experimental study sites, field camps, or supplies.

Be Safe

Be prepared for severe and changeable weather. Ensure that your equipment and clothing meet Antarctic standards. Remember that the Antarctic environment is inhospitable, unpredictable and potentially dangerous.

1. Know your capabilities the dangers posed by the Antarctic environment and act accordingly. Plan activities with safety in mind at all times.
2. Keep a safe distance from all wildlife, both on land and at sea.
3. Take note of and act on the advice and instructions from your leaders; do not stray from your group.
4. Do not walk onto glaciers or large snow fields without proper equipment and experience; there is a real danger of falling into hidden crevasses.
5. Do not expect a rescue service, self-sufficiency is increased and risks reduced by sound planning, quality equipment, and trained personnel.
6. Do not enter emergency refuges (except in emergencies). If you use equipment or food from a refuge inform the nearest research station or national authority once—the emergency is ove.
7. Respect any smoking restrictions particularly around buildings, and take great care to safeguard against the danger of fire. This is a real hazard in the dry environment of Antarctica.

Keep Antarctica Pristine

Antarctica remains relatively pristine, and has not yet been subjected to large scale human perturbations. It is the largest wilderness area on earth. Please keep it that way.

1. Do not dispose of litter or garbage on land. Open burning is prohibited.

2. Do not disturb or pollute lakes or streams. Any material discarded at sea must be disposed of properly.
3. Do not paint or engrave names, of graffiti on rocks or buildings.
4. Do not collect or take away biological or geological specimens or man-made articles as a souvenir, including rocks, bones, eggs, fossils, and parts or contents of buildings.

EUROPEAN TOUR OPERATORS ASSOCIATION: GUIDELINES FOR THE VISITOR

- Respect the privacy of residents.
- Be aware of the customs and cultures of the region you are visiting.
- Support the local economy wherever possible by buying local produce.
- Preserve the environment: do not harm historical sites and natural areas.
- Leave no waste.
- Use local transport wherever possible.

SAVE OUR PLANETS GUIDELINES FOR LOW-IMPACT VACATIONS

- Plan your entire trip carefully.
- Save energy when leaving home for a trip by turning off lights, lowering heating temperatures in winter and turning off air conditioning in summer.
- Rediscover the leisure of walking, hiking and bicycling during your vacations.
- Observe the posted speed limits.
- Minimize your impact on tourist attractions.

CREDO OF THE PEACEFUL TRAVELLER

Grateful for the opportunity to travel and to experience the world and because peace begins with the individual, I affirm my personal responsibility and commitment to:

- Journey with an open mind and gentle heart.
- Accept with grace and gratitude the diversity encounter.
- Revere and protect the natural environment which sustains all life.

- Appreciate all the cultures I discover.
- Respect and thank my hosts for their welcome.
- Offer my hand in friendship to everyone I meet.
- Support travel services that share these views and act upon them and, by my spirit words and actions.
- Encourage others to travel the world in peace.

The IIPT First Global Conference:
Tourism—A Vital Force for Peace
Vancouver, British Colombia,
Canada, 27 October, 1988.

ICOMOS—CHARTER OF CULTURAL TOURISM: ADOPTED BY ICOMPS, NOVEMBER, 1976

I. Basic Position

1. Tourism is an irreversible social, human, economic and cultural fact. Its influence in the sphere of monuments and sites is particularly important and can but increase because of known conditions of the activity's development.
2. Looked at in the perspective of the next twenty-five years, in the context of the phenomena of expansion which may have heavy consequences and which confront the human race, tourism appears to be one of the phenomena likely to exert a most significant influence on Man's environment in general and on monuments and sites in particular. In order to remain bearable, this influence must be carefully studied, and at all levels be the object of a concerted and effective policy. Without claiming to meet this need in all its aspects, the present approach which is limited to cultural tourism constitutes, it is believed a positive element in the global solution which is required.
3. Cultural tourism is that form of tourism whose object is, among other aims, the discovery of monuments and sites. It exerts on these last a very positive effect insofar as it contributes—to satisfy its own ends—to their maintenance and protection. This form of tourism justifies in fact the efforts which said maintenance and protection demand of the human community because of the socio-cultural and economic benefits which they bestow on all the populations concerned.

4. Whatever, however, may be its motivations and the ensuing benefits, cultural tourism cannot be considered separately form he negative, despoiling or destructive effects which the massive and uncontrolled use of monuments and sites entails. The respects of the latter, just like the elementary wish to maintain them in a state fit to allow them to play their role as elements of tourist attraction and of cultural education, implies the definition and implementation of acceptable standards.

In any case, with the future in mind, it is the respect of the world, cultural and natural heritage which must take precedence over any other considerations however justified these may be from a social, political or economic point of view.

Such respect cannot be ensured solely by policies regarding the siting of equipment and of guidance of the tourist movement based on the limitation of use and of density which may not be disregarded without impunity.

Additionally one must condemn any siting of tourist equipment or services in contradiction with the prime pre-occupation due to the respect we owe to the existing cultural heritage.

II. BASI. For Action

Resting on the Foregoing

- The bodies representing tourism, on one the hand, and the protection of the natural and monumental heritage on the other, deeply convinced that the protection and promotion of the natural and cultural heritage for the benefit of the many cannot be ensured unless it be in an orderly fashion, i.e. by integrating cultural assets in to the social and economic objectives which are part of planning the resources of the states, regions and local communities.
- Acknowledge with the greatest interest the measures which each of them states it is prepared to take in its own sphere of influence as expressed in the appendices to the present Declaration.
- Appeal to the will of the states to ensure the fast and energetic implementation of the international Convention for the Protection of the World Cultural and Natural

heritage adopted on 16 November, 1972 and of the Nairobi Recommendation.

- Trust that the World Tourist Organization fulfilling its aims and UNESCO, in the framework of the Convention mentioned above, shall exert all efforts in co-operation with the signatory bodies and all others who in future may really to ensure the implementation of the policy which the signatory bodies have defined as the only one able to protect Mankind against the effects of tourism's anarchical growth which would result in the denial of its own objectives.

They express the wish that the states by the means of their administrative structures; shall adopt all appropriate measures to facilitate the information and training of persons travelling for tourist purposes inside and out of their country of origin.

Conscious of the acute need which prevails now to change the attitude of the public at large towards the phenomena, they express the wish that from school age onwards children and adolescents be educated to understand and respect the monuments, the sites and the cultural heritage and that all written, spoken or visual information media should thereby efficaciously contributing to affective universal understanding.

Unanimous in their concern for the protection of the cultural patrimony which is the very basis of international tourism, they undertake to help in the fight initiated on all fronts against the destruction of said heritage by all known sources of pollution; and they appeal to the architects and scientific experts of the whole world so that the most advanced resources of modern technology be used for the protection of monuments.

They recommend that the specialists who shall be called upon to conceive and implement the tourist use of the cultural and natural heritage should receive training adapted to the multi-faceted nature of the problem, and should be associated from the outset in the programming and performance of the development and tourist equipment plans.

They solemnly declare that their action is to respect and protect the authenticity and diversity of the cultural values in developing regions and countries as in industrialized nations since the fate of Mankind's cultural heritage is of the very same nature everywhere in the face of tourism's likely expansion.

'WELCOME TO AUSTRALIA': AUSTRALIAN TOURIST COMMISSION

Australia has a proud history of National Parks. We were the first country in the world on proclaim a "National Park." Royal National Park in Sydney in 1879.

More than 50 million years of isolated evolution has made the Great South Land (as it was known in Cook's days) a country of contrasts; Our koala, kangaroo, platypus, wombat and echidna are but a few of the 140 native marsupials which join with an equally unique collection of trees and plants to make up the Australian "Bush." For Australians, the Bush is anything outside a city from rolling farmlands to luxuriant rainforests and the sparse malices scrub of the Great Outback.

The global significance of Australia's natural treasures has been recognized by the declaration of nine world heritage areas covering such distinct features as the Great Barrier Reef, Uluru (Ayers Rock) the Queensland rainforests and the ancient, mist shrouded peaks of south-west Tasmania.

Visitor Guidelines for the Protection of Australia's Environment and Heritage

Australia is a beautiful and ancient land hosting a remarkable diversity of unusual plants, animals and landscapes.

We ask you to help us establish a harmony between people and the natural environment so that fragile habitats and places of cultural importance are conserved for future generations. Please observe the following.

Australia's Native Plants and Animals Cultural Sites and Landscapes

- Photograph but do not remove or mark any feature of the natural environment and cultural sites.
- Be careful not to drop any non-native seeds, fruit or plants within the natural environment.
- Move quietly and carefully as noise can disturb native birds, animals and reptiles.

Travelling Tips

- Observe all signs and information boards which are there to ensure your safety and enjoyment.

- Seek advice on road conditions, walking tracks, equipment and extremes of climate before setting out.
- Where possible keep to defined roads and tracks and avoid fragile areas such as wetlands, alpine zones or vegetated sand dunes.
- Observe local fire restrictions and be careful with cigarette butts and matches.
- Detour around areas being rehabilitated or where scientific research is occurring.
- Experience the natural environment by waling, canoeing or bicycling, and generally minimized motorized transport.

Litter and Pollution

- Place litter in receptacles or carry it with you back to base.
- Water is scarce in this arid country so practice conservation and avoid pollution.
- If toilets are unavailable bury waste away from water.
- Respect your fellow travellers, right to peaceful enjoyment of our beautiful environment.

The Privacy of Others

- Permission may be required to visit some cultural sites.
- Seek permission before photographed other people.
- Consider the privacy, cultural heritage, habits and traditions of host communities.
- Respect your fellow travellers, rights to peaceful enjoyment of our beautiful environment.

Encourage Others to Protect our Environment

- Seek advice and co-operation of your tour guides and other tourism personnel in following these guidelines on how to protect Australia's unique and natural environment.

By following these guidelines, you will actively help to preserve Australia's unique environment for the pleasure for future Australians and our visitors.

We are proud to share our country. Please visit us again.

IMPLEMENTATION OF ENVIRONMENTAL CODES OF CONDUCT FOR TOURISM

Codes of conduct must be implemented if their potential beneficial are to be realized. In most industries, including tourism, codes are often poorly implemented.

If real changes are to be made, the organizations that develop codes must take responsibility for implementing them. Since codes are usually developed by governments and industry associations as part of an overall environment policy, implementation is rarely directly only to the codes but is part of a larger process.

This chapter provides examples of the tools and the programmes which both the public and the private sectors have found useful in implementation.

Making a Start

The implementation process is best begun by appointing a working group or task force to plan and carry out implementation of the code. Indeed, working groups of this kind, comprising all the various stakeholders, are often used to prepare the code in the first place, and this makes implementation easier. In the United Kingdom, for example, the Secretary of State for Employment commissioned a task force to investigate environmental conflicts related to tourism, and to identify the retroactive action that had taken place. The work of the task force, which concentrated largely on the practical aspects of visitor management, was published and subsequently triggered off many other initiatives. In Finland, a working group of government representatives, including members of the Finnish Tourist Board, were made responsible for the development and dissemination of the environmental code for tourism. This group has now been expanded to include industry representatives, and will spearhead the implementation of the code.

Methods of Implementation

A number of tools can be used to support the implementation of the codes. These tools, which are used by government, non-government and industry organizations alike, are listed below:

- dissemination and publicity campaigns;
- publications;
- seminars and conferences;
- pilot projects;
- awards;
- education and training; and
- technical assistance.

These tools will prove more effective when they are combined in an integrated package. Examples of such packages are given in the boxes to this chapter, which deal separately with packages designed by national organizations, tourism associations and non-governmental organizations.

Dissemination and Publicity Campaigns

The first, and most important, step in implementation is to let people know of the existence of the code. Attention should be directed at both the industry and the general public. This can be done through announcements in the national and local press, on radio and television, and by the production of videos, brochures and books. Special lectures can be arranged in schools, universities and industries. A particularly effective means of raising public awareness is the use of awards and the donation of insignia for special achievements.

The World Travel and Tourism Council, for example, launched a campaign of this kind called GREEN GLOBE. This combined a global awareness programme with an environmental management programme aimed at all organizations within the industry. Its aims were to increase environmental responsiveness throughout the industry, obtain participation from all sectors, emphasize that good environmental practice is good business, demonstrate the commitment of the industry through the use of the GREEN GLOBE logo, and highlight examples of best practice and outstanding progress.

WWF is an organization which has the raising of public awareness of environment issues as one of its main goals. To do this it produces many public service announcements, video news releases and documentary films, some of which deal with travel and transport issues. Other organizations that have used publicity campaigns as part of their implementation process are the ICC, PATA (with its Gold Awards) and ASTA. The Tourist Authority of Thailand has also launched a publicity campaign to raise environmental awareness amongst local populations. Dissemination of the Finnish codes was supported by a publicity campaign and the Tourism Development Authority of Trinidad and Tobago aims to create public awareness or environment matters through the national press and by launching national competitions.

Publications of codes of conduct is nor in itself a sufficient means of implementing codes, though a well written code that is published and then widely disseminated will be partially implemented. Additional techniques, however, are nearly always required.

INTEGRATED PACKAGES: NATIONAL ORGANIZATIONS

Costa Rica

The Costa Rican Tourist Bureau, in co-ordination with the Ministry of Natural Resources, Mining and Energy, and the National Parks Service, prepared general management plans for the country's protected regions. These studies are being carried out by the University of Costa Rica.

To ensure that communities near the protected areas receive real benefits from tourism, a Tourism Micro-Business organization was founded with representation from a number of tourism sectors. The organization supports training and educational programmes on tourism and the environment for young people in these communities.

England

The Country Code has been implemented with the production of publications, government appointed task forces, seminars and workshops, and pilot projects.

The English Tourist Board (ETB), together with the Countryside Commission and the Rural Development Commission, has published *The Green Light,* which provides guidelines for the development, management, and marketing of sustainable tourism. This was followed in September 1993 by a National Demonstration Project which produced an environmental audit kit for tourism businesses.

The ETB has also focused in tourism issues in sensitive areas with the publication *Tourism in National Parks—A Guide to Good Practice* and a green tourism award. Following a seminar on Tourism and the Environment in August 1990, the Secretary of State for Employment commissioned a task force to examine the environmental difficulties and challenges surrounding the development and management of tourism, and what counteractive measures are currently in practice. The work of the Task Force is published in *Tourism and the Environment-Maintaining a Balance.* This document discusses tourism development and management, presents ways of tackling problems, and recommends solutions. Subsequently, several seminars were held to stimulate local action. Several pilot projects were also launched to demonstrate techniques of environmentally responsible tourism.

Finland

Codes of conduct were originally developed by the Finnish Tourist Board (FTB) together with a working group which was chaired by the FTB and included representatives from the Finish Rural Tourism Group, the Ministry of Environment, the National Board of Water and the Environment, the Finnish Municipal Association, the Association of Rural Centres, and the Finnish Association of Rural Centres, and the Finnish Association for Nature Protection. A publicity campaign accompanied the dissemination of the code.

In 1993, this group was enlarged to include industry representatives, and four sub-groups were formed; hotels and restaurants, travel agencies, rural tourism and the public sector. In this context, the Association of Finnish Travel Agents has published a leaflet called *Green Ideas for Your Trip.*

Meanwhile, the Ministry of Environment has received a number of project proposals from the private sector. These proposals will be examined with a view to mounting pilot projects as examples of good sustainable tourism practice.

Scotland

The Tourism and Environment initiative of the Scottish Tourist Board (STB) has published two brochures.

The first, *Guidelines for the Development of Tourism Management Programmes,* seeks to encourage the development of environmentally-sensitive tourism. The implementation of these guidelines is spearheaded by a task force which comprises representatives of the STB, Scottish Heritage and other organizations. Help will be provided by government bodies but the STB hopes that the major responsibility and commitment will come from local bodies. Private sector involvement will also be encouraged.

Pilot projects for the implementation of the guidelines have been established at Callanish, Loch Ness, Trossachs, Loch Doon, St Andrews and Kilmartin. Other sectoral initiatives are being investigated for caravans, footpaths coastal erosion and tourist routes.

The second publication, *Going Green* seeks to encourage environmentally sound practices in the tourism industry. This publication is intended to make people think about what they can do to ensure that their tourism enterprise treats the environment in a sensitive manner.

Thailand

The Tourism Authority of Thailand (TAT) is carrying out an Environmental Awareness Programme (EPT) for tourism promoters and developers. A handbook has been produced on the development of different tourist destinations such as temples, caves, mountains, waterfalls, reservoirs and coastal areas. These guidelines are intended to minimize conflicts between tourism development and the environment.

Training programmes and lectures on tourism and conservation are provided for civil servants, private sector employees, students and other interested parties. Though the Annual Training Programme for 200 Youth Leaders, the TAT launches a high-profile publicity campaign designed to raise public awareness of environmental issues related to tourism.

Other functions of the EAP include environment research and impact studies, budgetary support for sustainable tourism and conservation efforts, and the establishment of the Foundation for the Protection of the Environment and Tourism.

INTEGRATED PACKAGES: INTEGRATED BODIES

The International Chamber of Commerce (ICC)

The ICC Business Charter for Sustainable Development, now translated into 24 languages, has the support of 1200 companies around the world. To help its members implement the Charter, the ICC has developed a number of tools including a guide to effective environmental auditing, a question-and-answer leaflet explaining the charter, and a quarterly bulletin. The Global Environment Management Initiative (GEMI) has published the *Environmental Self-Assessment Programme* help business assess their progress.

The ICC and UNEP have formed in Advisory Panel to promote partnership and cooperation in support of the charter.

Pacific Asia Travel Association (PATA)

PATA set-up a task force comprising travel, tourism and related industry specialists to analyze destinations, products and services, and make recommendations on how they could be improved. It has also created the PATA Foundation, a non-profit organization which awards scholarships and grants, including the Duncan Sandys Scholarship which are UK-based, custom-made programmes for manages from the Pacific Asian region; and the EDIT Scholarships, which provide funding for an executive, development course at the School of Travel and Industry Management at the University of Hawaii.

PATA sponsors workshops and conferences to raise awareness and highlight the importance of sustainable tourism. Train-the-trainer workshops are conducted to teach management, marketing, communication and planning skills.

In 1994, PATA launched its Green Leaf programme which offered companies the opportunity to affirm their support for the PATA codes. Participating companies received stickers, logos for use on stationery, and a certificate.

World Travel and Tourism Council (WTTC)

The World Travel and Tourism Environment Research Centre was established by the WTTC to create an academic centre for travel and tourism environmental issues, and databases of industry and government action. The rationale is to ensure that programmes can be analyzed objectively and best practice identified, the WTTC environmental guidelines were used as a framework for analyzing corporate practices in 1992 and 1993. The databases were started with information collected through questionnaires addressed to members of the WTTC.

The centre publishes an annual review, which includes a state of the art of environmental Travel and Tourism worldwide, as well as bi-annual newsletters.

In 1994, the WTTC launched an environmental management improvement and public awareness programme, named GREEN GLOBE, which provides participating companies with continuous support, education and training, information on best practices, and access to a global environment database.

Participating companies can display the GREEN GLOBE logo to acknowledge their commitment to environmental best practice. They are also eligible for the GREEN GLOBE Achievements awards.

The International Hotels Environment Initiative (IHEI)

The IHEI has published *Environmental Management for Hotels—the industry guide to best practice* and established its first regional chapter, the Asia Pacific Hotels Environment, intended to promote environmental awareness and action in hotels in Asia. With UNEP/IE and the IHA, it has also prepared an environmental tool-kit for small and medium-sized hotels.

American Society of Travel Agents (ASTA)

ASTA and the *Smithsonian* magazine jointly sponsor annual awards for individuals, companies or countries that have shown extraordinary efforts to preserve the environment while furthering responsible travel and tourism. The wards are announced at ASTA's annual world congress.

The International Youth Hostels Federation (IYHF)

The IYHF has developed guidelines and a work plan to help national associations implement its 1992 Environmental Charter, Guidelines and check lists are provided for national associations which include advice on:

- incorporating the charter in national policies;
- responsibility for implementation;
- developing a work plan;
- supporting hostel managers; and
- monitoring and reporting;

The work plan also lists minimum standards and advanced activities for each of the issue with which the charter deals. These are:

- consumption of resources;
- waste minimization;
- recycling;
- control and reduction of pollution;
- encouraging use of public transport;
- energy conservation;
- conservation and protection; and
- environmental education.

Australian Tourism Industry Association (ATIA)

Building on its Code of Environmental Practice, ATIA has developed guidelines for specific sectors, the first called *Environmental Guidelines for Tourist Developments* (1993). An annual Tourism Scholarship Programme is organized jointly with the

WTTC. ATIA participated in the development of the Australian National Eco-tourism Strategy and is now serving on the steering committee for the development of the National Accreditation Scheme.

Publications

Publications are one of the main ways of supporting the implementation of codes.

Examples include:

- *The Green Light,* published by the English Tourist Board, the Countryside Commission and the Rural Development Board in the United Kingdom;
- *Tourism in National Parks* published by the English Tourist Board;
- the findings of the Task Force commissioned by the UK Secretary of State for Employment were published in *Tourism and the Environment-Maintaining a Balance;*
- the Environment Initiative of the Scottish Tourist Board has published *Guidelines for the Development of Tourism,* and *Going Green;*
- the Tourism Authority of Thailand has produced a handbook on the development of different types of tourist destination;
- the WTTC/WTTERCE produces reports, occasional publications and newsletters;
- the International Hotels Environment Initiative (IHEI) has published a manual called *Environmental Management in the Hotel Industry—an Industry Guide to Best Practices;*
- based on the ICC Charter, the Global Environment Management Initiative (GEMI) published in 1992 the *Environmental Self-Assessment Programme* which is intended to provide helpful ideas for assessing and developing management programmes and improving environmental quality performance; and
- the International Conference on Monuments and Sites (ICOMOS) has produced a publication called *Management of Tourism in World Heritage Sites.*

Seminars and Conferences

Seminars and conferences are a popular means of implementing codes of conduct. The tourism development authority of Trinidad and Tobago, for example, organizes seminars and workshops to increase environmental awareness of the local population. PATA sponsors workshops and conferences to raise awareness and highlight the importance of sustainable tourism. Train-the-trainer workshops are conducted throughout the region to teach essential research, management, marketing, communication and planning skills.

Other organizations that seek to implement their codes in this way include the English Tourist Board, the Scottish Tourist Board, the Ecotourism Society, ICOMOS, the World Wide Fund for nature (WWF) and the World Conservation Union.

Pilot Projects

Pilot projects are usually used to demonstrate, test and put into practice development and management strategies. They are often the final step in the implementation process.

In an effort to demonstrate the issues highlighted in nation's ethics and environmental code of conduct, the Costa Rican Tourist Bureau has, in coordination with the Ministry of Natural Resources, Mining and Energy and the National Parks Service, developed General Management Plans for protected regions in the country. In the United Kingdom, following publication of the *Green Light* by the English Tourist Board, the Countryside Commission and the Rural Development Board, a national demonstration project was initiated. This resulted in the production of an environmental kit for small and medium-sized tourism businesses. Also, in the United Kingdom, following the publication of the findings of the task force commissioned by the Secretary of State for Employment, several seminars were held to stimulate action on a local level. This was followed by pilot projects to explore and further demonstrate techniques of environmental management and responsible tourism. Pilot projects have also been set-up on Scotland.

INTEGRATED PACKAGES: NON-GOVERNMENTAL ORGANIZATIONS

A number of international organizations are involved in the implementation of concepts and guidelines related to sustainable development. While not all those described below deal specifically with transport and tourism, their experience in implementing environmental codes is relevant to the tourist and transport industry.

International Council for Monuments and Sites

ICOMOS provides development and management advice, opportunities for education, and engages in some promotional activity. It also maintains specialized international committees on a number of topics including cultural tourism, rock art, archaeological heritage management, historic towns, and historic gardens and sites.

The council is involved in the development of management techniques for cultural properties and training programmes. It organizes expert missions and sponsors the International Day for Monuments and Sites (April 18).

ICOMOS' many publications include *Management Guidelines—for Cultural World Heritage Sites.*

World Wide Fund for Nature

WWF promotes public awareness of conservation problems and raises funds for the protection of threatened species and environments. It has a number of specific activities related to tourism.

WWF's principles of sustainable tourism development have been recently published in *Beyond the Green Horizon.* This publication discusses each principle, and provides a number of case studies to demonstrate their use.

WWF produces many public service announcements, video news releases and documentary films, some of which deal with travel and transport issues.

The World Conservation Union

The IUCN has supported many conservation and sustainable development programmes throughout the world for more than a decade. The IUCN Joint Programme on Strategies for Sustainability consists of two components:

- the conceptual component, which supports the exchange and analysis of experience concerning the development and implementation of strategies for sustainability; and
- field services, designed to strengthen local capacities to prepare and implement strategies for sustainability.

The Joint Programme is carried out by:

- Establishing regional networks of strategy practitioners;

during 1992-93 networks were started in Africa, Asia and Latin America, and they are now being set-up on the Pacific, Europe, North America and the Caribbean. The formation of these networks begins with regional workshops which are used to share and analyze experience. This experience is then disseminated in the form of guides, regional reviews, and training programmes.

- Publishing guides on preparing and implementing strategies for sustainability at national and local levels. A guide on the monitoring and evaluation of sustainable development strategies is being prepared. Additional guides are planned on indigenous peoples, environmental education, environmental assessment, economics, participation and communication and environmental law.
- Synthesizing the lessons learnt from work on strategies, and then distributing the result to practitioners, decision makers, governments and donor agencies.
- Applying the lessons learnt through field assistance to new and on-going projects, via partnerships with governments, NGO's communities and agencies, IUCN provides short- and long-term field assistance in all elements of the development, implementation and monitoring of sustainable strategies.
- Running a database on strategies. A related database is being developed on the processes and results of strategies.

Awards

Awards are a way of both implementing codes and monitoring their effectiveness. As consumer demand for 'greener' tourism increases, awards often prove to be a valuable marketing tool and method of public disclosure. Examples of organizations which have launched environmental awards include:

- the Green Tourism Awards scheme (later renamed The Tourism and Environment Award) developed by English Tourist Board;
- the GREEN GLOBE environmental management, implementation and public awareness programme of the WTTC has an achievement awards programme;
- the Pacific Area Travel Association (PATA) makes its 'Gold' awards annually; and

- the American Society of Travel Agents (ASTA)/ Smithsonian also makes annual environmental awards.

Education and Training

Education and training are essential for all members of the tourism industry if environmental performance is to be improved. Several tourism organizations are now making serious efforts to provide appropriate education and training.

PATA provides education scholarships through the PATA Foundation, and conducts 'train-the-trainer' workshops throughout the Asia Pacific region. PATA was also instrumental in founding the Travel and Industry management school at the University of Hawaii. Training programmes and lectures are also provided by the Tourism Authority of Thailand for government and private sector employees. Training for 200 youth leaders on environment and conservation management is provided on an annual basis.

The WTTC has recently opened its World Travel and Tourism Human Resource Centre (WTTHRC) in Vancouver, Canada. In one of its first projects, WTTHRC will work closely with the WTTERC to develop practical GREEN GLOBE education and training packages on travel, tourism and the environment.

In Costa Rica, the Tourism Micro Business organization was set-up as part of the pilot project to demonstrate the issues highlighted in the country code. This organization supports educational programmes on the environment for young people living near protected areas.

The International Conference on Monuments and Sites (ICOMOS) also provides technical and management training on the conservation and management of monuments and cultural sites.

The World Wide Fund for nature (WWF) uses educational techniques in its field projects. In Jamaica a project to diversify tourism in one particular area was achieved by a workshop in which participants included all the relevant stakeholders who examined the different tourism scenarios for 'best fit' in terms of level and profile, and then produced a strategy to implement it.

Technical Assistance

PATA operates task force for tourism and related industry specialists to analyze destinations, products, and services, and make recommendations on how they could be improved. The World Travel and Tourism Council provides technical assistance through its GREEN GLOBE project, as does PATA through its Green Leaf programme.

ICOMOS conducts expert missions at the request of international and national organizations and governments. Many NGOs also conduct expert missions at the request of international organizations and governments.

In an industry as fragmented as tourism, research networks play an useful rule in catalyzing to environmental management and examples of best practice. For this reason, The World Travel and Tourism Council (WTTC) established the World Travel and Tourism Environment Research Centre (WTTERC) to create an academic centre for travel and tourism issues, and a database for government and industry action.

Monitoring and Reporting

The Importance of Monitoring and Reporting

After making a commitment to put a code into action, it is essential to measure the progress achieved and to share the results. Approval and signature of codes are largely meaningless unless performance against agreed practices can be assessed and reported. The governments and organizations that develop codes and overall environmental policies have an essential role to play in following up the results, aggregating the information and providing a useful information exchange with others, thus leading to further improvements.

The importance of monitoring environmental performances is now widely recognized particularly in highly environmentally sensitive sectors. Tools such as environmental audits and total quality management approaches are now acknowledged as essential components of good environmental management in a growing number of sectors. However, they are only starting to be developed in most services sectors and in particular in tourism. Codes could play a significant role in accelerating their development.

Monitoring and reporting, though two distinct processes, are in fact one function. However, most industries give much higher priority to monitoring than to reporting.

The reporting of environmental performance is still at a very early stage of development. There is also controversy as to how reporting information should be verified independently by a third party or by other members of the same organization. However, the importance of reporting for sustainable development was stressed in Agenda 21 which states that Business and Industry should be encouraged to report annually on their environmental records, as well as on their use of energy and natural resources. The existence of codes may play a significant role in promoting such practices.

Several codes have stressed the importance of monitoring and reporting.

- the ICC Business Charter for Sustainable Development, in particular principle 16. To measure environmental performance; to conduct regular environmental audits and assessments of compliance with company requirements, legal requirements and these principles and periodically to provide appropriate information to the Board of Directors, shareholders, employees, the authorities and the public;
- the WTTC Guidelines: "targets for improvements should be established and monitored"; and
- the WWF/Tourism Concern *Principles for Sustainable Development* state that "on-going research and monitoring by the industry using effective data collection and analysis is essential to help solve problems and to bring benefits to destinations, the industry and consumers."

Green Globe

The World Travel and Tourism Council (WTTC) has launched a global environmental management improvement and public awareness programme, named GREEN GLOBE. Built on the WTTC environmental guidelines, GREEN GLOBE calls for the adoption of positive environmental goals and practices by all sectors and individual organizations of the industry.

The guiding principle behind GREEN GLOBE is on-going environmental management, implementation and improvement. Participating firms are encouraged to develop, implement and improve on their environmental performance.

The participating tourism companies are provided with a range of support services, including:

- expert advice from Green Flag International and the World Travel and Tourism Environment Research Council (WTTERC) on the development, implementation and monitoring of environmental management systems to cult-individual needs; and

- continuous support, education and training, information on best practices, and access to a global environment database.

Provided continuous improvement is demonstrated, participating companies are able to display the GREEN GLOBE logo, which publicly acknowledges their commitment to environmental best practice.

THE GREEN EVALUATION PROGRAMME

The Eco-Tourism Society

The Green Evaluation Programme, designed and developed by the Eco-tourism Society (TES) is an environmental assessment programme, which was launched in 1994. The programme is designed to monitor the performance of nature tourism companies according to the standards articulated in the Eco-tourism guidelines for nature tour operators.

TES believes that as eco-labelling becomes increasingly popular and better executed, the Green Evaluation Programme will prove of great interest to the entire travel industry.

Most nature tour operators work independently of travel agents either because they are able to market the tours themselves or because they work with counterparts that can provide this service. As a result, no programme exists to educate travel agents on how to select a responsible nature tour for their clients.

TES believes that the Green Evaluation Programmes will be useful to travel agents because it provides the background information agents need to select genuine ecotours for their clients. In addition this programme will bring tourists a deeper understanding of the issues involved in responsible eco-tourism.

The programme is based on consumer questionnaires and educational packages which will be distributed by participating tour operators to their clients in designated countries. Consumers who decide to participate will be asked to answer questions objectively not according to their level of satisfaction with a tour's services. For example, travellers will be asked to evaluate the information they receive before the tour, the ability of their guides to prepare them for limiting their impacts in each fragile habitat they visit, and the environmental impacts they can observe while on trails or in the water. These and many other questions will be included in the questionnaires, which will be returned directly to TES in sealed envelopes.

This process will be carried out over one year so that valid samples can be taken for statistical analysis. Highly negative or positive responses elicited by circumstances that may arise on just one particular tour will be screened out, producing a fairer view of the overall product.

TES does recognize the limitations of consumer evaluation, particularly when dealing with difficult questions of specific environmental and cultural impacts. However, TES decided to use consumers as evaluators because they are the only group that is always present on a wide variety of tours.

Countries designated for evaluation are selected on the basis of requests from governments or the private sector. Ecuador is the first destination to be evaluated with the participation of the Ecuadorian Ecotourism Association and Clemson University.

The Benefits of Monitoring and Reporting

The ICC Business Charter for Sustainable Development suggests that environmental monitoring offers three major advantages.

- *The Improvement of Policy and Performance*: Monitoring provides organizations with a means of improving policies, programmes and environmental performance taking into account the use of new technologies, the application of scientific advance, consumer needs and community expectations.
- *The Promotion of Openness*: Openness and dialogue with employees and the public is stimulated by monitoring. Organizations should anticipate and respond to concern about the impacts of their operations on the environment by addressing the concerns of employees, customers, consumers and communities.
- *The Assessment of Progress*: Monitoring enables environmental performance to be measured, and leads to the internal and external reporting of this information. Organizations can then assess their progress in attaining environmental objectives, and the degree to which this progress complies with legislative requirements.

These principles have been adapted to suit the specific needs of the tourism industry by the industry's leaders, with active support from industry organizations and non-government organizations.

Other benefits of environmental reporting include:

- an opportunity to inform customers of the environmental efforts being made by companies, and of the environmental sensitivity of its products;
- improvement of the corporate image; and
- ability to assess customer awareness and attitudes to codes.

The fact that many businesses in most sectors of the tourism industry are small and medium-sized enterprises makes the existence of codes particularly important for achieving an industry-wide consensus and improving practices.

A number of organizations and industry associations have issued publications to raise awareness on the importance of monitoring and reporting, provide examples of initiatives in the field and furnish practical information on how to monitor and report on environmental performances. These publications make recommendations as to how firms can define and implement their own policies in the field.

These efforts have often addressed industry as a whole, rather than the tourism industry in particular. They include:

- *The Environmental Self-Assessment Programme* (based on the ICC's Business Charter for Sustainable Development) published by the Global Environmental Management Initiative (GEMI) in 1992. This publication has been designed to evaluate and improve environmental management and performance over time, with a focus on corporate-level policy, systems and performance measurement programmes which are relative to the 16 principles of the ICC Charter. GEMI also published, in 1993, a document called *Total Quality Environmental Management* which outlines the methods of applying total quality management to corporate environmental strategies.
- The 1988 issue *of Industry and Environment* (published by UNEP/IE) devoted to environmental auditing.
- *Company Environmental Reporting* explaining the need to report, summarizing the ingredients of reporting and

providing examples of reporting in various sector (UNEP/IE, 1994);

- *The ICC Guide to Effective Environmental Auditing* (1991);
- *Environmental reporting a manager's guide* published in 1994 by the World Industry Council for the Environment (WICE, a global coalition of enterprises initiated in 1993 by the ICC);
- The Public Environment Reporting initiative (PERI) comprised of some major US companies also published guidelines on environmental reporting in 1994.

For the travel and tourism sector, special mention should be made of the WTTERC Newsletter *Environment and Development,* No. 2, November 1993, devoted to "The self-regulatory option" which includes in account of British Airways' environment programme. Other publications produced by WTTERC also provide information about the initiatives taken by companies to manage their environmental performance.

For the hotels sector, UNEP/IE/IHEI and the IHA will publish in 1995 the *Environmental Tool Kit for Small and Medium-Sized Hotels.* This will explain to hotel managers how to develop, implement and maintain an environmental management system and how to monitor environmental performance.

The Monitoring and Reporting Process

Monitoring can be used to:

- measure the response, and the level of acceptance, of the contents of the codes;
- measure the extent of implementation of the code—the activities have been initiated as direct response to the code, and
- identify the areas where implementation efforts failed or had poor results, and why, and take appropriate measures to reach the goals defined.

Monitoring is an on-going process, which should ideally be begun when the code is disseminated. The Australian Government, for example, integrated ecologically sustainable development strategies into its National Tourism Strategy. Within this framework the Australian Tourism Industry Association adopted similar guidelines, and performs regular monitoring to ascertain the overall response to its code.

The two most important monitoring initiatives in the tourism industry have been made by "The World Travel and Tourism Council and the Ecotourism Society."

The WTTC has launched a global environmental management improvement and public awareness programme; named GREEN GLOBE participating firms are encouraged to develop, implement and, above all, monitor and report on their environmental performance.

The FATA Green Leaf programme provides checklists that will help companies and organizations to assess their environmental practices and the implementation of the PATA code.

The Eco-tourism Society (TES) has published ecotourism guidelines for nature tour operators. These cover pre-departure visitor education and information, guiding, management and monitoring programmes. The latter provide guidelines on the prevention of accumulated impacts of tourism on the environment. Also included are recommendations about how services should be delivered, with what objectives, and for whose benefit.

When it disseminated these guidelines, TES launched a continuous monitoring programme to evaluate the general response to and the level of acceptance of this effort. Tour operators are encouraged to comment through an evaluation from which is included with the guidelines. The form also provides an opportunity to suggest new ideas on guidelines.

Looking further ahead, the next stage, after monitoring and reporting, may be to monitor customer awareness. Only by monitoring what actual tourists think will tourism bodies really be able to understand the likelihood of change. The industry may also eventually be forced to adopt or will decide to promote some form of code enforcement.

Recommendations

The case for the tourism to develop its voluntary codes of conduct on the environment is overwhelmingly strong. This industry, above all others, depends primarily on conserving and improving the environment which is its main trading asset. Since the industry is composed of a great many small and medium-sized firms, it makes sense for it to opt as far as possible for self-regulation, and voluntary codes are one of the best ways of achieving this.

For this reason, voluntary codes of conduct are likely go grow in importance as the tourism industry increasingly realises the advantages that self-regulation have to offer over direct government and international controls. Although most codes are relatively recent, more are therefore likely to be produced in the years to come, and a further review of the state of codes in a few years time is likely to be extremely illuminating. However, a warning note should be sounded too many codes, especially if they carry conflicting messages, could be almost as dangerous as too few—the duplication of codes in some areas could result in confusion rather than purposeful action.

Environmental codes of conduct for the tourism industry serve a number of functions over and above the obvious ones of helping to preserve the environment on which the industry depends, preserving biodiversity and reducing pollution. Codes are also in important means of raising general awareness about the relationship between the industry and the environment and about the industry's concern for the environment. In addition, some codes have been compiled not for the industry but for the tourists themselves. Such codes are important in helping preserve the environment particularly in sensitive areas. They also help raise the awareness of tourists that their actions may have environmental implications.

Codes are important to the industry in their own right. Developing succinct and effective codes in an important and for businesses trying to develop and manage their activities in an environmentally sound way. In this sense, codes must be placed in their proper context, which is as one tool in the development of sound business policies and strategies. Eventually, codes may need to become, to some degree, enforceable if they are to become primary management tools. The Antarctic Tour Operators, through their association, are already influencing developments in Antarctica since they are determined on expelling any members which do not adhere strictly to the association's code.

Since about 1990 many international and national organizations, tourist organizations and NGOs have produced codes of conduct. Some of them are reproduced in this publication. However, the analysis of the codes assembled during the UNEP/IE survey, and the views of the workshop held later to discuss the survey and this publication, indicate a number of important points about codes.

First, they must be positive, specific and action-oriented. If codes are too vague they have to bite and signatories commit themselves to very little when adopting them. Real change requires real codes, with real objectives.

Although codes must be tailored specifically to the situation they confront, most have several features in common. These are:

- the need to make an overall commitment to the physical and human environmental, to accept responsibility for environmental damage and take corrective action where necessary, and to promote and reward outstanding environmental performance;
- the need to develop policies and strategies that take account of land use planning regulations and the need to protect some areas from further development;
- the need to develop management policies that enhance beneficial and minimize adverse impacts on the environment; and
- the need to cooperate with other firms sectors and countries.

It is important that codes are not developed in isolation. All codes should be the result of partnerships with other businesses, with tourists themselves or with potential host communities as appropriate.

Secondly, code are nothing more than words on paper if they are not implemented. It is essential to consider the implementation and monitoring of codes from the very beginning, even at the time when they are being drafted. While many organizations have already prepared, codes, far fewer have given serious thought to implementation and monitoring. Those that have, however, have developed interesting packages of measures which comprise:

- publicity and dissemination campaigns;
- publications of all types;
- the provision of expert services to signatories of the code;
- the provision of networks to improve communication between participants;
- the organization of conferences and seminars for the exchange of ideas;
- the provision of awards for outstanding environmental behaviour; and

- the organization of demonstration projects to set examples for others to follow.

To be most efficient, measures such as publications, seminars and conferences must be practical in orientation and directed at specific audiences.

Finally, there is an important need to monitor, report and evaluate the implementation of codes. Since few codes have been in existence for more than three or four years, there has been little progress in this area to date. Nevertheless, some organizations are monitoring progress, or requiring adherents to the codes to monitor their own performance or to make their own reports on progress. Monitoring and evaluation, just like the production of codes, should incorporate the reactions of people directly affected by the codes.

The most important conclusion of all is simple: an overall management strategy is needed which will integrate all the activities involved-code preparation, implementation, reporting and evaluation.

Because of the importance of the tourism industry in many countries, and of the relationship that exists between the tourism industry and the environment, the business industry is now developing environmental codes with some speed. It is to be hoped that these developments will be able to serve as a model for other industries, an event which will in turn enhance the overall image of the tourist industry.

CONSULTANCY IN ENVIRONMENTAL TRAINING: A CASE STUDY

Focusing on our strengths: experience, use of practical solutions, and commitment to our clients; Capaccio's mission is to help industry and the environment prosper.

Our consulting services encompass all stages of environmental management, including audits and assessments, permitting and planning, pollution prevention and abatement, facility start-up and closure, remediation, developing and implementing integrated environmental management systems, identifying cost-effective solutions to meet environmental and business goals, and helping our clients to meet current regulatory requirements and be prepared for future requirements such as the EU Hazardous Material Declarations. We understand that regulations are no longer the only drivers which influence your environmental programmes. Banks may be driving a site assessment for refinancing, facility relocation or new facility construction. Your customers may be adding new disclosure requirements in order to meet world market needs. Capaccio is ready to help you meet these new challenges.

Our engineering services also cover all of your facility needs, from industrial process modifications to industrial water/ wastewater, air, and soil pollution control/remediation systems. We design cost effective solutions that work because our engineers come from industry and understand the needs and concerns of the end user.

Ten reasons you should choose Capaccio:

1. Industry specific experience to environmental issues.
2. Knowledgeable and easy to work with technical staff.
3. Undying customer service.
4. Competitive rates.
5. Use of most current technologies in engineering design.
6. Computer-based tools to facilitate environmental compliance.
7. Classroom and computer-based environmental training.
8. Collaborative team effort to create environmental consulting and engineering solutions.
9. Frequent updates to inform you of regulatory changes.
10. Great rapport and reputation with regulatory agencies.

Environmental Articles

Establishing Objectives and Targets

Any worthwhile Environmental Management System (EMS) will have at its core objectives and targets or goals with metrics. Most EMS models stipulate that these objectives be developed, managed, tracked and communicated. Simply, these objectives will detail what an organization intends to do to improve its environmental performance, and provide an objective measurement to insure that the goal is met. When an EMS is initiated, there is typically an abundance of low hanging fruit that can serve as objectives and targets that can be easily plucked. This is important so that the system can demonstrate initial success, and the organization can practice and learn how to effectively manage environmental projects. Management can see these readily achieved goals as a stepping-stone to tackling the more complex or costly environmental issues that may face an organization.

The ISO 14001 Standard requires that an organization consider a number of variables when establishing objectives and targets. In practice, the following questions should all be considered in the process used to establish objectives and targets:

- *Compliance Issues*: Does the objective address an area that is not in compliance with regulations? Will it create a new compliance issue?
- *Significant Environmental Impacts*: Does the objective relate to an impact your system has determined to be significant?
- *Technology:* What are the technical options for modifying or replacing existing equipment or processes?
- *Financial Limitations*: Will the objectives fit into the operating budget of the organization?
- *Personnel Resources*: Does the organization have the people to implement and manage the project?
- *Operational Requirements*: Will the objective enhance (or decrease) productivity or streamline the environmental activities?

A good method that could simplify the process of establishing objectives is to create a template listing these and other pertinent questions. The real work behind developing the objectives is to research and answer these questions, which can prove to be a time consuming task. A good example would be establishing the cost of equipment and installation versus return on investment for various technical options. This could require significant effort, not always with the anticipated result. Another interesting facet of this process is that targets can either be exceeded or fall short. In the case of an objective not meeting expectations, or being prohibitive due to a lack of resources, it must be kept in mind that the effort expended was not a total waste. In an ISO EMS, most auditors can accept an objective not meeting the target if the effort was made to follow through using the established project management procedures, and document these activities. Simply put, some projects do not work out the way you plan them, yet you should still take credit for having made the attempt.

Another question that often arises is how many targets and objectives should my organization be pursuing at one time? The straightforward answer to that would be to base it on the resources of your company, especially when it comes to people. There is no strict requirement in the ISO 14001 Standard that all significant environmental impacts need to be simultaneously addressed by an objective and target in order to reduce them. Some impacts are simply technically or financially not feasible for an organization to address. A good strategy may be to address one feasible, technically complex project related to a significant impact coupled with addressing less technical issues that could involve the general population of an organization. In this strategy, the technical staff would be pursuing what they do best while involvement in continual environmental improvement could be shared with people that want to do something positive, but lack the necessary skills to perform complex environmental tasks such as redesigning a piece of equipment or a process to reduce an impact. Typical projects that could involve anyone with a willingness to participate would be recycling or community clean-up activities. These could also be linked into the communication element of the system, in dealing with shared environmental issues with neighbours of an organization.

Involvement in the EMS by as many employees as possible is key to the long-term success of the system. People need to feel that they can contribute to the success of the system, rather than just hearing about the efforts of the environmental or process engineering departments. The morale improvement associated with these short-term non-technically driven projects should not be underestimated. Involvement in "feel good" projects that offer recognition to employees will enhance the importance of the EMS in the organization. Most companies want their employees to believe they are doing the right thing towards the environment, and these sorts of activities will serve to enhance those beliefs. The environmental reputation of an organization truly begins with its employees, and can play a role in future expansion, recruitment of top caliber staff and global image. Complex, long-term projects that do not necessarily involve the general population can potentially benefit the environment by reducing a significant impact, but the technical details are often not well-understood and the extended time line typical of these projects could cause interest in the EMS to wane if these were the only types of objectives under consideration.

A pitfall that organizations should be aware of is to not take on more objectives or establish goals beyond the resources available. The idea that an organization should have multiple complex objectives and targets in order to satisfy a register may be risky without sufficient resources being dedicated to the task.

There is a fine line for an organization between over commitment and doing what you can with what may be available. By establishing objectives and targets beyond the capabilities of an organization, you could be setting the stage for failure, which would subsequently paint the EMS in a negative light to both the management of an organization, and the general population, who would view the system as ineffective at making progress. An organization has to "live within its means" when establishing objectives and targets, but continually should strive to consider alternatives and unique methods to approach opportunities to improve that may exist.

Compliance and EMS Services

The services provided by the Compliance and Environmental Management Systems (EMS) Group are designed to assist clients with environmental regulatory compliance issues and with the development of Environmental Management Programmes and Systems. The Staff can assist with individual tasks or can help you in developing programmes and systems that will help to ensure continued compliance and improvement toward specific goals. Compliance services include: permitting and licensing, regulatory reporting, emergency planning (e.g., contingency plans), managing hazardous materials, pollution prevention planning, developing record keeping and documentation systems, training, and auditing. The Group provides hands-on assistance with flexible approach to meet your compliance and EMS needs.

The Compliance and EMS Staff includes Certified Hazardous Materials Managers, Certified Environmental Trainers, Certified Environmental Auditors, Toxics Use Reduction Planners, Registered Environmental Managers, and ISO 14000 RAB auditors.

Environmental Training Services

ISO 14001 General Awareness

Capaccio offers on-site courses to help companies increase the awareness of ISO 14001 among their employees. This training can be customized to meet specific needs of each client. Environmental Management System (EMS) Awareness training is a requirement of ISO 14001. Capaccio's training can fulfill this requirement for companies pursuing registration and those already registered.

Environmental Products/Tools

As Capaccio consistently attempts to find new ways to stay current with technology, we have used technology to develop innovative tools to assist our clients. For the past few years we have been offering Computer-based Environmental Training as a cost-effective alternate to live training. This new development has lead to research and design of other technological tools to assist in our clients' environmental tasks.

Our Informational Technology (IT) staff is always researching for new tools to assist our clients. From web development to Microsoft Access database design services, we offer innovative products to guide your Environmental Department through the 21st century.

Capaccio performs a training needs analysis with each training project, including evaluation of a facilities specific environmental training requirements, as well as consideration of the methods of training and effective means of tracking and implementation. All of our courses are offered as both on-site and off-site live classroom training with our experienced staff who provide technical information in formats that help maintain interest and topical focus.

In an effort to find new efficient ways to meet training needs—we also offer self-paced Computer-Based Environmental Training (CBET) via CD-ROM or Online. Our CBET is highly interactive with targeted feedback to help ensure important concepts are understood and retained. Pertinent graphics are used to demonstrate concepts and examples. Both customized and standardized courses are available.

Capaccio's training staff consists of professional personnel experienced in various environmental disciplines.

Introduction to Engineering and Design

Engineering is defined as "contriving, planning, constructing and managing with skills and craft."

The *environment* is defined as the "complex of physical, chemical, and biotic factors that act upon an ecological community and ultimately determined its form and survival."

Environmental Engineering is therefore the branch of engineering concerned with the environment and its proper management, and is a critical function to ensuring a cleaner, safer world for our generation and those to follow.

Environmental Engineering and Design requires skills and craft from essentially every other engineering discipline, such as chemical, civil, mechanical, structural, industrial, electrical and controls. Capaccio has built its reputation as a leader among engineering firms by effectively integrating these disciplines to provide innovative solutions to industry's environmental problems.

Our mission statement is to *help industry and the environment prosper.* In applying this guiding principle to every engineering and design project we undertake, Capaccio has been able to serve the needs of our clients while preserving the integrity of our environment for more than ten years.

Computer-based Environmental Training

In response to our client's needs for flexible and effective delivery of environmental training, Capaccio Environmental Engineering, Inc. has developed a series of interactive computer-based environmental training courses.

Demonstration Available

Understand how Computer-based Environmental Training could help your facility—view a sample course now. The sample course will demonstrate what our CBET products are about. The sample includes examples of highly interactive excises and list the benefits of using Computer-based Training.

***ISO 14001 General Awareness Training*—Fully Customized for the Facility**

This course is designed to train all employees of an organization undergoing ISO 14001 registration and/or surveillance audit. In addition, this training can be used to train suppliers, contractors, and others about the company ISO 14001 Environmental Management System (EMS). Implementation of this course will cost-effectively help organizations to address the training and awareness requirements of Section 4.4.2 of the Standard (Section 4.4.2 of the ISO 14001 standard requires that personnel receive training on environmental policy and procedures, environmental impacts, and roles and responsibilities).

What is Included

The course contents are customized to include company-specific information on environmental policy, objectives and targets, programmes, EMS, etc. The course is geared towards those persons who may have a less active role in ISO 14001 implementation at the company, but who still need to have a general understanding of what it means and what the company is doing in order to meet the training and communication requirements of the ISO 14001 Standard. As part of registration/certification audit and subsequent surveillance audits, the registrar may ask any employee in the facility about ISO 14000 and the company environmental management system policy, objectives and programmes. This training will also help prepare company personnel for registration and surveillance audits. In addition, this training can be used to train suppliers, contractors, and others about the company EMS.

Instructional graphics, animations, and interactive exercises, questions and games are incorporated into the course to help engage the user. For those with sound cards, narration, music and other sound options are available. The course also includes a review section that can later be used for reference purposes after the initial training is completed.

6

Tourism Product: Development Strategy, Management and Research

Tourism—the practice of travelling for pleasure, the business of providing tours and services for tourists.

Recreation—"refreshment of one's mind or body after labour through diverting activity; play."

To "recreate" is to "impart fresh life to; refresh mentally or physically; to take recreation."

Tourism products are a combination of two components:

- Activity
- Setting.

Settings

- Natural Environments
- Built Environments.

Built Environments

- Theme parks
- Resorts
- Casinos
- Cruise ships.

Natural Environments

Public lands cover 85 per cent of Alaska and it is these resources that attract most of our visitors.

Which Setting is the Best Fit for Alaska?

When you have a tourism product that is dependent on a unique, high quality natural environment or setting, the highest priority and concern is to maintain the high quality of that natural environment, since without that you have no product.

The next distinctive aspect of natural-setting tourism is that these settings are primarily publicly owned lands, held in common by all state or national citizens.

This factor alone creates a whole list of tourism planning and development issues and challenges.

Commercial Activities on Public Land

Tourism businesses cannot expect to simply serve their own personal business growth and development goals.

Public Land Managers need to provide well-thought out management and permitting plans that support the needs of these businesses.

Commercial Recreation Analysis

This is a cooperative effort by:

- Alaska Department of Community and Economic Development
- Alaska Department of Natural Resources
- Alaska Department of Fish and Game
- U.S. Forest Service.

To integrate planning on the state's tidelands and the Forest Service shorelines and uplands in Southeast Alaska. Our goal is to:

- identify and prioritize facility improvements needed to support commercial recreation use.
- determine the appropriate levels of recreation facilities, business services, use areas, and access points needed on public land.
- identify areas of existing or potential conflict between commercial user groups.
- apply appropriate land use designations to those areas that have the greatest value to the industry; and which are compatible with the interests of nearby communities.
- identify opportunities to streamline permitting requirements for commercial recreation use.

Carrying Capacity

- Built Environments
- Natural Environments.

Natural Setting

Many tourists are accepting of a small number of people around them, but generally travel to natural settings to experience some degree of solitude and quiet.

Economy of Scale

Built Setting Tourism—large outlay of capital and high operating costs require highest volume possible to minimize cost per customer and maximize profit.

Result—The bigger, the better—Businesses have to be large to be successful.

Natural Setting Tourism

- small outlay of capital and low operating costs
- expectation for smaller group experience in high quality natural setting, with none to minimal development.

Result— Businesses are successful by setting limits on numbers of customers to keep quality of experience high. Costs are kept low by having smaller, "leaner" businesses.

SEA Trails

South-east Alaska Trail System Mission:

To facilitate planning, construction, and maintenance of a regional South-east Alaska trail system which will enhance economic development, quality of life and transportation.

MODEL TOURISM PRODUCT STRATEGY FOR RURAL ACCOMMODATION

Criteria	*Interpretative orientations*
Situated in the countryside, in a village, or in a small-town	*< 5000 inhabitants in the village/town, or in very typical/ traditional quarters*
Rural surrounding, with evident characteristic of traditional farming, agriculture, or high nature values	*high nature values = Nature Park or similar. "Traditional farming" excludes predominance of industrial farming (greenhouses etc.)*
Tourism is not the main or dominant activity or source of income in the closer area	*Maximum relation "tourist beds, inhabitants": 1/1*
Good conservation of environment, quiet and "peaceful" setting no noise or pollution	*Smell and noise resulting from traditional farming are acceptable*
Authenticity of the accommodation and ambience	

(*Contd.*)

Criteria	*Interpretative orientations*
Hospitality—Personal attention by the host	
Small-scale capacity of the accommodation unit	*upper limit, around 40 bed places*
Social and environmental sustainability in the context of a multi-functional activity in the countryside	*(some criteria should be specified)*
Connection with the local community and traditional culture	*Minimum integration of the activity into the surrounding community, guests have possibility to get in contact with the local reality if they want*
Local products and gastronomy	*to be available in the surrounding*
Culture (folklore, crafts, traditions, heritage,..)	*to be available*
Excluding criteria are:	
• urban or industrial setting or surrounding	*rural-typical impacts are accepted*
• mass-or highly developed tourism areas	
• noise, risk/danger, visual and other pollution	

The above criteria should be incorporated by the supporting organizations and organisms into their respective guidelines and product descriptions.

NATURE AND CULTURE AS TOURISM PRODUCTS

The initial phase of the study consisted of a series of interviews with about ten entrepreneurs in Varmland in the field of nature tourism and with a number of municipal officials who were interested in developing this form of tourism. These interviews took place in the spring of 1989 and the objective was collect some material in order to start an analysis of nature tourism in Varmland. Gradually, our area of interest was extended to cover the growing field of culture tourism in the region.

The object of the study was to analyze these social phenomena from a sociological standpoint, which meant they should be related to a social context and changes in this context. Regional nature and culture tourism which aims at transforming nature and culture into tourist products' becomes intelligible if we place it in a broader tourist and social context.

The analysis presented in this thesis should be seen as a first step in a process since more empirical material and greater theoretical precision are needed if we are to study tourism as a social phenomenon in a sufficiently scientific manner. The thesis is thus only 'a tentative sociological analysis.'

The methodological points of departure for the study largely derive from discovery and reflection; discovery because tourism, particularly nature and culture tourism, is a social phenomenon which has to be scientifically described, and reflection because a major feature of this study is the conscious effort to exercise systematic control over the various choices that are made in the attempt to capture the phenomenon theoretically and empirically.

The statistical data used to describe the structure and significance of Swedish tourism are primarily drawn from the structural plans of the former Swedish Tourist Board. It should be noted that there are shortcomings in the tourist statistics partly because of the complex and extremely fragmentary nature of the tourist industry and partly because of the practical difficulties in collecting statistics.

The historical sources used are purely secondary. This is sufficient since the main aim is merely to understand present-day tourism in the light of the history of tourism and travel.

This study has been conducted very much along the lines of Pierre Bourdieu's epistemological programme which entails conquering, constructing and confirming sociological facts. The work has involved a scientific conquest of the field of tourism and the construction of fruitful scientific concepts for analyzing tourism. The collection of data on tourism has been used as a tool in the processes of conquest and construction rather than as a means of confirming hypotheses.

One may define tourism in three different ways: one semiotic, one in terms of social science theory and one in politico-administrative terms.

Etymologically the word tourism is derived from the educational journeys of the seventeenth and eighteenth centuries, 'le Grand Tour', where the term 'tour' designates a journey from one's hometown to another place and back. In tourism research and the debate on tourism the term has various connotations ranging from the negative to the positive. Somebody has attempted to treat the term in a neutral manner.

In terms of social science theory tourism can be seen as an anti-everyday activity which may concentrate on what one may term either educational and self-developing tourism or on carnival tourism. These two ideal types of tourism can be practiced either in central places, primarily big cities or on the periphery, for instance in Varmland's natural and cultural landscape.

The politico-administrative definition shows that tourism is difficult to operationalize in official statistics, for instance to unambiguously distinguish recreational tourism. Someone problematize the concepts of leisure and recreation, which are often used in these contexts. Activities which are not normally considered as part of leisure time may be significant touristic activities, such as staying at a hotel, eating in a restaurant or travelling to a big city to shop. Leisure away from home covers more than leisure at home. Recreation is an ambiguous concept which is closely related to the instrumental, disciplinary view that the authorities have of people's leisure time. As it is generally used, it excludes many activities which form part of carnival or pleasure tourism.

A study of the history of tourism shows that tourism is a social product which is intertwined with other aspects of social development. The embryonic analysis presented here primarily deals with travel and tourism in the nineteenth and twentieth centuries where modern tourism has its roots. The historical survey considers three aspects: which class or classes were of major importance for the shaping of tourism, what were the tourist attractions and what means of transport were used. Nineteenth and twentieth century tourism was very much a middle-class phenomenon. Tourism among the working class started in the period between the wars arid became particularly significant in the post-war period. Major attractions in both centuries have been coastal and mountain regions and the culture of Dalecarlia. Writer and artist milieus have also been very attractive. Charter tourism has become important since World War II. At first it was an escape from the urban environment, but today big city tourism is more prominent. The history of modern tourism is very closely linked with developments in transportation; the steamer and the steam locomotive shaped tourism in the nineteenth century and the cycle, car and aeroplane in the twentieth century. The last two have played a decisive role since the war.

Available statistics show that present-day tourism is a major industry, both internationally, nationally and regionally. It is one of the world's biggest industries as regards numbers employed. Its turnover represents about 6 per cent of world trade and the future looks very bright. In Sweden, the turnover was about 3 per cent of the BNP in the early 1990s. The industry employs about 5 per cent of the total workforce. In Varmland tourism provides employment equivalent to somewhere between 2000-3000 man years. The net surplus in the early nineties was estimated at more than 400 MSEK. The impact of tourism differs from municipality to municipality. In some Varmland municipalities, such as Sunne, Torsby, Munkfors and Arjang, tourism is a relatively significant economic factor.

A scrutiny of the former Swedish Tourist Boards structural plans for 1987, 1989 and 1990 revealed that the Swedes are very much a nation of tourists but that Sweden is not a major tourist country as regards the number of foreign tourists. The Germans, Dutch, English and Americans dominate. The Swedes themselves travel abroad a great deal, particularly in Scandinavia. Germany, Spain, Austria and Greece are also major tourist goals. The main reasons for travelling abroad are 'to relax', 'to meet friends and relatives' and 'for entertainment/pleasure.'

Swedes make about 100 million domestic journeys per year which entail an overnight stay and are longer than 200 km 75 per cent of these are leisure trips. The most common reasons for leisure trips with overnight stays are 'to visit friends and relatives', 'to visit one's holiday cottage' and 'to get peace and quiet/relaxation.' The predominant means of transport is the private car. Leisure trips without overnight stays are also of major economic importance for the industry since they are mainly shopping and pleasure trips. Business journeys and official journeys, both those with or without an overnight stay, are also of considerable economic importance since the people travelling often use more expensive types of transport and accommodation. The tourist industry has five components; restaurants, accommodation, transport, distribution, and activities and events. It largely consists of small enterprises, the big companies being mainly in transport, accommodation and distribution. The restaurant trade is the largest component both as regards turnover and employment.

The growing economic significance of the tourist industry has led to an increase in its political significance. Tourism policies have three main objectives: a recreational policy one, a currency policy one, and a regional and employment policy one. Briefly, the first is to enable as many people as possible to enjoy tourism, the second to attempt to improve the balance of payments and the third to achieve a regional balance in Sweden and to improve the level of employment, particularly in rural areas.

It is doubtful whether any of the objectives have been attained. There are many people who never make tourist trips. 'Sweden is bleeding tourist currency.' The regional policy objective is considered more closely in this study, primarily from a Varmland perspective. From a number of official reports and from political and administrative decisions at both national and regional level, it is clear that tourism has become increasingly important for achieving a regional balance in the country and in the various regions. During the 1980s and 1990s tourism policy has undergone a re-orientation, focusing increasingly on commercial goals, a policy pursued by the right-of-centre political parties in the face of opposition from those left of centre. Among other things this has led to the Swedish Tourist Board being replaced by Next Stop Sweden, primarily a marketing company. At the regional level in Varmland, the growing emphasis on commercial goals can be seen, for instance, in the Varmland Tourist Board's wavering between social and commercial goals and in the fact that many of the municipalities that are important from a tourism viewpoint are adjusting their tourist activities to the market in the form of foundations, economic associations and companies. This is an example of the process referred to in this study as commodification, which is a major point of discussion in the following more theoretical sections.

A Sociological Frame of Reference

In this section of the study we set out a sociological frame of reference, which is then used as a point of departure for understanding tourism. A survey of the analyzes made by two tourism researchers, Jost Krippendorfand John Urry, shows how valuable it is in theoretical terms to deal with tourism in relation to the surrounding society.

The major building blocks in present-day society are economic, political, socio-cultural and socio-material. In line with the materialist approach to history, we maintain that the economic sphere is the most significant for the nature of and changes in other social spheres. In this sphere it is not only material resources that are commodified or commercialized but also immaterial ones such as tourist attractions. Dominating the modern welfare state is the opposition between commodification, for instance the commercialization of experiences of nature and culture, and what we term decommodification, emphasizing non-commercial goals such as the social objective of tourism policy of 'tourism for everybody.' The socio-cultural sphere mainly covers the reproductive everyday and non-everyday, for instance leisure trips to another place. This sphere is being increasingly affected by the economy and politics. The socio-material sphere is the man-made environment, for instance the shape of urban environments and the cultural landscape. These are of great importance for the nature of tourism and are in their turn affected by tourism.

In the study we use Scott Lash's and John Urry's theory of the transition from organized to disorganized capitalism to characterize the changes that are at present taking place in society. In economic terms the trend is towards greater commercialization. The service class or the new middle class is growing in importance. The postmodernist paradigm, which is primarily distinguished by greater integration between, for instance, elite culture and popular culture, is having an increasing cultural impact.

As an industry, tourism can be divided, for analytical purposes, into production, distribution and consumption. This study only deals with production and consumption. The actors in these sectors are considered in terms of both their structural location and their cultural affiliation.

The Productive Sector of the Tourist Industry

In this section the production of tourism is considered from three angles: what resources are used, in what forms are they used, and how are these forms commodified.

A resource is something which is in demand or for which a demand is created. The resource is thus related to the social context in which the demand is created. The national and regional resources which, according to many of the official plans and reports, are to be exploited are nature and culture. We use the term nature tourism in this study for activities involving the commodification of various types of genuine and artificial natural phenomena, for instance rafting down the Klara river in Varmland and so-called survival courses. The laws on the use of natural resources and on environmental protection indicate the areas in Sweden which are most suitable for this type of tourism, roughly speaking the mountain and coastal regions and along some of the big rivers. The public right of access is a major resource in this context. The Swedish climate produces a two-season tourism model, summer tourism and winter tourism. On the basis of the social-science definition of culture, where virtually all collective consciousness is termed culture, all tourism with this orientation should be termed culture tourism. However, established culture tourism takes a narrower view, concentrating on the so-called aesthetic elite culture and the so-called cultural heritage.

It is clear that the form of production for both national and regional nature and culture tourism is small-scale. In fact, it is very similar to what is often termed handicraft production, work which concentrates on a specific assignment where so-called silent knowledge plays a major role, especially in the contact with tourists. The producers very much live for their work. It seems to be the case that entrepreneurs from outside are better able to see the opportunities for exploitation, particularly in the local landscape.

Using a concrete example, a company producing rafting voyages down the Klara river in Varmland, we discuss the theoretical significance of commodification, where utility value, particularly the psychological and social value of natural and cultural experiences, is transformed into exchange value, a monetary price, and where selling can be distinguished from buying. The exchange process may be an independent process with the traders primarily interested in the process itself. Small-scale producers seem to make every effort to avoid becoming traders to any extent.

With concrete projects in Sweden and in Varmland as a point of departure, we discuss the commodification of culture in culture tourism, in recent years an expanding field. Culture tourism differs from nature tourism in that it is more frequently arranged by official institutions and organizations, such as county authorities, museums and local folklore societies.

The Life-Style Producing Tourism Consumer

This section is more concerned with discovery and hypothesis than the rest of the study. The overarching aim is to develop a fruitful sociological point of departure for analysing present-day tourism consumption.

A survey of Swedish data on tourism reveals distinct differences between different socio-demographic groups. Somewhat over 30 per cent of the population of Sweden between the ages of 16 and 74 reported in 1990/91 that they had not made a holiday trip lasting more than a week during the past year, more than 50 per cent said they had not been abroad. Women more tourist trips than men; students and those gainfully employed more than pensioners; the better educated more than those less educated; households without children or with older children more than households with young children; urban residents more than rural residents; upper classes more than lower classes.

In this part of the study we hypothesize that there are class differences as regards the consumption of tourism. The middle class is more interested in what was earlier termed educational and self-developing tourism whereas the working class prefers carnival tourism. What is here termed the new middle class, where the so-called welfare-state professionals and the market professionals are prominent groups, seem more to unite the two forms of tourism. British studies suggest that it is people in this class that are the main consumers of the products of nature and culture tourism. It is reasonable to assume that the situation is similar in Sweden. According to many present-day sociological consumer researchers, it is primarily the new middle class that forms the new consumer society, which should also be true of the consumption of tourism.

This class defines what is good taste and what signs should be used to indicate the lifestyle one wishes to be seen as belonging to. It is also this class that shapes the consumption which will satisfy the need for relaxation from the boredom of work and everyday life. Consumption occurs in special socio-material space in society, for instance at tourist resorts and in the city of big cities, and this has an impact on the spatial design of society.

The cultural paradigm which many researchers see as justifying the current consumer culture is what is termed postmodernism. The main feature of this paradigm is the integration between different social spheres, for instance between elite culture and popular culture and between various sectors of 'the cultural economy.' Signs, primarily figurative, and code systems play an increasingly important role in social life. In some cases they form a hyperreal world which constitutes a reality in itself.

In the study the theoretical analyzes of consumer culture and postmodernism are formed and exemplified by means of two different travelogues and a number of concrete examples from the tourist industry in Varmland.

The Consequences of Tourism

This section begins with a brief survey of what is meant in theoretical terms by consequences, in particular unintentional consequences, functional or dysfunctional feedback consequences, and functional or dysfunctional consequences for the survival of the system. When it comes to tourism, all these types of consequences, including unintentional and dysfunctional environmental consequences are of importance.

TOURISM PRODUCT DEVELOPMENT STRATEGY: A CASE STUDY OF KWAZULU-NATAL

Introduction

Research for the preparation of the Tourism Product Development Strategy has included the consortium tourism working group reviewing an extensive array of reports on earlier relevant tourism research, as well as marketing surveys produced at local, provincial and national levels. In summary, it was found that the provincial tourism industry has declined, particularly in terms of tourism revenue, over the last four years.

It was also found that, whilst there was generally a high-level of support for tourism development and growth, this was mainly occurring in an ad-hoc and independent manner. It also appeared to be more 'product driven' aimed at existing tourist-source markets, as opposed to the 'market driven' nature of the Tourism Industry, which could deliver an increase in tourist numbers. The absence of a cohesive tourism strategy or master plan for the province was believed to be the main cause in this respect. As a result, a strategic framework (Chart 1) was developed, which identified the various components requiring investigation as part of arriving at the recommendations for inclusion in the overall Tourism Product Development Strategy.

Chart 1: Strategic Framework for the KZN Tourism Product Development Strategy

One of the key areas for the preparation of the overall strategy has been the contextualization of the above framework within which

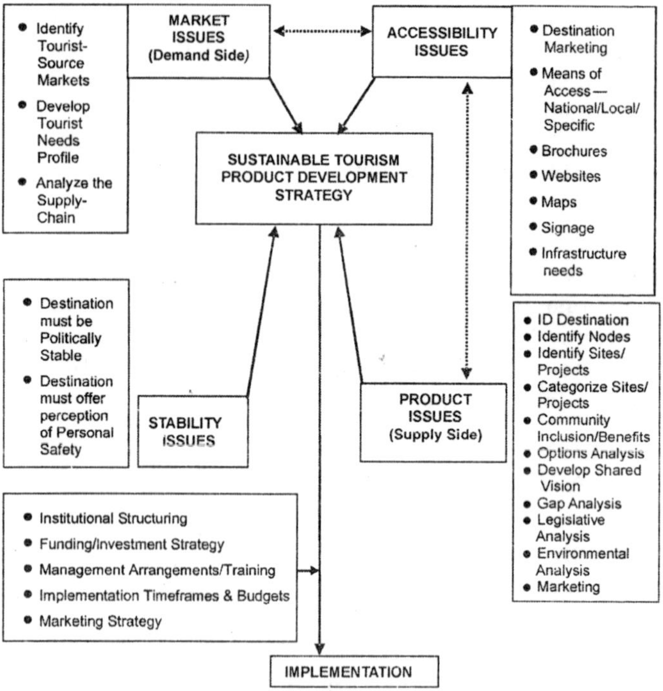

the tourism industry is dependant for its sustainability. This area has been addressed at length within the full report, and Chart 2 on the following page is an attempt to 'paint the picture' and its particular relevance to KwaZulu-Natal. This chart links both the Domestic and Foreign Tourist-source Markets with each of their own Marketing needs; their two Supply-chains; Accessibility—both international and local; and the need for understanding the levels and roles of Primary and Secondary Tourist Attractions as well as Tourist Facilities.

Chart 2: Tourism Accessibility and Attraction Flow Model

In conclusion, it has been found that the Tourism Product Development Strategy must primarily focus on infrastructure and product that will enable the growth of tourist numbers. In turn, it was determined that the largest sectors of both domestic and foreign tourist-source markets are seeking a coastal destination for their leisure holidays. Furthermore, it was found from market research that the two main disappointments for departing foreign tourists was their lack of ability to interact with traditional culture and heritage, as well as wildlife.

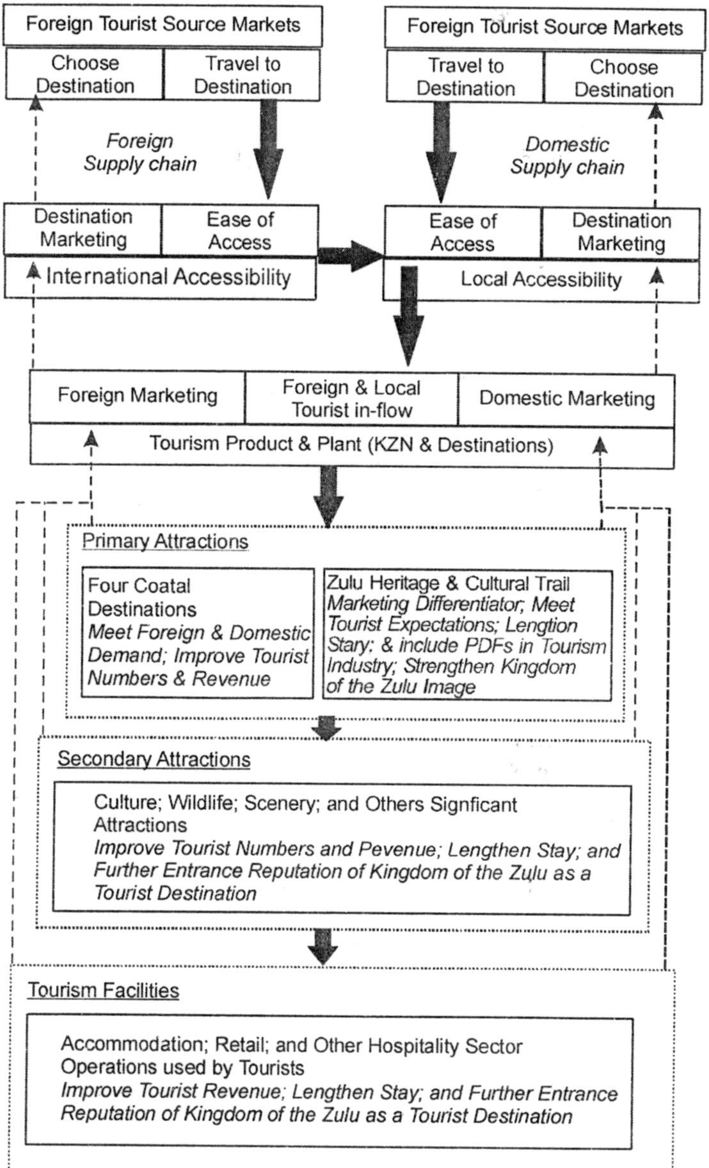

The Tourism Product Development Strategy has therefore focused on strategic interventions that will hopefully re-address the above shortcomings, as well as addressing the needs identified by the KZNTA within the Terms of Reference.

This has led to the Tourism Working Group recommending that a focus be given to the following strategies for crafting of the Tourism Product Development Strategy.

A Primary Tourism Product Development Strategy for KZN to build a reputation for its 'Coastal Destinations', which will include the need for a more focused 'Destination Marketing' strategy on KwaZulu-Natal's potential for growth as a domestic, as well as an international, coastal destination, with the objective of maximizing tourist numbers and associated tourism revenue.

The potential increase in tourist numbers will then provide the necessary justification, through the improved opportunity of sustainability for;

A parallel Tourism Product Development Strategy for the establishment of a Zulu Heritage and Cultural Trail, which will provide the enabling environment for broadening of ownership within the tourism sector, particularly within the rural and previously disenfranchized sectors. It is also considered that this will compliment and improve the existing product mix within the context of the 'Kingdom of the Zulu' branding.

As well as;

Policies for Strategic Intervention for inclusion of a 'Zuluness' within other tourism product development initiatives, particularly within the destinations of:

- *Durban/Pietermaritzburg/Midlands Tourism Corridor and linkage to the Southern Drakensberg.*
- *The Thukela Gateway—linkage to the Ukhahlamba-Drakensberg World Heritage Site; Wildlife; Heritage and Culture; and the Battlefields.*

Spatial Framework

From an overall review of KZN, in terms attaining the KZNTA goals and targets for tourism growth, it is recommended that the focus for both tourism product development and associated marketing should be aimed at the following 'Destinations':

The planning and implementation of a 'Zulu Heritage and Cultural Trail', focusing initially on a spatial corridor from just north of Durban through to Northern Zululand, but eventually 'meandering' throughout the whole province, thereby linking together the diversity and variety of heritage and cultural tourism sites of interest. This proposal, we believe, will truly underpin the branding of the Kingdom of the Zulu.

Four spatial 'Coastal Destinations', each with its own differentiation in terms of product attraction, targeted tourist-source markets, and ability to create its own image/branding within the overall context of the Kingdom of the Zulu. The four Coastal destinations are:

- Maputaland/St Lucia (Coastal linked to Wildlife)
- Dolphin Coast (Coastal linked to Zulu Heritage and Culture)
- Durban (Cosmopolitan Beachfront and Culture)
- South Coast (Coastal linked to Wild Coast)
- Two spatial 'Interior Destinations', the Durban/ Pietermaritzburg/Midlands Corridor and the Thukela Gateway/Ukahlamba-Drakensberg.

Tourism Node Identification and Product and Infrastructure Prioritization

The process for identification of the Nodes as well as the prioritization of the Sites/Projects/Infrastructure has been informed and analyzed by using the following criteria:

- How the Node/Site/Project relates to being, or facilitating, a Provincial/Local Primary Attraction, in that it will significantly increase the potential of attracting more domestic and/or foreign tourists in accordance with the product/visitor characteristics as defined for the destination.
- How the Node/Site/Project relates to being, or facilitating, a Provincial/Local Secondary Attraction, in that it will significantly increase the potential of attracting more domestic and/or foreign tourists, together with lengthening their stay, in accordance with the product/ visitor characteristics as defined for the destination.
- How the Node/Site/Project relates to being, or facilitating, a Provincial/Local Visitor Facility, in that it will significantly increase the potential of lengthening the stay of domestic and/or foreign tourists, in accordance with the product/ visitor characteristics as defined for the destination.
- Does the Node/Site/Project offer the potential of including rural and/or previously disadvantaged people in order to gain significant benefit by their involvement in the proposed tourism products?

- Does the Node/Site/Project meet the needs of untapped tourist-source markets, in being a significant coastal/ wildlife/heritage/cultural tourism asset, thereby encouraging tourism revenue growth, as opposed to only tapping into existing tourists already visiting KZN?

The Nodes/Sites/Projects/Infrastructure were identified from a variety of sources, particularly District and Local Government structures. Close to 500 projects were captured onto a database with as much relevant information as could be ascertained. Each project was then given individual scores against the above criteria, with the highest scoring projects then being put forward for prioritization. The full Tourism Product Development Strategy Report contains a full listing of each project, together with its score per Destination and per Node.

More comprehensive details on the proposed spatial framework recommendations are contained in the detailed Tourism Product Development Strategy.

Strategy to Develop Tourism in Rural Areas

The key attraction to draw tourists into rural areas has been identified as primarily being associated with Zulu Heritage and Culture. The creation of the Zulu Heritage and Cultural Trail is therefore considered as the principal development initiative in order to create a focus on strategic rural tourism product development. The development of this tourism route, which has the potential eventually to meander throughout KwaZulu-Natal, is considered as the 'glue' that will join together the wide diversity of rural cultural tourism attractions and sites of historical importance. More importantly it is anticipated that it will act as a catalyst for the opening up of previously disadvantaged areas for further tourism product development.

As stated above, it has been recommended that the initial Zulu Heritage and Cultural Trail commences just north of Durban and runs through to Northern Zululand. An initial scan of potential sites of interest and attractions include the following:

- Bambatha Rebellion
- Border Cave
- eMakhosini Valley
- Hlobane
- Inanda Tourism Route
- Isandlawana

- Isibayi—Nongoma
- Kambule
- King Shaka Tourism Route around KwaDukuza
- KwaBulawayo
- Lilani and Shu Shu Hot Springs
- Ndondakasuka
- Nkandla
- Ondini
- Ongoye Forest
- Ophathe Game Reserve
- Shakaland
- Thukela Frontier
- Zulu Heritage and Cultural Interpretive Centre.

The above list is not intended to be fully inclusive, but rather provide an example of the variety of product that can be initially included within the Zulu Heritage and Cultural Trail. The location of such attractions within the proposed Zulu Heritage and Cultural Trail will lead to a number of these projects, together with associated infrastructure, needing to become prioritized for development as a result of the key issue of accessibility having been addressed.

Key to the sustainability of the proposed strategy for the development of tourism within rural areas is the need to ensure growth of tourist numbers, together with tourism revenue yield, into KwaZulu-Natal, which will then be attracted to explore the Zulu Heritage and Cultural Trail.

The Tourism Product Development Strategy has identified, amongst other issues, the need to focus on coastal destination product development and marketing, in order to widen access into relatively untapped foreign tourist-source markets. These markets' primary choice for leisure holidays are coastal destinations, but they also need to be offered unique additional activities associated with wildlife, heritage and culture, when viewed within the African context. Similarly, the largest sector of domestic tourists also seeks coastal destinations. It is for this reason of sustainability that the Tourism Product Development Strategy identified the need for a parallel and inter-related coastal tourism product development strategy.

Identification of Key Tourism Destinations, Nodes and Sites for Public Sector Funding

Each of the spatial destinations referred to above have been analyzed with a view to identifying the key nodes and sites for inclusion with the Tourism Product Development Strategy. The following provides a summary of the findings and recommendations for each of the proposed destinations:

Maputaland/St Lucia (Umlalazi River Mouth to Kosi Bay)—Linkage to Wildlife

Product Description: Approximately 250 kilometres of mostly pristine beaches, including the Greater St. Lucia Wetland Park World Heritage Site, and stretching up to Kosi Bay. Wildlife areas of Mkhuze, Phinda, Tembe, Ndumu, Pongola, Itala and Hluhluwe-Umfolozi are included within this destination. These all contribute to the potential of creating a world-class unique coastal and wildlife destination and tourism cluster within the Kingdom of the Zulu.

Potential Market

Due to the potential uniqueness and product clustering of this destination, it is proposed that the focus of tourism product should be on high quality/mid to high income/low-density tourism, offering exclusive individual beach and wildlife destinations with sensitive environmental management. This should be targeted at 'A' income domestic and foreign tourists arriving by scheduled flights and connecting local charters to airstrips in close proximity to the destinations. Spinal corridor routes need to be able to provide close road vehicle accessibility without spoiling the perception of the exclusiveness of the destination.

Proposed Key Nodes

The Key Nodes of this destination are recommended as follows:

Primary Node

The Greater St Lucia Wetland Park (World Heritage Site), stretching from Cape St Lucia in the South to Kosi Bay in the North and inland, generally using the N2 as the Western Boundary.

Secondary Nodes

- Hluhluwe—Umfolzi Park
- Itala/Pongola
- Richards Bay Waterfront and Marina
- Linkage to the Zulu Heritage and Cultural Trail

Proposed Key Sites

Coastal

- Kosi Bay
- Mabibi and Lake Sabayi
- Sodwana Bay
- Greater St. Lucia Wetland Park
- St. Lucia
- Mapelane
- Richards Bay Waterfront and Marina Wildlife:
- Tembe Elephant Park
- Ndumu Game Reserve
- Jozini/Ghost Mountain/Pongola Reserve
- Mkuze and Phinda Reserves
- Itala Nature Reserve
- Hluhluwe-Umfolozi Park
- Royal Zulu Reserve and Biosphere.

Cultural/Rural

- Border Cave
- Grave of King Dingane
- Maqonqgo
- Ongoye Forest.

Recommendation for Public Sector Funding

Due to the advanced stage of the Lubombo Spatial Development Initiative, and the knowledge that KZNTA have been involved in the processes to date, research into the individual projects and infrastructural needs of this destination has not been undertaken. However, it is recommended that this destination should continue to be considered as a key priority for tourism product development in the province by KZNTA. Dolphin Coast (Westbrook to Umlalazi River Mouth—The 'King Shaka Region' and Gateway to Zulu Heritage and Culture.

Product Description

Approximately 50 to 70 kilometres of superb beaches and coastline, which has already been identified as probably having the best prospects for re-attracting higher-income domestic and international tourism, given careful environmental management. With this stretch of coastline acting as the Primary Attraction, it is proposed that the development of Secondary Attractions and Visitor Facilities that will complement the destination as a major domestic and international coastal resort be investigated. This is closely identified as being linked to the Kingdom of the Zulu through providing direct linkage and accessibility to the proposed Zulu Heritage and Cultural Trail.

Potential Market

It is proposed that the focus of tourism product should be on medium to higher quality/lower middle to higher middle income/ medium to high-density tourism, offering a range of beach resort style individual destinations. These should be targeted at 'A' and 'B' income domestic and foreign tourists arriving either direct by road or air via Durban, with international scheduled and/or charter flights for the foreign market.

Proposed Key Nodes

The Key Nodes of this destination are recommended as follows:

Primary Node

The coastal stretch of beach from the Tongati River in the South to Tinley Manor in the North (King Shaka Coast).

Secondary Nodes

Linkage to Zulu Heritage and Cultural Trail Linkage to The Valley of 1000 Hills.

Proposed Key Sites

Coastal

- Zimbali
- Ballito
- Shaka's Rock
- Salt Rock
- uMhlali Beach
- Tinley Manor
- Blythedale Beach
- Zinkwazi Beach
- Thukela Mouth
- Amatikulu
- Mtunzini/Umlalazi

Recommendation for Public Sector Funding

Not including recommendations for the Zulu Heritage and Cultural Trail, which have been included elsewhere in this report, the key recommendation is for the establishment of a major coastal resort development, but within the context of an overall coastal development master plan. The project, which has been identified in conjunction with the Lembe District Municipality, is located on the northern banks of the Tongati River at the river mouth. A comprehensive report has been prepared for this development, which sets out the extent of Public Sector support and finance.

Gaps Opportunities and Priorities in Tourism Product Development and Management

GAPS	Viewers' expectations to see the generic component of the wildlife viewing product, Bald Eagles, are unfulfilled in non-winter months. Viewers' expectations to view wildlife, birds and flowers are generally not met by wildlife viewing products other than Bald Eagles. Education/interpretive components of tourism products do not meet the expectations of wildlife viewers. Trail systems and viewing platforms in Squamish do not meet the expectations of wildlife viewers and are inadequate from social and environmental standpoints. Viewers' expectations of experiencing local cuisine are not met due to lack of knowledge about such establishments. Squamish is unsure as to whether mere are adequate campground facilities to meet wildlife viewers' accommodation expectations. Outstanding scenery is not adequately incorporated into the development and promotion of wildlife viewing products. The variety of outdoor activities that Squamish has to offer is not adequately incorporated into the development and promotion of wildlife viewing products. Infrequent market research has led to insufficient knowledge about wildlife viewers' characteristics and expectations. Knowledge about demand has not been incorporated into product development. Enhance, develop and promote tourism activities in the Squamish Estuary.
OPPORTUNITIES	Develop and promote salmon viewing and the Return of the Salmon Festival.
	Develop wildlife-related cultural tourism products. Develop the area where the Royal Hudson passengers disembark.

(Contd.)

PRIORITIES	Ensure that all wildlife viewing development first considers the sustainability of wildlife and their habitat. Further efforts should be made to eliminate hostilities between the forestry and tourism industries. Efforts should be made to reduce the confusion among residents and tourists as to whether Brackendale or Squamish is the primary host for eagle viewing. The District should become more involved in the planning, development and promotion of wildlife viewing.

TOURISM PRODUCT DEVELOPMENT AND RESEARCH

Tourism Industry Resource Centre

The Tourism Industry Resource Centre is designed to meet research and information needs of clients and staff by providing tourism related research tools and guidance. The Centre is operated by the Tourism Product Development and Research unit, Department of Tourism and Culture, Government of Yukon.

Located at 100 Hanson Street on the 1st Floor of the Tourism Business Centre in Whitehorse, the Centre is open from 9.00 a.m. to 4.30 p.m. Monday through Friday except for holidays. It offers a quiet comfortable place for research. Staff are available to help clients access and use the information in the Centre. Clients who require specific assistance may book appointments with Product Development and Research staff by calling 867-667-3053 or 1-800-661-0408 (within Yukon). We can also be reached via e-mail at tirc@yknet.yk.ca.

Tourism Product Management

The Opportunity

By participating in Tourism BC's widely recognized inspection and registration programme, accommodation properties become eligible for inclusion in the Approved Accommodation Guide and can also apply for "approved accommodation" signage. The 2006 Approved Accommodation Guide, with approximately 2,938 properties, is the most comprehensive directory of inspected accommodations for the province, including British Columbia Provincial Parks. Tourism Product Services is also responsible for designating artisans, attractions and accommodations for the purpose of highway signage.

Quality Assurance also inspects and rates properties for Canada Select (for fixed roof properties), Camping Select (for campground/RV Park properties), the national star-rating programme, and for Access Canada, a programme that rates properties for accessibility for mature travellers and persons with disabilities.

Tourism Product Development Company (TPDCo)

The Tourism Product Development Company is the product development agency of the Tourism Division of the Office of the Prime Minister.

Mission

To develop and improve the tourism product in order to position Jamaica as a preferred destination and to ensure that tourism is sustained as a major contributor to the development of the economy.

Activities

TPDCo develops and implements projects in resort areas, and develops and promulgates standards and guidelines for the industry as well as coordinates and implements human resource development policies for the tourist industry.

In collaboration with government ministries and agencies, TPDCo manages the Sustaining the Environment and Tourism Programme (SET). This is a project of the Government of Jamaica to clean, upgrade and maintain resort towns. SET is designed to have a positive impact on beatification, visitor safety, comfort and convenience. It has been implemented in Ocho Rios and Montego Bay.

While the TPDCo does not presently certify ecotourism developments it has developed eco-tourism guidelines and a checklist for environmental sustainability practices for nature attractions.

Our Mission

To facilitate the diversification, development and improvement of the tourism product utilizing an experienced and qualified staff to enhance visitor experience by building consensus and strategic alliances with industry stakeholders in order to engender socio-economic growth.

The Tourism Product Development Company (TPDCo) is the central agency mandated by the Government of Jamaica to facilitate the maintenance, development and enhancement of the tourism product.

TPDCo has been in operation since April 5, 1996, and is registered as a private company under the jurisdiction of the Ministry of Industry and Tourism. A Board of Directors oversees the company's policies and strategic plans. The Executive Director reports to the Chairman of the Board and has a functional relationship with the Minister of Industry and Tourism, the Permanent Secretary and the Director General in the Ministry of Industry and Tourism.

The company is designed to support government and quasi-government agencies in the development of the tourism industry, particularly by coordinating and facilitating prompt action between public and private sector interests.

Members of TPDCo's Board are drawn from both the public and private sectors, and include representatives of the Jamaica Hotel and Tourist Association (JHTA), JAVA and each resort area. TPDCo's Chairman is appointed by the Government.

Resort Boards were established in each resort area in an advisory capacity to TPDCo. These boards are legally empowered to function within certain parameters and with TPDCo's authority.

The Resort Areas are categorized as follows:

- *Kingston Metropolitan Area*: Covering the parishes of Kingston, St. Andrew, Thomas and St. Catherine.
- *South Coast*: Covering the parishes of Clarendon, Manchester, and St. Elizabeth up to the Ferris Crossing of Westmoreland.
- *Negril*: Covering Hanover and parts of Westmoreland through to Ferris Crossing (the border of the South Coast Resort Area).
- *Montego Bay Resort*: Covering the parishes of Trelawny and St. James.
- *Ocho Rios*: Covering the parishes of St. Ann and St. Mary.
- *Port Antonio*: Covering the parish of Portland.

The Resort Boards Ensure

The development, improvement and sustainability of the Tourism Product within the Resort Area.

TPDCo and The Tourism Master Plan

Jamaica's tourism development is presently being guided by the recommendations of the Tourism Master Plan, which was formulated in 2003 and which projects a timely increase in visitor arrivals and earnings up to the year 2010. The Master Plan points the industry to long-term sustainable development by the implementation of a number of strategies that bring into focus a generic vision to:

- Develop Jamaica's competitiveness;
- Enhance the visitor experience;
- Build an inclusive industry by fostering closer integration of our people; and
- Develop and sustain the environment.

The Master Plan is designed to increase earnings in the sector from the current figure of US$ 1.3 billion per annum to US$ 2.9 billion by 2010. The growth is to be spurred by the investment of US$ 1.6 billion in the industry by 2010, with private sector contributing US$ 1.4 billion through the construction of hotels and attractions.

TPDCo is now implementing a comprehensive plan of action that will guide its mandate to deal with the projected increase in business over the short, medium and long-terms. The company has redefined its objectives and has strengthened and streamlined its existing organizational structure for greater efficiency. Fundamental to this strategy will be a high level of people involvement and compliance to achieve objectives in the following areas:

Improved Product Quality

- Compliance to standards set by international benchmarks—achieved through licensing of tourism operations.

Product Enhancement

- Tourism training
- Beautification
- Health and Wellness Tourism (spas, HIV control, retirement tourism)
- Heritage tourism.

Product Diversification

The company acts as a catalyst, facilitator and coordinator for:

- Development through Sports
- Community-based development (with emphasis on culture, heritage and eco-tourism)
- Tourism for Prosperity Entrepreneurship Drive.

CRITERIA FOR RESORT DEVELOPMENT AND MANAGEMENT

Physical Infrastructure and Services

Environment

- All environmental laws to be enforced.
- Operators both public and private to comply with environmental regulations.

Security/Safety/Law Enforcement

- Ensure that all laws are enforced with emphasis on municipal laws in respect to parking, solid waste, traffic controls, littering and harassment.
- Ensure that crime is reduced and swift response capabilities are in place to deal with incidents.
- Ramps are put in place to accommodate the disabled.

Safety

- Ensure all public buildings have requisite Fire Safety Certification.

Traffic Flow

- Transport centres should be in place for public transportation.
- Regulated traffic flow systems to be in place and documented.
- Efficient traffic control mechanism to be in place.
- Adequate parking facilities to be in place and regulations adhered to by the public.
- Parking zones to be implemented and enforced.

Pedestrian Zone (Safety)

- Pedestrian zone to be allocated for resort areas.
- Ensure that the resort has adequate space for pedestrians.

Health

All operators require certification from the Ministry of Health:

- There should be strict compliance with food safety requirements and laws.
- Health facilities must be up to standard in order to service the community.
- Public facilities are to be in good working order.
- There should be adequate health infrastructure for the homeless, mentally ill and indigent.

Sanitation

- Solid waste regulation and laws to be enforced.
- Solid waste collection to be consistent and effectively maintained on a daily, hourly basis.
- Effective maintenance of streets, sidewalks and buildings. All derelict structures to be discarded.
- Drainage to be in good working order.

A Focus on Three Tourist Resorts

Falmouth

Falmouth, considered by many as one of the Caribbean's finest example of a colonial Georgian town, is Jamaica's newest tourist resort. This town was given resort status in September 2005 which is seen as a strategic move in light of major development plans for the parish of Trelawny of which it is capital.

The historical facade of Falmouth with its rustic architecture; beautiful Georgian structures, remnants of the colonial past, and its almost sleepy disposition, makes it an anachronism as it located between two bustling metropolitan resorts, Montego Bay in the west and Ocho Rios in the east. Falmouth is also well positioned along a major highway connecting the major resort towns, and it is in close proximity to an international airport and a cruise ship pier.

The granting of resort status to Falmouth is timely, as the parish of Trelawny is poised for major multi-million dollar development—Harmony Cove, a 1000 room upscale hotel expansion, and the new Greenfield Stadium which will host the opening ceremony for Cricket World Cup 2007. The town's development will also fall within TPDCo's heritage development thrust.

These major developments will provide a stimulus for wide-ranging opportunities in the areas of accommodations, attractions development, entertainment and transportation. Opportunities for employment will also be an added benefit.

Portland

Portlanders began this Winter Tourist Season (December, 15-April 15) on a high note with the arrival of the first of thirteen cruise ships. Some 13,000 passengers are expected to visit the town during the season, spending in the region of $180 million. The town's people are busy getting their town and its attractions in shape to deal with the influx of visitors over the period, as they begin implementation of a three-year development plan for Portland, spearheaded by TPDCo. Projects to be completed on a phased basis include:

The Beautification of Cenotaph Square

- Painting of buildings in the commercial district.
- The upgrading of facilities at the Musgrave Market for both visitors and locals to patronize local craftspeople and fruit vendors.
- Upgrading of the facilities for rafting on the Rio Grande as well as training and uniform provision for the rafts men.
- Establishment of a Travel Halt at Boston Jerk Centre.
- A Heritage Tour to Folly Ruins.
- A Walking tour of Titchfield Hill.
- Improvements to facilities at Boston Beach and Long Bay Beach.

Appropriate signage at major entrances to the towns, roadways, at attractions and places of interest, and the establishment of information kiosks for visitors, will also form part of the upgrading of the town. Residents are being trained as tour guides and tourism ambassadors.

TPDCo is working to set the tone for improved interaction between the relevant agencies, local authorities and stakeholders in the community to facilitate these improvements, build commitment and create ownership.

South Coast Sustainable Development Programme

A draft project document has been completed for the *South Coast Sustainable Development Programme* and is now awaiting budgetary support for implementation.

The programme aims to meet the economic, social and cultural needs of the people of the South Coast, through a strategy of sustainable and orderly development, in the areas of: *Tourism development and environmental management* which respects the unique natural resources of the South Coast, and *Fisheries Management* to preserve the biological diversity of the area, and to sustain the social and economic benefits to those communities active in the fisheries sector.

The tourism development plan will span the restoration of Black River to a heritage theme town, community-based tourism development, and the development of a heritage trail in the project area.

The programme which will be implemented over a four-year period is being funded jointly by the Inter-American Development Bank, The Global Environment Facility and the Government of Jamaica.

Tourism Enhancement

Promoting Standards throughout the Tourism Industry

TPDCo, through its Product Quality department, seeks to strengthen the overall standards and quality of entities in order to facilitate the competitiveness of the tourism industry. This is implemented via the dissemination of quality standards and systems designed to upgrade the health, safety, and security of product offerings.

International Benchmarks

The Product Quality department conducts inspections and monitoring of the industry and makes recommendations to guide the development of standards in operations as well as inform on international benchmarks.

The department has been instrumental over the years through its linkages with other agencies and associations in encouraging operations towards *HACCP (Hazard Analysis Critical Control Points)* systems in the food safety areas, *Green Globe* certification in the accommodations sector and which is also geared to environment management systems, and *Blue Flag* for the beaches.

Checklist for standards and guidelines are available for the following sectors:

- Hotels

- Non hotels
- Nature attractions
- Eco attractions
- Water sports
- Contract carriage operations
- Car rentals
- Craft markets
- Heritage attractions
- Ground transport systems for cruise ship piers.

Operations Audit

TPDCo's Consultation Unit conducts operation audits for entities seeking incentives under the Hotel and Attraction Incentive Programme. This audit also seeks to develop and upgrade existing operations and offer guidance for specific projects.

The Unit comprises trained personnel in HACCP Certifications, auditing of benchmarks inclusive of Environmental Management Systems, for the accommodation and attractions sectors.

International Standards

TPDCo seeks to strengthen the overall standards and quality of entities in order to facilitate the competitiveness of the tourism industry. This is implemented via the dissemination of quality standards and systems designed to upgrade the health, safety, environment and aesthetics of the product offerings.

Standards and systems are based on international benchmarks as cited below:

- Blue Flag www.blueflag.org
- Green Globe www.greenglobe 21.com
- ISO 14000 www.iso14000.com
- ISO 9000 www.iso.org

New Growth in Tourism

Jamaica's tourism is continuing on a positive growth path and final figures for 2005 should confirm this trend. The sector has been recording positive growth in stop-over visitors, cruise passengers and overall earnings since the precipitous decline in 2002, caused by the terrorist attacks on the United States, which is the major source of visitors to the island, as well as the impact of Hurricane Ivan in 2004.

The year 2003 was an impressive and record-breaking year for the industry. The sector experienced growth of over 30.9 per cent in cruise passenger arrivals, welcoming over 1.13 million cruise ship passengers over 2002—a first in the history of Jamaica. During the same period, stop-over visitors grew by 6.6 per cent to 1.35-million increasing gross foreign exchange earnings by 13.2 per cent to US$1.350 billion.

	2002	2003	2004	2005	2006	2010
Stop-over Visitors	1,266,366	1,350,285	1,414,786	1,467,363	1,614,099	2.2 m
Cruise Passengers	865,419	1,132,596	1,099,775	1,144,235	1,225,240	2.2 m
F/X Earnings US$ m	$1,192,900	$1,350,000	$1,437,000	$1.5 m	$1.780 m	$2.9 m

Data Source—Jamaica Tourist Board

By the year 2010, the Tourism Master Plan envisages an annual target of 2.2 million of stopover visitors and a similar number of cruise ship passengers resulting in earnings in the region of US$ 2.9 billion.

The growth is to be spurred by the investment of US$ 1.6 billion in the industry up to 2010, with private sector contributing US$ 1.4 billion through the construction of hotels and attractions.

Investment Activity

A major US$ 600,000 expansion programme is now underway with the construction of 13 new hotels, to provide 5,000 additional rooms. This will result in the creation of an additional 10,000 jobs.

The Harmony Cove Project in Trelawny will add four five-star hotels, including a 1000 room facility. The US$300 million Cinnamon Hill development in the vicinity of Montego Bay, will also add hotel rooms, villas and a shopping village.

Blue Flag

The Blue Flag is an exclusive eco-label awarded to over 3200 beaches and marinas in 36 countries across Europe, South Africa, Morocco, New Zealand, Canada and the Caribbean in 2006.

The Blue Flag Programme is owned and run by the independent non-profit organization Foundation for Environmental Education (FEE).

The Blue Flag works towards sustainable development at beaches/marinas through strict criteria dealing with water quality, environmental education and information, environmental management, and safety and other services.

The Blue Flag Programme includes environmental education and information for the public, decision makers and tourism operators.

Blue Flag Beaches/Marinas

On these pages you can find lists of Blue Flag beaches and marinas in different countries/regions.

Please note that the information about awarded sites will be updated each year on June 5 for Europe, Canada, Morocco and new countries nearby, and on November 1 for the Caribbean, New Zealand, South Africa and other new countries in the vicinity.

Number of Blue Flag beaches and marinas in each country awarded by the International Jury in 2006.

Country	*Beaches*	*Marinas*
Belgium	6	6
Bulgaria	11	0
Canada	5	0
Caribbean	9	2
Croatia	103	19
Cyprus	49	0
Denmark	211	77
Estonia	2	4
England and N. Ireland	85	6
Finland	6	30
France	269	84
Germany	39	123
Greece	411	5
Iceland	2	3
Ireland	81	3
Italy	216	52
Latvia	6	1
Lithuania	6	0
Montenegro	15	0
Morocco	4	0
Netherlands	40	45

(Contd.)

New Zealand	0	1
Norway	0	4
Poland	2	3
Portugal	207	11
Puerto Rico	4	0
Romania	8	1
Scotland	8	1
Slovenia	8	2
South Africa	20	0
Spain	480	82
Sweden	45	58
Turkey	192	14
Wales	43	4

History

The Blue Flag was born in France in 1985 where the first French coastal municipalities were awarded the Blue Flag on the basis of criteria covering sewage treatment and bathing water quality.

Blue Flag on European Level in 1987

1987 was the "European Year of the Environment" and the European Commission was responsible for developing the European Community activities of that year. The Foundation for Environmental Education in Europe (FEEE) presented the concept of the Blue Flag to the Commission, and it was agreed to launch the Blue Flag Programme as one of several "European Year of the Environment" activities in the Community.

The French concept of the Blue Flag was developed on European level to include other areas of environmental management, such as waste management and coastal planning and protection. Besides beaches marinas also became eligible for the Blue Flag.

In 1987, 244 beaches and 208 marinas from 10 countries were awarded the Blue Flag.

The Blue Flag Success

Since 1987, the Programme has year after year increased in numbers of Blue Flags. The criteria have during these years been changed to more strict criteria. As an example, in 1992 the Programme started using the restrictive guideline values in the EEC Bathing

Water Directive as imperative criteria, and this was also the year where all Blue Flag criteria became the same in all participating countries.

The Blue Flag Programme Outside Europe

In 2001 FEE decided to become a global organization by changing the name from FEEE to FEE (Foundation for Environmental Education).

Several organizations and authorities outside Europe have made applications to FEE, wishing for co-operation on spreading the Blue Flag Programme to non-European countries. FEE has been co-operating with UNEP and WTO on extending the Programme to areas outside Europe. The Blue Flag Programme has already been implemented in the Republic of South Africa, Canada, Morocco, New Zealand and in four countries in the Caribbean region. Chile is currently in the pilot phase of the programme and interest has also been expressed by the USA, Argentina, Brazil, Ecuador, the United Arab Emirates and countries in South East Africa.

FEE has made the overall decision that the beach criteria within a region should be similar. The beach criteria has however varied from region to region reflecting the specific environmental conditions of the region. As of 2006 an international set of criteria is being used with some variation within.

The Programme Today

In 2006 over 3200 beaches and marinas were awarded the Blue Flag.

Thirty-six countries are currently participating in the Blue Flag Programme: Bahamas, Belgium, Bulgaria, Canada, Croatia, Cyprus, Denmark, Dominican Republic, England, Wales and Northern Ireland, Estonia, Finland, France, Germany, Greece, Iceland, Ireland, Italy, Jamaica, Latvia, Lithuania, Montenegro, Morocco, the Netherlands, New Zealand, Norway, Poland, Portugal, Puerto Rico, Romania, Scotland, Slovenia, South Africa, Spain, Sweden and Turkey.

Brazil, Chile and Russia are currently running the programme in the pilot phase.

Blue Flag in a New Country

The Foundation for Environmental Education (FEE) and the Blue Flag Co-ordination often receive requests about how to implement the Blue Flag Programme in a new country. First of all, FEE and the Blue Flag Co-ordination should be contacted in case of interest for starting up the Blue Flag Programme in a new country/region.

Membership of Fee

In order for a new country to start up the Blue Flag Programme, a suitable organization must be identified to carry out the task as national Blue Flag operator. In order to be suitable, the organization must be a non-profit, non-governmental, independent organization and it must have environmental education and protection as important objectives. It is an obvious advantage if the organization has a history of environmental work related to local authorities and also experiences with national initiatives. If there is no suitable organization, a new national organization can be founded.

Once such an organization is found or founded, it must become a member of the Foundation for Environmental Education (FEE). This in turn means that the organization must be in accordance with the statutes of FEE, be able to raise the necessary funds to pay the subscription fee, be able to run the Blue Flag Programme and lastly be ready and willing to participate in the other activities of FEE as well. It is the FEE General Assembly that considers and approves applications for membership and it puts a great deal of emphasis on whether the organization is generally sharing the objectives of FEE.

Please contact the FEE Secretariat in order to be informed about the procedures for applying for FEE membership and in order to receiving the membership application form.

Implementation of the Blue Flag Programme in a New European Country

FEE and the Blue Flag Co-ordination have good experiences in implementing the Blue Flag Programme in a new European country. The Programme started with 10 participating countries in 1987 and today has the Blue Flag Programme implemented in 29 European countries. Furthermore, work is taking place on implementing the Blue Flag in other European countries.

In order to implement the Blue Flag Programme in a new European country, the FEE member organization must go through the following four steps in the implementation process:

1. Organizing a Blue Flag workshop/meeting.

2. Establishment of a Blue Flag national committee.
3. Carrying out the Blue Flag feasibility phase (production of national and local feasibility report).
4. Running the Blue Flag pilot phase (testing the compliance at pilot sites, filling out the gaps).

Implementation of the Blue Flag Programme in a New Country Outside Europe

FEE and the Blue Flag Co-ordination have in the recent years begun the implementation of the Blue Flag Programme in countries and regions outside Europe. South Africa, Morocco, Canada, New Zealand and four countries in the Caribbean have already implemented the Programme, Chile currently has a beach in the pilot phase, and work with the implementation of Blue Flag is taking place in Brazil, Barbados and Turks Caicos Islands.

The four steps in the implementation described above are also applicable for countries outside Europe. It is a good idea to consider how the Blue Flag implementation process can be started in several countries in a non-European region at the same time as this would strengthen the implementation work.

Appendix

Guidance Document[1]

Worksheets for implementing quality supporting systems in a local tourism destination.[2]

Guidelines for tourism destination managers, planners and officials.[3]

PRELIMINARY NOTE

Before you start working with the sheets and undertake to complete the checklists that follow, you are invited to consider the following premises on which any design and implementation of a quality supporting system should be based:

Need to Establish an Own Quality Approach

Should your destination consider applying a quality system already existing and used elsewhere, it should not be merely a copy of such a system. Every time the purpose should be to identify the quality features that are specific to your destination. This approach pretends to provide you with an opportunity to personalize" such a system. This will also help compare (benchmark) your destination to its competitors and, if necessary (in most cases), differentiate it from others.

---

1. Prepared on the basis of World Tourism Organization regional seminars held in Oaxaca, Mexico, May 2001 and Mamaia, Romania, June 2001.
2. A local tourism destination has been defined by the "Think Tank" of the WTO Education Council as a space having "physical and administrative boundaries defining its management, and images and perceptions defining its market competitiveness."
3. Additional explanations of concepts and terms used will be provided in the WTO manual (under preparation) "Towards Quality in Tourism." Guidelines for Planners, Officials and Managers," notably in chapter 2 of section 2.2 ("Logical framework for quality system design and implementation"). On request, the WTO Secretariat may also provide a conceptual example illustrating the worksheets.

Need to Establish a Quality Type and Level

These must be established by the destination itself and must correspond to the legitimate expectations of the actual and potential visitors within the integral approach to quality in tourism as specified in the WTO working definition of quality. It should be understood that at a given moment there may be varied levels of compliance—not necessarily full compliance—with quality criteria given in said definition, but that the destination must be clear on the existing levels and assume consequences, thus allowing itself to relate the product to the real and expected visitors and, if necessary, to design a roadmap leading to the desired or optimum types and levels of quality in the future.

Convenience of Obtaining an Independent Audit and Certification

As it is implicit in the guidelines that follow, it is becoming more and more important for tourism companies in a destination to obtain, from an independent institution, an assessment, audit and certification of the quality system that has been implemented. This independent and confirmed assessment may be significant for transparency and especially when communicating quality to your actual and potential visitors, otherwise your destination may not be duly rewarded by the market for all the efforts made towards quality improvement.

Please note that certification of a company does not intervene in its quality level, neither it ensures management excellence. Certification is just a starting point of a whole process aiming at streamlining companies' operations in a tourism destination and eventually rewarding it with a quality product.

The following questions referred to:

- Product/Service Certification (PSC), such as grading, rating or classification systems[4] based on standards.[5]
- Quality Management Certification (QMC).

---

4. *Grading systems*: Their application scope could be "basic", establishing minimum requirements or tangible standards for classification by type of tourist establishment (for instance, hotel, apartment, etc.) and by categories (stars or other symbols). Rating systems can also address an assessment of the quality "performance" (facilities, services, people, etc.), including intangible standards like services speediness and effectiveness, customer attention, cleanliness level, etc.
5. *Standards*: Describing levels of attainment against which performance may be measured. Attainment of a standard usually implies a measure of fitness for a defined purpose.

Does your destination feature suppliers of tourism services applying quality supporting systems and certification?

Yes ☐ No ☐

If "yes", please specify which type of systems and to which extent they have been implemented.

System certification	*Levels of implementation in your destination*			
	Hotels	*Other accommodation*	*Other services supplied by private sector*[6]	*Services supplied by public sector*[6]
1. Product/services standards				
1.1. Basic grading/ classification by category like stars or similar				
1.2. Classification according to tangible and intangible standards				
1.3. Other types of classification or system of product/services standards[8]				

(*Contd.*)

6. Services supplied by the following companies and establishments:
   - — tour operators, travel agents, tour services, tourist information and reservation offices (including CRS/GDS);
   - — e-commerce firms;
   - — passenger transportation companies (including cruise companies);
   - — marinas;
   - — transporation rental and leasing companies;
   - — air terminals and other passenger transport terminals;
   - — food and beverage companies;
   - — convention centres and meeting planners;
   - — suppliers of trade fair and exhibition organization services;
   - — theme parks and other public attractions;
   - — health, spa, leisure and other activity organizers and centres;
   - — travel insurance and assistance companies;
   - — tourism public services;
   - — other companies and establishments supplying services predominantly to visitors.
7. *Other types of systems:* For instance specialty or differentiation labels used by tour operators, tourism guidebooks, or reservations systems, such as "families with children", "golf", "all inclusive", "heritage" to highlight special features of facilities and/or services for specific clientele segments.

System certification	*Levels of implementation in your destination*			
	Hotels	*Other accommo-dation*	*Other services supplied by private sector*[6]	*Services supplied by public sector*[6]
2. Quality management				
2.1. Basic tools for controlling and supporting quality[8]				
2.2.				
• ISO 9000-2000				
• EFQM[9]				
• TQM[10]				
2.3.				
• HACCP[11]				
• ISO 14000				
• Other system(s)				

If "no" please explain why?

- Our destination is not required to apply such systems.
- Our destination does not need such systems.
- We need something, but have not made a clear decision yet what systems to promote.
- We know what we want to achieve, but we have not yet reached an internal agreement among tourism stakeholders on the design and/or the implementation of any quality systems.

Whether your answers have been affirmative or not, you may wish to take sometime to go through the logical framework proposed below. It is a helpful tool for a decision-making process in a tourism destination, regarding the implementation or extension of quality supporting systems.

---

8. *Basic tools*: Such as customer survey, complaints and suggestions box or forms, department management meetings to discuss and solve quality issues, etc.
9. *EFQM*: European Foundation of Quality Management.
10. *TQM*: Total Quality Management.
11. *HACCP*: Hazard Analysis Critical Control Points system.

Technical Approach

This area refers to all the technical components of the quality supporting systems in which your destination is or may get involved. *Identify and assess your current situation and specify the desired situation (if applicable).*

Five main Variables (V) have been identified, all of which implying a decision-making process on behalf of the destination planners.

Variables (V)	*Implementation Status*		*Specifications of current and/or desired situation*
	YES	*NO*	
Variable 1: Certification of product/ services standards or quality management certification			
V1a: Product/service quality certification			
V1b: Quality management certification			
Variable 2: Application in specific activity or all-sector scope			
V2a: Activity application[12]			
V2b: All-sector Application[13]			
Variable 3: Application to underlying factors			
V3a: Quality of basic infrastructure			
V3b: Quality of environment			
V3c: Other fields (like hygiene, security, etc.)			
Variable 4: Standards to assess tangibles and/or intangibles			
V4a: Tangible standards[14]			

(Contd.)

12. *Activity application*: Applying a quality supporting system to one or more tourism activities within the tourism sector. For instance, hotels; other types of accommodation; other services supplied by private sector; services supplied by public sector, etc. (see also note 4).
13. *All-sector application*: All types of private and public services related directly or indirectly to the tourism sector within one destination.
14. *Tangible standards*: Requirements for facilities and services that cannot be subjected to interpretation. They relate to the existence, lack and working order of these facilities and services.

Variables (V)	*Implementation Status*		*Specifications of current and/or desired situation*
	YES	*NO*	
V4b: Intangible standards[15]			
V4c: Combined (tangible + intangible)			
Variable 5: National versus international endorsement			
V5a: Local or national endorsement of quality			
V5b: International endorsement of quality			
V5c: Combined local-national-international endorsement			

Management and Funding Variables

This area refers to all the management and funding components of the quality supporting system in which your destination is or may get involved. *Follow the decision-making frame below.*

Six main Variables (V) have been identified, all of which implying a decision-making process on behalf of the destination planners.

Variable (V)	*Implementation Status*		*Specifications of current and/or desired situation*
	YES	*NO*	
V1: Design of Quality Supporting System by			
• Public sector			
• Private sector			
• Foreign entity			
• Public-private group			
V2: Nature of System			
• Obligatory			
• Voluntary			
V3: Implementation			
• Training plan			
• Technical assistance to local managers			
• Technical assistance to companies			

(*Contd.*)

Variable (V)	*Implementation Status*		*Specifications of current and/or desired situation*
	YES	*NO*	
• Design and follow-up of quality-related indicators			
• Other			
V4: Audit			
• By whom?			
• Frequency			
• Method			
V5: Certification			
• By whom?			
• Frequency			
• Method			
V6: Funding and Resources			
• Public sector			
• Private sector			
• Special incentives			

Promotion Variables

This area refers to all the promotion components of the quality supporting system in which your destination is or may get involved. *Follow the decision-making frame below:*

Two main variables have been identified, each implying a decision-making process on behalf of the destination planners:

- Internal promotion among stakeholders within the destination to grant the following objectives: to raise awareness, to explain, to sell the benefits, and/or to get formal applications to the system, etc.
- External promotion among actual or potential visitors, travel intermediaries, opinion leaders, etc.: to ensure a positive perception of the quality supporting system adopted in our tourism destination; and to make sure that stakeholders use ("buy-in") our systems in their decision-making process (choosing our destination).

Variable (V)	*Implementation status*		*Specifications of current and/or desired situation*
	YES	*NO*	
V1: INTERNAL PROMOTION (awareness raising and targets)			
• Tourism activity corporate bodies			
• Tourism companies			
• Tourism executives, professionals and staff			
• Tourism-related sectors and professionals (petrol stations, taxi drivers, souvenir shops, etc.)			
• Non-Tourism-specific trades (shopping, personal services, etc.)			
• Public services (police, first-aid, etc.)			
• Local population			
V2: EXTERNAL PROMOTION (awareness raising and targets)			
• Potential individual and corporate customers in their home country or region			
• Actual visitors and customers on site (when they are already visiting our destination and using our services)			
• Travel agencies and tour operators external to the destination (in the country and abroad) and other professional intermediaries (CRS/GDS, etc.)			
• Media both at home and abroad			
• Other stakeholders (opinion leaders, local population and similar, both at home and abroad)			

Draw your own conclusions from the results of this assessment:

(*a*) Have we done everything possible to offer quality to our visitors and customers?
(*b*) We need to promote quality supporting systems.
(*c*) Have we done anything wrong?
(*d*) We need to improve the following aspects of our current quality supporting systems.
(*e*) We need to implement the following new systems.

Our next top priorities *(choose three or more important and urgent ones from the former conclusions)*:

1.	....
2.	....
3.	....

Bibliography

Allan Jacobs and Donald Appleyand: "Toward an Urban Design Manifesto," Journal of the American Planning Association, Winter pp: 112-20.

Ash Worth, G. J.: Urban Tourism: An embalance in attention in C.P. Coopier, Progress in Tourism, Recreation and Hospitality Management, London: Ballhaven.

Bale, J.: Sport and Local Economic Development: A view of the literature. Paper presented at the IBG Annual Conferences Sheffield, January 1991.

Bamberger, R.J. and Parham, D.W.: Leveraging Amenity Infrastructure: Indiapoles, economic development strategy. Urban Land, 43(11), 12-18.

Bassett, K.: Economic Restructuring: Spatial ambition and Local Economic Development Strategy, a case study, Bristol, Political Geography Quarterly, 5 (Supplement), 163-178.

Berkowitz, B.L.: Rejoinder to down town Redevelopment. Journal of Urban Affairs, 9(2), 133-38.

Berry, B.J.L.: Urbanization and Counter Urbanization. Beverly Hills; Sage.

Blank, U. and Petkovich, M.D.: Research on Urban Tourism Destinations. In: JRB Rithie and C. Goeldner (eds). Travel, Tourism and Hospitality Researchers, Chapter 14, New York: John Wiley.

Bradford Metropolitan: District Council Economic Development Strategy, Brandford: Bradford Metropolitan District Council.

Bull, A.: The Economics of Travel and Tourism, Melbourne: Pitman.

Cillenge M.: Tourism and Urban Regeneration. Vision for Cities Conference Paper, London: English Tourist Board.

Cooper C.P.: Progress in Tourism, Recreation and Hospitality Management, Vol. 2, London: Belhaven.

Daniel H. Burnham, Jr. and Robert Kingery: Planning the Region of Chicago: Chicago Regional Planning Association, p. l8.s.

Donnison, D. and Middleton A: Regenerating the Inner City Glassgow Experience, London, Routledge and Regan Paul.

Drabble, M.: A Vision of the Real City. In: M. Fisher and U. Owen (eds). Whose Cities? London: Penguin.

English Tourist Board/LDR.: Manchester Salford, Trafford Strategic Development Initiative: A Framework for Tourism Development: London, English Tourist Board.

Ford, L.R.: Urban Preservation and the Geography of the City in the USA, Progress in Human Geography 3, 211-38.

Frieden, B. and Sagalyn, L.B: Downtown Inc: How America Rebuilds it Cities? Cambridge, MA: MIT Press.

Getz, D. Festival: Special Events and Tourism, In: D.E. Hawkins and JRB Ricnie, World Trand and Tourism Review, Vol. I, pp. 183-84. Wallingford: CAB International.

Go, F.: The International Conventions and Meeting Markets, In: D.E. Hawkins and J.R.B. Ritchie, World Travel and Tourism Review, Vol. 85, pp. 127-28. Walling Ford: CAB International.

Goodall, B.: Tourist Accommodation: A Destination Area Perspective Built Environment 15, 78-81.

Hall, P.: Urban Development and the Future of Tourism Management, 8, 129-130.

Hendon, W. and Show, D.: The Arts and Urban Development In: G. Gappert (ed.) The Future of Winter Cities; Beverly Hills: Sage.

Hughes, G.: Conceiving of Tourism, Area, 23, 203-07.

Hughes C.G.: The Employment and Economic Benefits of Tourism, Reappraised Tourism Development, 3, 167-76.

Jack, L. Nasar: "The Evaluative Image of the City", Journal of American Planning Association, Winter, p. 44.

Jansen-Verbakea, M.: Inner City Tourism, Resources, Tourists and Promoters: Annals of Tourism Research 13, 79-100.

Jeffrey, D.: Monitoring the Growth of Tourism-related Employment at the Local Level: The Application of a Census Based Survey Method in Yorkshire and Humberside, 1981-87. Planning Outlook 33, 108-17.

Johnson, P. and Thomas, B.: Measuring the Local Employment Impact of a Tourist Attraction: An Emperial Example. Regional Studies, 24, 395-403.

Kent, W.E., Shock, J. and Snow, R.E. Shopping: Tourism's, Unsuing Hero (inc): Journal of Travel Research 21(4) 2-4.

Law, C.M.: Urban Tourism: Selected Care Studies, Urban Tourism Project Working Paper, No 1: Department of Geography, University of Salford.

Le Corbusier: The City of Tomorrow and Its Planning, New York: Dover Publication.

Levine, M.V.: Downtown Redevelopment as an Urban Growth Strategy: A Critical Appraisal of the Ballimore, Renaissance, Journal of Urban Affairs, 9(2) 103-23.

Morrell, B.: Employment in Tourism, London: British Tourism Authority.

Negi, Jagmohan: Himalayan Heritage: Gitanjali, New Delhi.

Negi, Jagmohan: Tourism Development and Resource Conservation: an environmental ecological, socio-economic and cultural approach to tourism in developing countries. Metropolitan, New Delhi.

Owen, C.: Tourism and Urban Regeneration Cities, 194-201.

O Toole, M. and Robinson F.: Gorden Festivals and Urban Regeneration, New Castle: University of New Castle Upon Tyne.

Plog, S.C.: Understanding Psychographics Tourism. In JRB Ritchie and C.R. Goeldner (eds.), Travel Tourism and Hospitality Research, New York: John Wiley.

Pysarchik, D.T.: Tourism Retailing. In: S.F. Wilt and L. Mauntinho (eds.) Tourism and Management Handbook; Engle Wood Cliffs, NJ: Prentice Hall.

Rines, M.: The Business of Conferences Management Today, February 19-108.

Richards, G.: English Conference Venues: Market Trends and Prospects. Investing in Tourism (ETB), Jan-June; 29-23.

Rosentraub, M.S. and Nunn, SR.: Suburban City Investment in Professional Sports, American Behavioural Scientist, 21, 393-414.

Smita, S.L.J.: Restaurant and Dining Out; Geography of a Tourism Bureau Annals of Tourism Research, 10, 515-49.

Stevens, T. Barcelona: The Olympic City, Leisure Management 12(6) 26-30.

Susan Carey: Tourist Spits Developing; 'Green Images', Wall Street Journal, p. A7.

Tibbalds, Colbaurne: Karski Cardiff Tourism Study. Final Report London: Tibbalds, Catborne, Karski.

Tighe, A.J.: Cultural Tourism in the USA, Tourism Management, 6, 234-51.

Trinity Research: The UK Short Break Holiday Market: Trinity Research.

Vaughan, R.: Does a Festival Pay? A Case Study of the Edingburgh Festival in 1976, Tourism Recreation Research Unit, Working Paper No. 5: University of Edingburgh, Edingburgh.

Wishart, R.: Fashioning the Future; Glasgow. In: M. Fisher and V. Owen, Whose Citied? London: Penguin.

Wynne D.: The Culture Industry, The Arts in Urban Regeneration Aldershot: Avebury.

Index